LADIES OF RICHMOND

LADIES *of* RICHMOND

Confederate Capital

BY KATHARINE M. JONES

With an Introduction by Clifford Dowdey

 THE **BOBBS-MERRILL** COMPANY, INC.
A SUBSIDIARY OF HOWARD W. SAMS & CO., INC.
Publishers • INDIANAPOLIS • NEW YORK

973.782

CONTENTS

325541

ILLUSTRATIONS

following page 92:

Confederate White House at Richmond

Mrs. Jefferson Davis

Mrs. Clement C. Clay

Mrs. James Chesnut

Mrs. Robert E. Lee

Mrs. Lee's bedroom at 707 East Franklin Street,
Richmond

Sally Buchanan Campbell Preston

following page 243:

St. Paul's Church

The Davis children, Christmas 1864

Little Joe Davis' grave, Hollywood Cemetery,
Richmond

Miss Elizabeth Van Lew, Union spy

Captain Sally Tompkins

Miss Louise Wigfall

Miss Mary Triplett

Miss Hetty Cary

INTRODUCTION

By Clifford Dowdey

When I was a child in Richmond, I grew up in the neighborhood of the once-beautiful mansion in which Miss Van Lew, the Union spy, had lived during the war. The formal garden of the days of splendor was overgrown with shrubbery and vines, which well served the purpose of Dr. Parker, who was then using the great house as a small, private sanatorium. To children, the slumbrous walls of vines enclosed all the mysteries associated with Betsy Van Lew, including a secret tunnel through which Federal prisoners had escaped from Libby.

Once, in 1864, when the Federal raider Dahlgren had been killed outside Richmond, his father, Admiral Dahlgren, had requested the Confederate authorities to return his son's body. Soldiers discovered that the grave was empty; for some weird purpose of her own, Miss Van Lew had directed several Negroes to dig up Dahlgren's body and hide it somewhere. When we played outside the enclosed grounds at dusk, the ghost of Dahlgren somehow joined the Federal prisoners (some of whom we imagined to be still hiding), and a more haunting place could scarcely be conjured up in the minds of children.

Miss Van Lew and her contemporaries were never historic figures to us. They peopled the mythology of our childhood, and we had no impression of a different time in which they had lived. They belonged in perpetuity to the world we knew, and, indeed, some still strolled under parasols over the red brick sidewalks and drove in carriages on the then changeless streets. At St. Paul's Church, they spoke as of a recent event in describing the "beautiful bride," Hettie Cary, who stood at the altar with General John Pegram and, a month later, returned to the same altar to look down upon his coffin.

With new generations and the changing city—the old landmarks giving way to anonymous utilitarian buildings of progress —the famous ladies of the wartime capital have grown dim in memories. A stone marker stands on the brow of a hillside park where Phoebe Yates Pember was the matron of nurses at Chimborazo Hospital, reputed then to be the largest military hospital in history; a new window in St. James Church commemorates "Captain Sally," Miss Tompkins, who was officially commissioned in order to continue the operation of her private hospital; The Confederate Museum displays its fine collection in the parlors of the White House of the Confederacy, where the Cary girls and Mattie Ould danced at the President's levees, and Mrs. Chesnut and Mrs. Mallory and Mrs. Wigfall visited with the President's lady (and developed their private feuds with the wives of other dignitaries). All this, of course, does not evoke the flavor of their dramatic hours in a besieged city, nor communicate the ethos of the brief empire to which they brought all their aspirations, and in which they suffered the anguish of fear, despair, and finally defeat.

Now it is only in the words of the ladies themselves that the sense of mortal life is recaptured during that rarest experience that has ever come to American women—existence in a wartime city under four years of attacks and nearly one year of siege. In all American history, only the ladies of Richmond lived through the birth and death of a nation in its capital.

In recording their reactions to this existence, these ladies made no attempt to write for the ages. They wrote in private letters, in diaries, and even their memoirs were written essentially to record the experience while it was fresh in their minds and emotions. Miss Katharine Jones has made her selections from these documents of the heart to distill the essence of the times.

Few of these ladies were natives of Richmond. They came from all over the South, and could claim varied backgrounds of experience in Washington, New York, and faraway places. Since many were strangers, they wrote of their impressions of the Confederate capital. Others were the wives of generals and cabinet members, so they recorded their impressions of the government. All of these ladies were intensely involved with the nation's fortunes, as reflected through the government and the armies, and for this reason they wrote more personally, more passionately, than is usual for observers of great events in our history. For them, the consequences of the Confederate government's actions could mean victory or defeat and, more often than not, the grief attendant upon the death of a dear friend or loved one.

Yet, the most moving quality in their confidences is concerned with the day-by-day minutiae of life—the strategems against hunger and want, the pathos of their efforts to sustain the spirit by social gatherings and diversions, their determination to turn themselves out attractively in defiance of all destitution and blockades. A strong strain of gaiety, sometimes even frivolity, ran through the city's life until near the very end. This embattled merriment was but another face of the courage that maintained the city as one enormous hospital, as an industrial and supply center, and as the vortex of the government's operations. For these ladies worked in munitions plants, government offices, hospitals and powder mills; they knitted socks and made bandages out of old sheets; they found comfort in a cup of sassafras tea and invented the most ingenious substitutes for food.

Through Miss Jones' sympathetic hand and patient research into the enormous amount of available material, the life in America's one besieged capital is re-created through the unstudied words of the ladies who gave Richmond its spirit, its mood, and its memories.

AUTHOR'S PREFACE

Once upon a time—from May 1861, to April 3, 1865, to be exact—Richmond, Virginia, was the capital of the Confederacy. A French visitor called it a miniature Paris, and a world traveler observed, "I should say there is no more brilliant capital among all the nations."

Campaign after campaign was planned by Lincoln and his military advisers to capture this city, and general after general went down in defeat and disgrace. General Winfield Scott boasted that he would capture the city before the Confederate Congress met there on July 20, 1861. His boast was empty. Generals Irvin McDowell, George B. McClellan, John Pope, Ambrose E. Burnside and "Fighting Joe" Hooker tried and failed. Then General Grant launched his assault in the spring of 1864. Stoneman, Dahlgren, and Kilpatrick attempted cavalry raids. Thousands upon thousands of invaders were killed and wounded in the prolonged effort to take Richmond, and thousands upon thousands died in its defense.

The ladies of the city played an important part in its Confederate history. After First Mannassas, they threw open the doors of their homes to the refugees and the wounded. From all parts of the South, women arrived to fill positions in the many government departments; to volunteer their services to the always-crowded hospitals, or to nurse members of their own families. They strengthened the morale of their men in office and in the field. Sometimes they went hungry; sometimes they had champagne at $350 a dozen. A gentle-born lady who worked in the Treasury Department was without shoes. She fainted one morning, and "Her feet were found wrapped in long pieces of lint, as she had no shoes, and just clothes enough to cover her.'

When the victorious army finally entered Richmond, Charles A. Dana reported much suffering among the population. "The rich as well as the poor are destitute of food," he said.

Here is the ladies' own story of what they saw and heard, thought and felt and did, as they set it down in letters, diaries, or memoirs. Long after the war, one of them—Mrs. Robert E. Lee—spoke of "the glorious old times of the Confederacy." They relished the glory, whetted the spirit of resistance, endured the ultimate tragedy. Often they wrote to the accompanying rumble of great guns.

LADIES OF RICHMOND

*To the Memory of
the Ladies of Richmond*

PROEM

Washington, D. C., November 8, 1860—
April 22, 1861

"It was while I was in Florida, on November 11, that (alas) my husband resigned his seat in the Senate of the U. S.," said Mary Boykin Chesnut, wife of James Chesnut, Jr., of South Carolina. "I might not have been able to influence him, but I should have tried."

Within six weeks, South Carolina passed an Ordinance of Secession from the Union. "This was the tremendous event," wrote Mrs. Roger A. Pryor, wife of the Virginia Congressman, "which was to change all our lives—to give us poverty for riches, mutilation and wounds for strength and health, obscurity and degradation for honor and distinction, exile and loneliness for inherited homes and friends, pain and death for happiness and life. "

Efforts toward peace and compromise between the North and the South came to nothing. As early as December 13, Senator Clement C. Clay, of Alabama, had said, "Many and various efforts are being made to compromise existing difficulties and patch up the rotten concern. They will all be futile."

Each day the Capitol galleries were crowded with "ladies assembled together like a mosaic of flowers."

"We begin to feel we are to be scattered like chaff before the wind," said Mrs. Eugene McLean, "and we go to meet our fate in our best bonnets and with smiling faces."

Southern women and children were advised to leave Washington before Lincoln's inauguration, and, day by day, wharf and railway station were crowded with baggage and passengers, all heading south.

"To wrench oneself from the ties of fifteen years is a most distressing effort," said the wife of Senator Jefferson Davis of Mississippi.

Our story begins in Washington before Southern women of official life moved down to Richmond, capital of the Confederate States of America.

1. MARGARET SUMNER McLEAN

"Where Will It All End?"

> Margaret Sumner McLean, daughter of General Edwin Vose and Hannah W. Forster Sumner, of Massachusetts, was the wife of Captain Eugene McLean, West Point, 1842. Her husband was a native of Maryland, and his sympathies were with the South. Mrs. McLean, whose sympathies were apt to change from day to day, began a diary two days after "Election Day."

Washington

November 8, 1860. Terribly exciting day—State after State going for rail-splitting abolitionism and Lincoln—Black Republicans triumphant—radical Southerners equally so—conservatives thoughtful. "Where will it all end?" I asked Colonel de Russey, who had spent the evening with us. *"Mon Dieu,* who knows? Let us not spoil our digestion and our evening in contemplating it. A game of euchre will give us a better night's rest and fewer wrinkles." And so we played till twelve, when the ringing of bells announced the election *un fait accompli.*

Moved our lodging to Brown's Hotel, the headquarters of the Disunionists, and already the irrepressibles are pouring in. For the first time I hear the disunion openly avowed, and feel as much shocked as if the existence of a God were denied; but reflection and history teach me that there is nothing inherently divine in republics.

It is becoming evident that a broad line will be drawn this winter between Northerners and Southerners, even in social life. What am I to do, with so many friends on both sides? Have seriously canvassed the propriety of getting ill to avoid unpleasant *contretemps*, but with so much to be seen and heard have not the resolution to shut myself up, and have decided to act naturally and take the consequences "like a man."

December 3. Congress meets to-day. The most exciting session ever known predicted—the question of slavery in the Territories to be decided. Northern men cool, calm, and determined; Southern men vehement, passionate, and threatening. Sympathize more with the latter; cannot at all comprehend the cold-blooded policy of the former, some of whom look as if born to be the natural enemies of mankind. The President's message satisfies no one—too simple a diet.

Went to the Senate to-day with Mrs. Jefferson Davis; more pleased with her conversation than anything I heard. She is as full of feelings as of wit, and there are times when both are called into play, though I fear she has too much of the former to make her a happy woman in a revolution where she will play so prominent a part as the wife of the acknowledged Southern leader. Mr. Davis's talents and character alone give him this unenviable notoriety, as he has said very little so far, and what he has said has been marked by a temperance and moderation unusual in the Southern man. I believe he would willingly effect a compromise to-morrow were it in his power.

Mr. Douglas[1] to-day, in a clear, emphatic voice, painted the horrors of a war we are bringing on ourselves, and was equally severe on the radicals of both sides. It seems now as if we were to drift into a civil war without one helping hand to save us. . . . Every place was crowded and the ladies generally in full

---

[1] Senator Stephen A. Douglas, of Illinois.

visiting toilette. . . . We begin to feel we are to be scattered like
chaff before the wind, and we go to meet our fate in our best
bonnets and with smiling faces. If we must secede, let us do so
becomingly. There is very little outside gaiety; not one large
party so far, and our evenings are our dull times, so unlike the
Washington of other days.

2. CATHERINE PATON JONES THOMPSON

"Straws Tell Which Way the Wind Blows"

After attending school in Paris, in 1836, Catherine Jones
of Oxford, Mississippi, married Jacob Thompson, a native of
North Carolina who had come to Mississippi to practice law.
He was elected to Congress in 1839 and served until 1851.
For four years beginning with 1856, he had been Secretary
of the Interior.

Mrs. Thompson wrote the following letter to her friend
Mrs. Howell Cobb, who had returned to her Georgia home
after her husband's resignation as Secretary of the Treasury.

It was well that she could not know the answer to her
question, "What are we all coming to?"

On January 9, 1861, her husband resigned his Cabinet post,
and they went back to Mississippi. He would take an active
part in the affairs of the Confederacy, and she would divide
her time between Oxford and Richmond. After serving in
the Confederate Army and as Inspector General of the Confederacy, Jacob Thompson was sent by President Davis on a
diplomatic mission to Canada in the spring of 1864. Along
with Jefferson Davis, Clement C. Clay, and others, he was
charged with having plotted "the atrocious murder of the
late President Abraham Lincoln." A reward of $25,000 was
offered for his arrest.

Washington City, Dec. 15/60

My Dear Mrs. Cobb, . . . I did not see Gov. Cobb after you
left. Mr. Thompson went to see him every day and often invited

him to take dinner with us but he never could spare the time. His resignation created great excitement here. Mr. Thomas[2] has entered upon the discharge of his duties but I have not seen any of the family since their new laurels have fallen upon them. There is great excitement now that Genl. Cass[3] has resigned, and before I finish this letter I will see Mr. Thompson and write you the truth about it.

The same gloom and depression is still over this city—no parties, no dinners, every body looks sad—but I think we Southern people ought to be looking up, for all seems to be going well with us, but I am afraid to hollow until I am entirely out of the woods. I think if you could have heard some of the Black Republican speeches that have been made here even your devotion to this *Union would* have given away. You will read the President's proclamation for fasting and prayer on the 4th of Jan. That tells whether he sees danger or not. Miss Lane[4] and I continue *our* silence on political questions. I go to see her and the President as often as I can because I know they feel their old friends are many of them deserting them. I will do all I can to stand by them until the 4th of March, and hope that day may come quickly. . . .

Mr. Thompson has received an appointment from the Gov. of Missi. to go as Commissioner to N. Carolina, and leaves here on Monday the 17th and I am going with him; he will be absent a week or ten days and I can't stay here by myself. The President approves of his going. Mr. Lamar[5] has returned home to be a candidate for the State convention. He is very reasonable on the secession question, does not go as far as your husband

---

[2] Philip F. Thomas, of Maryland, Secretary of the Treasury *ad interim.*

[3] General Lewis Cass, of Michigan, Secretary of State.

[4] Harriet Lane, President Buchanan's orphaned niece and White House hostess.

[5] Lucius Quintus Cincinnatus Lamar was Professor of Mathematics at the University of Mississippi. He served as Confederate Commissioner to Russia in 1862.

nor mine, but he amuses me, telling me how delighted he is with his present home and position in the College and yet he can't stay there more than a month at a time. . . .

All your friends here enquire a great deal about you. The Gwins are all well and go up to the Capitol every day. I have been up twice, the galleries crowded. I have made no Senatorial calls except upon old friends. I shall not call upon or leave cards upon a single B. Republican or *Douglas*. "Straws tell which way the wind blows," and to be prepared for any emergency. I had ½ doz. packs of cards for Mr. Thompson struck off and left off the *Sec. of the Interior*, as I have no idea of his cards ever being left anywhere as *Mr. Ex. Sec.* as some of the old broken-down politicians here do. Gov. and Mrs. Floyd[6] came over to spend the evening with us last evening and I enjoyed it very much. I find I have a great deal of time to stay at home since you left, as I have no place to go to that fills up your house. I felt like some duty was left undone if I did not go to see you every day for several weeks before you left. Some company has just come in, social visitors, this bad day, and I will lay my pen aside until they are gone.

After dinner.—Mr. Thompson returned from his office after 5 o'clock and brought Mr. Ashe[7] of N. Carolina home to dine with us; he gives good accounts of the secession movement in that state, and will go with us to Raleigh on Monday. Maj. McCulloch[8] has just left, and he has the steam high up for secession and war if we can't do better. Dr. Maynard[9] (the gun man) has been here two hours trying to sell Mr. Thompson 3,000 guns, so my head is nearly crazy and my heart goes *pit-a-pat,* at any sound I hear. What are we all coming to? Where is the end

---

[6] John B. Floyd, of Virginia, was Secretary of War in Buchanan's Cabinet.

[7] William Shepperd Ashe, president of the Wilmington & Weldon Railroad.

[8] Ben McCulloch, who led the famous Texas Rangers in the Mexican War.

[9] Dr. Edward Maynard, noted dental surgeon, who invented a tape primer for guns.

of all this trouble? I trust there is a kind Providence whose hand
is directing this great revolution and it will go down to His
glory and our happiness. . . .

P.S. Mr. Thompson says it is all true. Genl. Cass has resigned
and is a miserable man.

3. SARA RICE PRYOR

"Tremendous Event"

Sara Agnes Rice Pryor, wife of Congressman Roger A.
Pryor, of Virginia, was one of the most beautiful and popular
members of Washington official society. Described as a light
brunette with soft brown hair and eyes, she wore a distinc-
tive coiffure. "She carried her head charmingly," said her
friend Mrs. Clement Clay. Born in 1830, the daughter of the
Reverend Samuel Blair Rice, of Halifax County, Virginia,
she had spent her early days at "Cedar Grove," twenty-five
miles from Richmond, with her uncle and aunt, Dr. and
Mrs. Samuel Pleasants Hargrove. Later she lived in Charlottesville.

At the age of eighteen she married Mr. Pryor. For a while he
practiced law in Charlottesville before moving to Richmond to
be editor of the Richmond *Enquirer*. He was involved and
fought in many duels; and this earned him the nickname of
"Harry Hotspur." In 1857 he founded *The South* and contributed to *The States,* newspapers of Washington, to give vent
to his strong Southern views. Mrs. Pryor and her three young
sons were with him in the Federal City when he was elected to
Congress in 1859.

Washington, D. C. Dec. 20, 1860

We were all in our places in November, setting our houses
in order, several weeks before the assembling of Congress.
Everything promised a season of unusual interest.

In Washington our social life did not begin before New
Year's Day. Among our first cards this winter was an invitation

to the marriage of Mr. Bouligny,[10] member from Louisiana, and Miss Parker, daughter of a wealthy Washington grocer. Mr. Parker's large house was to be converted into a conservatory filled with blossoming roses and lilies. Fountains were to be introduced, new effects in lighting. The presents were to be magnificent, the bridal dress gorgeous.

Upon arriving at the house I found the President seated in an arm-chair at one end of the drawing-room, and the guests ranging themselves on either side. A crimson velvet curtain was stretched across the other end of the room. Presently the curtain parted and the bridal tableau appeared in position behind it. After the ceremony the crowd waited until the President went forward to wish the bride and her husband a great deal of happiness. Everybody remained standing until Mr. Buchanan returned to his seat. I stood behind his chair and observed that he had aged much since the summer. . . .

On the day of the wedding, December 20, he stoutly denied that he was ill. . . .

The crowd in the Parker drawing-room soon thinned as the guests found their way to the rooms in which the presents were displayed. The President kept his seat, and I stood behind him as one and another came forward to greet him. Presently he looked over his shoulder and said, "Madam, do you suppose the house is on fire? I hear an unusual commotion in the hall."

"I will inquire the cause, Mr. President," I said. I went out at the nearest door, and there in the entrance hall I found Mr. Lawrence Keitt,[11] member from South Carolina, leaping in the air, shaking a paper over his head, and exclaiming, "Thank God! Oh, thank God!"

---

[10] Representative John Edward Bouligny, of Louisiana, was opposed to secession. When war came, he retired to private life, and he remained in Washington until his death, on February 20, 1864.

[11] Lawrence Massillon Keitt was mortally wounded at the battle of Cold Harbor on June 3, 1864, and died the next day in Richmond. After serving in the Confederate Congress, he raised the 20th Regiment, South Carolina Volunteers, and served as its colonel until his death.

I took hold of him and said: "Mr. Keitt, are you crazy? The President hears you, and wants to know what's the matter."

"Oh!" he cried, "South Carolina has seceded! Here's the telegram."

I returned and, bending over Mr. Buchanan's chair, said in a low voice: "It appears, Mr. President, that South Carolina has seceded from the Union. Mr. Keitt has a telegram."

He looked at me, stunned for a moment. Falling back and grasping the arms of his chair, he whispered, "Madam, might I beg you to have my carriage called?"

I met his secretary and sent him in without explanation, and myself saw that his carriage was at the door before I re-entered the room. I then found my husband, who was already cornered with Mr. Keitt, and we called our own carriage and drove to Judge Douglas's. There was no more thought of bride, bridegroom, wedding cake, or wedding breakfast.

This was the tremendous event which was to change all our lives—to give us poverty for riches, mutilation and wounds for strength and health, obscurity and degradation for honor and distinction, exile and loneliness for inherited homes and friends, pain and death for happiness and life.

4. EMILY MASON

"Were Ever Circumstances So Complicated?"

On December 26, Major Robert Anderson, in command of Fort Moultrie in South Carolina, evacuated the fort and, under cover of darkness, moved across Charleston harbor to occupy Fort Sumter. South Carolina considered Major Anderson's move a hostile act.

Congress was still in session on the last day of 1860. The major event in Washington that day was a speech defending the right of secession by Senator Judah P. Benjamin, of Louisiana, who would shortly be named Attorney General of the Confederate States of America.

Emily Mason, member of an old and distinguished Virginia family, was an interested spectator in the Capitol galleries. She was the daughter of General John Thomson Mason, who had served in the War of 1812, and Elizabeth Moir Mason, of Loudon County, Virginia. Her friend Mrs. Robert E. Lee called her "Miss Em." Her youngest brother, Stevens, was the first governor of Michigan (1836-40).

On New Year's Eve, she wrote to "R," another brother, Major Robert Mason, who was then in Virginia.

Washington, New Years Eve, '60.

I dined at Major Buell's to-day. He does not see how the States can dissolve without bloodshed. Mr. Buchanan says it may come after his day but while he is in the President's chair, his whole task shall be to prevent one drop from flowing. Poor old man I do pity him. Was ever task so difficult as his? Were ever circumstances so complicated? The times so big with events, give nothing new to-night. I met Col. Cooper[12] to-day and finding him quite excited congratulated him upon being Secretary of War. It was reported this morning that he was acting Secretary and then that General Scott was to be, but Mr. Holt[13] is the man. The Colonel was hurrying to General Scott. He said he had just had a letter from you. Do you see the N. Y. papers? The *Tribune* has an article headed "Washington, Garibaldi, and Anderson!" Poor modest Major Anderson never expected to come in such juxtaposition. They are making a great hero of him for an act which seems to me a simple natural soldierly one. Nothing but what any other officer would have done in the circumstances. Mr. Benjamin's speech to-day was considered very eloquent and his conclusion most brilliant—the galleries rang with shouts of applause, so that they had to be cleared.

---

[12] Samuel Cooper, who became Adjutant General of the Confederate Army.

[13] Joseph Holt, of Kentucky.

5. MARGARET SUMNER McLEAN

"God Grant They May Succeed"

> For absent members of her family, Mrs. McLean recorded
> in her diary what she saw and heard in the Senate on the last
> day of 1860, and what she did on the following day.

December 31. Senate again to-day. Missed the South Caro-
linians, but felt a comfortable conviction that there would be
talking enough without them. Toombs, of Georgia, was the
lion of the house, pacing up and down in front of his desk
exclaiming, "If this be treason, then I am a traitor."

A number of the officers of the army from South Carolina
have resigned. If worse comes to worst I suppose they will all
go, though they say very little about it, and it is an understood
thing that so long as they wear the uniform of the United States
they are not Secessionists, even in opinion. I have no idea what
some of our most intimate friends are going to do, and am
amused at the persistence they show in avoiding all discussion
of the subject. Such a state of affairs cannot last long.

Every one is watching with interest almost two deep for words
the actions of the Committee of Thirteen, composed of Northern and Southern men, to endeavor to effect a compromise of
some sort. God grant they may succeed! Union men say there
is little probability of it.

Mr. Jefferson Davis announced that the compromise committee could come to no terms, and it was received by that
immense audience in a silence like death. His succeeding remarks made a deep impression, and he himself was evidently
much affected. He is by far the most interesting speaker in the
Senate; his voice alone makes him one of nature's orators—so
cold and sarcastic one moment, so winning and persuasive the
next, and again rising to tones of command that carry obedience

with them. If I did not know him in private life, and did not
know his high, honorable, and chivalric nature, I could well
understand the influence he exercises; he is one of the few public
men I have ever seen who impresses me with his earnestness.

New Year's Day. A good deal of visiting, but conversation
turns on the state of the country, and we cannot help asking
ourselves and one another, "Where shall we be next year?" Some
one has said anniversaries are the tombstones of time, and I
begin to see how they can be made so. The officers of the army,
in full uniform, went as usual to pay their respects to the
President, and as they passed, with the gallant Scott at their
head, a Georgia lady said with a sigh, "How many of them will
be our enemies?"

6. JULIA DUBOSE TOOMBS

"I Have Despaired of the Union"

Julia DuBose Toombs was the wife of Senator Robert
Toombs, of Washington, Georgia. Four years after their mar-
riage in 1840, her husband was elected Representative in
Congress; in 1851, he took his seat in the United States
Senate.

Mrs. Toombs addresses herself to "Little Ellick" Stephens—
Damon to Mr. Toombs's Pythias—who long since has de-
parted for his home, "Liberty Hall," in Crawfordsville,
Georgia. Alexander H. Stephens soon will be chosen Vice-
President of the Confederate States.

Mrs. Toombs accompanied her husband to Milledgeville,
Georgia, where he was a delegate to the Secession Convention
on January 16. On January 19, Georgia seceded from the
Federal Union. So sure was Toombs that secession would not
bring war that he promised to "drink every drop of blood
spilled." Later, he would be named Secretary of State in the
provisional Confederate Cabinet.

Washington, D.C., Jan. 1st, 1861

Dear Sir: I write a few lines to you this morning to ask you what I shall do with your furniture that is in our house. I have despaired of the Union and will begin to pack up my own things today. If you can do anything you must be at it. I have given up the ship notwithstanding your old friends' opinion in a telegram of the morning papers; I mean Messrs. Douglas and Crittenden.[14]

I shall go home with Mr. Toombs when he goes to the convention.

I will take great pleasure in having your things packed and shipped or will do anything with them that you desire. You have the following articles: a carpet, bedstead, feather bed, mattress, bolster and pillows, bowl and pitcher, bureau, couch, shovel and tongs, etc. Please let me know as soon as you can what to do with them. We will send the most of our things home, for we can't get one cent for them here. I hope you are well.

7. EMILY MASON

"Madness of Coercion"

> Miss Mason reports again from the Capitol galleries. Senator Douglas, whose talk was "like thunder," died less than two months following the outbreak of war. His wife was the niece of Mrs. Rose O'Neal Greenhow, the famous Confederate spy.
>
> Senator Stephen R. Mallory, who "has just written his brother," would soon be named Secretary of the Navy of the new Confederate States.

----

[14] Senator John J. Crittenden, of Kentucky, and Stephen A. Douglas wired citizens of Atlanta on December 30, 1860: "We have hopes that the rights of the South, and of every state and section, may be protected within the Union. Don't give up the ship. Don't despair of the Republic."

Okeley, Fairfax Co., Va., Jan. 6, 1861

I came down from Washington Thursday with N. J. . . . We heard Mr. Baker's[15] speech the other day. A new star in the Republican firmament—from Oregon. A very gentlemanly looking person with bad voice, who made no sensation except amongst his own crew. He quoted old state lines from Campbell and from Webster in most emphatic manner, and spoke rather to glorify himself, I thought, than for much else, though he purported to answer Mr. Benjamin.

Mr. Douglas got up after him and I never before realized his wonderful power. The other man's talk had been child's play. This was like thunder. We heard only a part of his speech, but it was very fine. Though against the right of Secession (like the President) he showed the folly, the madness of *coercion*. "Talk of your armies and your navies in the name of the Union" he cried and showed how there might be a war of forty years duration but never *one* Sovereign State subdued, much less fifteen. He said that coercion meant law, and how carry out law where no law was recognized? In the whole state of S. Carolina is not one person who recognizes the laws of the United States. How carry out laws where is no Judge? He showed how as in our own Revolution it was first Rebellion; then Revolution; then a Government *de facto,* which, while they warred against us, was recognized by our enemies. You may declare war against a State but she cannot be coerced. Such is the language of Mr. Madison and George Mason in the debates in the Convention which adopted the Constitution. And such is the spirit of the Bill of Rights. At this time Virginia, and ever more clearly, New York and Rhode Island reserved to themselves unequivocally the right to secede; and now people deny this. It seems to me that the Constitution bears as many interpretations as the Bible itself.

---

[15] Senator Edward Dickinson Baker.

They do say in Washington that Mr. Seward will soon offer some resolutions, the spirit of which will satisfy all parties. At present there seems little prospect of amicable adjustment. Mr. Hunter,[16] and Mr. Davis of Mississippi have some plan for peaceable separation which seems very well. The 4th of March will decide I suppose.

On New Years day V. and I called on poor Mr. Buchanan, whose day is declining in darkness and gloom. Had "a happy New Year" from the President. I could not say "Amen" in faith. . . .

All the world was talking of Mr. Pugh's[17] great speech. Such an effort was never heard on that floor—you could hear the sobs in the galleries, and they say that Mr. Douglas, Mr. Davis of Mississippi, and Mr. Wigfall[18] wept like children. There was not a dry eye in the Senate. How can people withstand such appeals as these? Everybody hopes there will be a better spirit manifested when Congress meets again. Going home for the holidays will give these men an opportunity to think of what is going on and to consult with their constituents. I talked with Mr. Mallory of Florida. He says he sees no light yet but had just written his brother who is in the Navy and was very uneasy, to take no steps toward resignation but patiently bide the issue which a few months would decide.

8. MARGARET SUMNER McLEAN

"Speed the Parting Guest"

While Mrs. Eugene McLean listened to Senator Seward's long speech on January 9, the *Star of the West*, bearing men

---

[16] Senator Robert Mercer Taliaferro Hunter, of Virginia. He had served in the U.S. House of Representatives 1837-1846, and in the U.S. Senate from 1847 until he resigned in 1861. He was Secretary of State of the Confederacy from July 25, 1861, to February 18, 1862, when he became a member of the Senate.

[17] James L. Pugh, of Alabama.

[18] Senator Louis Trezevant Wigfall, of Texas.

and supplies for Fort Sumter in Charleston Harbor, was turned back by fire from a battery on Morris Island.

January 9. Mr. Seward[19] drew a crowded house to-day. We went at nine o'clock in order to get seats, and found difficulty in obtaining them even at that early hour. We spend so much time in the Senate that many of the ladies take their sewing or crocheting, and all of us who are not absolutely spiritual provide ourselves with a lunch. The gallery of the Senate is the fashionable place of reunion, and before the Senate meets we indulge in conversation—sometimes very spirited, though generally the oposing factions treat each other with great reserve—a very necessary precaution. Mr. Seward spoke for nearly four hours, and I was sorry when he took his seat, yet for the life of me do not know what he said, what he did not say, or what he meant to say; either his speech was above vulgar comprehension or he is the Talleyrand of America, as I find no one knows any more than I do, and yet every one says it was a masterly effort. He chained the attention of a promiscuous audience of all classes and of every shade of opinion for four hours; he offered no compromises; he offered no prejudices; he expressed opinions, but did not commit himself. It was like a skilful fencer who shows great adroitness and dexterity in the use of his weapons, and does not hurt his opponent, only because he has taken the precaution to use blunted foils. It may be a sleight of hand to which politicians are accustomed, but to me it is wonderful and argues great reserved strength. Why does he not exert it to save the country? The North grows more and more unyielding every day; the South more and more defiant. Is there no Curtius to close the gulf?

Went to a levee at the White House last evening. A number of ultra Southerners there and all on the best terms, apparently,

---

[19] William H. Seward, Senator from New York, would soon be Lincoln's Secretary of State.

with the Administration. Miss Lane, as usual, handsome, well-dressed, and agreeable—Mr. Buchanan politic and polite.

Mississippi secedes, and I suppose the others will follow soon, as it seems to be the policy to "speed the parting guest." The tall, handsome, and belligerent Mississippi women in ecstasies, and the children making a Fourth of July of it with firecrackers, etc. I am becoming accustomed to it.

January 11. Alabama goes out. Another *feu de joi.* A caustic old gentleman remarks that they had better save their gunpowder. It would be an economy if they would all go out together.

Johnson, of Tenn.,[20] has consumed two days in his argument against the right of secession. A Southern man and a slaveholder, he is regarded as a renegade. He is a remarkable-looking man, with a piercing eye that might, I should judge, see as far into the millstone as any other that has tried to look. At all events, his arguments seemed to me unanswerable, and I came home convinced that people had a right to be rebels, but not right to be secessionists, which is just what I have felt all the time. The question being settled, it now behooves me (taking future contingencies into consideration) to cultivate rebel proclivities.

Mr. Crittenden spoke to-day in a trembling voice and with tearful eyes, beseeching those who could to save the Union. I could not control my feelings; it was sad to see that old white-haired man, who had devoted his best years to his country find himself powerless to help it in this its extremity, but, with piteous entreaties to deaf ears and hardened hearts, exhaust himself in the vain effort to bring about a single concession. . . .

Have seen the wives of some of the United States officers at Fort Sumter. When it was decided to abandon Sullivan's Island and retire into the fort the ladies were sent over to Charleston,

---

[20] Andrew Johnson, of Tennessee.

but could find no accommodations and were obliged to come North. Not a boarding-house would receive them, and one woman frankly said that if she did she would lose all her other boarders. I cannot imagine such a state of feeling, and am quite indignant with the Southern chivalry, though they say some few of the gentlemen of Charleston were very polite and offered them rooms in their private houses; but, with the enmity openly avowed toward their husbands, they could not, of course, accept any obligations. They feel very bitter and are ready for war. In the meantime they are receiving a great deal of attention as the first martyrs.

Have moved up to Willard's Hotel and am in the full odor of Black Republican sanctity. The South "dies daily," and, if I am to believe all I hear, is in just that helpless condition which would justify any generous soul in flying to its assistance. It is a fact, however, that when the Southerners were here they held their own remarkably well, and the accounts daily received of forts surrendered do not seem to argue weakness in anything but the United States army. . . . Am entirely disheartened, and have lost all the hope and enthusiasm with which I commenced the winter.

States going out and Mr. Lincoln coming in are the only topics of the day; and if the first is beginning to be looked upon as a matter of course, the latter is waited for with impatience by all parties. . . . I should like to place my platform on Mason and Dixon's line, but, not being a "solo" or a prima donna, am not considered entitled to one. . . .

9. VIRGINIA TUNSTALL CLAY

"The Saddest Day of My Life"

Virginia Caroline Tunstall, daughter of Dr. Peyton Randolph and Anne Arrington Tunstall, was born in North Carolina. After her mother died, the child was sent to Alabama to live with her uncle, Judge Henry W. Collier. She attended private schools at Tuscaloosa and at Nashville, Tennessee. In 1845, at the age of twenty, she married the Honorable Clement C. Clay, of Huntsville, Alabama. Following his service in the House of Representatives, in 1853, he was elected to the United States Senate. Mrs. Clay was a most popular Washington hostess; a contemporary called her "one of the brightest ornaments in Washington society."

Surely the saddest day of my life—January 21, 1861—when, . . . I saw my husband take his portfolio under his arm and leave the United States Senate Chamber in company with other no less earnest Southern Senators. For weeks the pretense of amity between parties had ceased, and social formalities no longer concealed the gaping chasm that divided them. When the members of each met, save for a glare of defiance or contempt, each ignored the other, or, if they spoke, it was by way of a taunt or a challenge. Every sentence uttered in Senate or House was full of hot feeling born of many wrongs and long-sustained struggle. For weeks, men would not leave their seats by day or by night, lest they might lose their votes on the vital questions of the times. At the elbows of Senators, drowsy with long vigils, pages stood, ready to waken them at the calling of the roll.

Not a Southern woman but felt, with her husband, the stress of that session, the sting of the wrongs the Southern faction of that great body was struggling to right. For forty years the North and the South had striven for the balance of power, and the admission of each new State was become the subject of bitter contention. There was, on the part of the North, a palpable envy of the hold the South had retained so long upon the Federal City, whether in politics or society, and the resolution to quell us, by physical force, was everywhere obvious. The face of the city was lowering, and some of the North agreed with us of the South that a nation's suicide was about to be precipitated. . . .

The incertitude of President Buchanan was alarming; but the courage of our people to enter upon what they knew must be a defense of everything they held dear in State and family institution rose higher and higher to meet each advancing danger.

The seizure by South Carolina of United States forts that lay, a menace, within her very doorway, acted like a spur upon the courage of the South. . . .

In those days men eyed each other warily and spoke guardedly, save to the most tried and proved friend. One evening early in 1861, Commander Semmes,[21] U.S.N., called upon us, and happened to arrive just as another naval officer was announced. The surprise that spread over the faces of our visitors when they beheld each other was great, but Senator Clay's and my own was greater. Neither of the officers appeared to be at ease, yet for hours neither seemed to desire to relieve the situation by taking his departure. Midnight had arrived ere our now forgotten guest rose and bade us "good night." Then Commander Semmes hastened to unbosom himself. He had resolved to out-sit the other gentleman if it took all night.

"As my Senator, Mr. Clay," he said, "I want to report to you my decision on an important matter. I have resolved to hand in my resignation to the United States Government, and tender my services to that of the Confederate States. I don't know what the intention of my brother officer is, but I could take no risk with him," he added. Many a scene as secret, as grave, and as "treasonable," took place in those last lowering weeks. . . .

To the last, alas! too few of our people realized that war was inevitable. . . .

Personally I knew of but one man whose ferocity led him to collect and secrete weapons of warfare. He was Edmund Ruffin,[22] of Virginia, with whom I entered into collusion. For months my

---

[21] Raphael Semmes, later the gallant captain of the famous *Alabama*.

[22] Agriculturist and publisher of Hanover County, Virginia. As a private soldier, he fired the shot that blocked the bridge over Cub Run at First Manassas.

parlour was made an arsenal for the storing of a dozen lengthy
spears. They were handsome weapons, made, I suspect, for some
decorative purpose, but I never knew their origin nor learned
of their destination. On them were engraved these revolutionary
words:

"Out of this nettle, danger, we pluck the flower of safety."

As Senator Clay's unequivocal position as a Southern man
was everywhere understood, our parlours were frequently the
gathering-place of statesmen from our own section and such
others as were friendly to our people and believed in our right
to defend the principles we had maintained since the administration of the first President of the United States. . . . Often the
"dread arms" deposited by Mr. Ruffin proved a subject of con-
jecture and mirth, which closed some weightier conversation.
As the day drew near, however, for the agreed upon withdrawal
of our Senators, the tension under which all laboured made jests
impossible, and keyed every heart to the utmost solemnity.

Monday, January 21st, was the day privately agreed upon
by a number of Senators for their public declaration of secession; but, as an example of the uncertainty which hobbled our
men, until within a day or two of the appointed time several
still awaited the instructions from their States by which their
final act must be governed. . . .

And now the morning dawned of what all knew would be a
day of awful import. I accompanied my husband to the Senate,
and everywhere the greeting or gaze of absorbed, unrecognizing
men and women was serious and full of trouble. The galleries
of the Senate, which hold, it is estimated, one thousand people,
were packed densely, principally with women, who, trembling
with excitement, awaited the denouement of the day. As, one
by one, Senators David Yulee,[23] Stephen R. Mallory, Clement C.
Clay, Benjamin Fitzpatrick,[24] and Jefferson Davis rose, the emo-

[23] Of Florida.
[24] Of Alabama.

tion of their brother Senators and of us in the galleries increased; and, when I heard the voice of my husband, steady and clear, notwithstanding his illness, declare in that Council Chamber, "Mr. President, I rise to announce that the people of Alabama have adopted an ordinance whereby they withdraw from the Union, formed under a compact styled the United States, resume the powers delegated to it, and assume their separate station as a sovereign and independent people," it seemed as if the blood within me congealed.

As each Senator, speaking for his State, concluded his solemn renunciation of allegiance to the United States, women grew hysterical and waved their handkerchiefs, encouraging them with cries of sympathy and admiration. Men wept and embraced each other mournfully. At times the murmurs among the onlookers grew so deep that the Sergeant-at-Arms was ordered to clear the galleries; and, as each speaker took up his portfolio and gravely left the Senate Chamber, sympathetic shouts rang from the assemblage above. Scarcely a member of that Senatorial body but was pale with the terrible significance of the hour. . . .

When Senator Clay concluded his speech, many of his colleagues, among them several from Republican ranks, came forward to shake hands with him. For months his illness had been a theme of public regret and apprehension among our friends. . . .

From the hour of this exodus of Senators from the official body, all Washington seemed to change. . . . Carriages and messengers dashed through the streets excitedly. Farewells were to be spoken, and many, we knew, would be final. Vehicles lumbered on their way to wharf or station filled with the baggage of departing Senators and Members. The brows of hotel-keepers darkened with misgivings, for the disappearance from the Federal City of the families of Congressional representatives from the fifteen slave-holding States made a terrible thinning out of its population. . . .

10. VARINA HOWELL DAVIS

"A Final Adieu"

Varina Howell Davis, wife of Senator Jefferson Davis, of "Brierfield" plantation, Mississippi, was born near Natchez, May 7, 1826. Her father was William Burr Howell, of New Jersey, who had settled in Mississippi some years earlier. Her mother was Margaret Louise Kempe, of Virginia.

Her husband was elected to Congress in 1845, the year of their marriage, and, thereafter, Varina led a busy life. Colonel Davis served in the Mexican campaigns, then became a Senator, a Cabinet member (he was Secretary of War under President Pierce), and, once again, a Senator in 1857. Their three children—Maggie, aged six; Jeff, Jr., aged three; and baby Joe—were familiar figures and great pets in Washington. The two boys had been born in the capital, and her eldest son, Samuel, was buried there.

A point of great pride to Mrs. Davis was near-by Cabin John Bridge, built by her husband during his term as Secretary of War. This bridge, with a span of 220 feet, was the longest in the world until 1903. The name of Jefferson Davis was deeply cut in the solid granite blocks; during the war it was erased.

Early in the New Year, it was reported from Washington that when Mrs. Davis visited the White House, she wore a badge inscribed "Jeff Davis No Seceder."

Mr. Davis had been ill for more than a week, and our medical attendant thought him physically unable to make his farewell to the Senate. On the morning of the day he was to address his colleagues, the crowd began to move toward the Senate Chamber as early as seven o'clock. By nine there was hardly standing room within the galleries or in the passway behind the forum. The Senators' cloak-room was crowded to excess, and the bright faces of the ladies were assembled together like a mosaic of flowers in the doorway. The sofas and the passways were full, and ladies sat on the floor against the wall where they could not find seats. There brooded over this immense crowd a palpitating, expectant silence which was afterward remarked as very unusual. I sent a servant at seven o'clock, who, with a friend of hers, kept my seat and that of my companion, until the morning hour had expired. The gallery of the reporters was occupied by the Diplomatic Corps and their respective families.

Mr. Davis told me that he had great difficulty in reaching his seat, as the ladies, of course, could not be crowded, and each one feared that the other would encroach on her scanty bit of room if an inch was yielded. Curiosity and the expectation of an intellectual feast seemed to be the prevailing feeling, and I, who had come from a sleepless night, all through the watches of which war and its attendants, famine and bloodshed, had been predicted in despairing accents, looked on this festive crowd and wondered if they saw beyond the cold exterior of the orator his deep depression, his desire for reconciliation, and his overcoming love for the Union in whose cause he had bled, and to maintain which he was ready to sacrifice all but liberty and equality. We felt blood in the air, and mourned in secret over the severance of tender ties both of relationship and friendship; but a cloud covered all the rest, and our hearts were "exceeding sorrowful even unto death"; we could even guess at the end.

Mr. Davis, graceful, grave, and deliberate, amid profound silence, arose to address the Senate for the last time as a member of that body. Every eye was turned upon him, fearful of missing one word. He glanced over the Senate with the reluctant look, the dying cast, on those upon whom they gaze for the last time. His voice was at first low and faltering, but soon it rang out melodiously clear, like a silver trumpet, to the extremest verge of the assembly. The music of his voice prevented the great volume of sound from jarring upon the ears of his audience. Unshed tears were in it, and a plea for peace permeated every tone. Every graceful gesture seemed to invite to brotherly love.

His manner suggested that of one who parts from his family, because even death were better than estrangement.

He was listened to in profound silence, broken only by repeated applause, which his face revealed he deprecated before the Vice-President called the audience to order. The orator was too grief-stricken and too terribly in earnest to think of the impression he might create upon others. Had he been bending over his bleeding father, needlessly slain by his countrymen, he could not have been more pathetic or inconsolable.

Not his wife alone, but all who sat spellbound before him knew how genuine was his grief, and entered into the spirit of his loving appeal.

With a plea for the indulgence of his colleagues who, in debate he might, in all the past years of heated and strenuous endeavors, have offended, he offered the hand of fellowship to each of them who might be willing to accept it.

There was scarcely a dry eye in the multitude as he took his seat. . . .

Inexpressibly sad he left the chamber, with but faint hope; and that night I heard the often reiterated prayer, "May God have us in His holy keeping, and grant that before it is too late peaceful councils may prevail."

Mr. Davis remained a week in Washington. A part of the time he was ill and confined to his bed. To him came Commodore Shubrick,[25] Captain Semmes, General Floyd,[26] Colonel Chesnut,[27] Senator C. C. Clay, and others too numerous to mention, as Southern men anxious about the fate of their country. I did not hear the conversations or know the purport of them from my husband, but was pained to see the deep depression under which he labored. The only time he ever seemed cheerful was when he

[25] William B. Shubrick, to whom James Fenimore Cooper dedicated *The Pilot* and *The Red Rover*.

[26] John Buchanan Floyd, of Virginia, Secretary of War.

[27] Senator James Chesnut, of South Carolina.

spoke of his hope that the moderation of the President and his advisers would restrain the ardor of the anti-slavery men. "If they will give me time," he said, "all is not lost; violence on one side and extreme measures of wrong on the other now, will dissolve the Union." And by telegrams and letters to every Southern State he endeavored to postpone their action.

To wrench oneself from the ties of fifteen years is a most distressing effort. Our friends had entered into our joys and sorrows with unfailing sympathy. We had shared their anxieties and seen their children grow from infancy to adolescence. To bid them farewell, perhaps to meet in the near future with a "great gulf between us," was "death in life." Mr. Davis was resigning an office which, of all others, was the most congenial to his taste, and conducive to the increase of his reputation. He anticipated a long and exhausting war, and knew that his property in cotton planting would be utterly destroyed in the course of the impending conflict. Deeply depressed and supremely anxious, he made his preparations to go home.

We left Washington "exceeding sorrowful," and took our three little children with us.

11. JULIA GARDINER TYLER

"This Peace Convention"

It had been more than sixteen years since Julia Gardiner Tyler, the wife of former President John Tyler, had presided as the youngest "First Lady" in White House history. She was born in 1820 on Gardiner's Island, New York, the daughter of the Honorable David and Juliana McLachlin Gardiner. As a young lady, she had attended Madame Chegary's boarding school in New York and had traveled in Europe. On June 26, 1844, she married the President. Upon leaving the White House in March 1845, the Tylers retired to Sherwood Forest, his estate on the James River, some thirty-five miles from Richmond.

The Peace Convention, of which Mr. Tyler was president, met in Washington on February 4. Twenty-one states were represented. Delegates debated and made propositions and counterpropositions.

Mrs. Tyler, who accompanied her husband to Washington, wrote the following letters to her mother in New York. It is interesting to note that she refers to her husband as "the President."

Brown's Hotel, Washington, D. C., Feb. 3, 1861

I hasten to write you this evening of my arrival, with the President, Alex, baby and Fanny. . . . I had several reasons for coming, apart from such enjoyments as you think I shall be disappointed in finding. To be on hand at such a trying and exciting time to the President, and observe and listen to the doings of the convention, has for me the most intense interest. Perhaps I am here during the last days of the Republic. Everything in the political world is calculated to interest me, and I do not expect or desire gay entertainments under such circumstances as exist. A note has just been handed in to a dinner at Douglas' on Tuesday. I don't know that we shall accept. I was really in hopes to find you here on our arrival, and am really sorry to have hoped in vain. I sent this evening to enquire for a box at the express office, but it is not open to-day. I must send in the morning; peradventure you may have forwarded one.

The President has been surrounded with visitors from the moment he could appear to them, after refreshing himself with clean linen, etc. All the Virginia delegation, and a number of others, have just left, and he has retired upon a dose of *hydrargum,* quite tired out with the fatigue of the day; but he is in a stronger condition to bear up than for many a day, and looks well. They are all looking to him in the settlement of the vexed question. His superiority over everybody else is felt and admitted by all.

It would interest you to see how deferentially they gather around him. They will make him President of the Convention, I presume, from what I hear; but whether he will accept or not, is a question which his feelings at the time will determine. All of the South or border States will enter upon the deliberations with very little expectation of saving the Union, I think—there seems such a fixed determination to do mischief on the part of the Black Republicans. General Scott's absurd and high-handed course here in Washington is very much condemned. The rumor to-day is afloat that he is collecting there troops to overawe Virginia and Maryland. If the President concludes so, upon observation, I think he will recommend the Governor of Virginia to send five thousand troops at once to Alexandria to stand on the defensive side, and overawe General Scott's menacing attitude; but this is *entre nous,* and a "state secret."

We are very handsomely accommodated here—private parlors, etc. I left the children at home well,[28] and as you may suppose, everybody charged concerning them. . . .

The President's centre-table is loaded with correspondence from every quarter. There seems to be a general looking to him by those anxious to save the Union. I wish it might be possible for him to succeed in overcoming all obstacles. They all say, if through him it cannot be accomplished, it could not through any one else. Mr. Rives[29] remarked this evening that it was admitted his influence in the country at this time is in advance of all others. Mr. Barringer,[30] of North Carolina, said to me to-day in the cars: "President Tyler has had the great happiness accorded him of living to see himself fully appreciated. All

---

[28] Mrs. Tyler was at that time the mother of seven children; baby Pearl had been born on June 20, 1860.

[29] William Cabell Rives, member of the Confederate Congress, former U.S. Senator from Virginia and Minister to France. He had been a classmate of Tyler at William and Mary and was a lifelong friend.

[30] Daniel Moreau Barringer, of Raleigh, North Carolina, former Congressman and Minister to Spain.

party feelings have faded away, and his old enemies are among
his warmest friends."

I could tell you of many interesting incidents, but I should
never get to the end of them on paper. I wonder if I shall meet
Mr. Seward, and how I shall be able to treat him. He approached
the President in the Senate Chamber to shake hands, but it was
done with a timidity he could not disguise. . . . Good night.
Write to me here.

Brown's Hotel, February 4, 1861

My Dear Mamma: I hastily write you a few lines before
retiring. The box by express came safely to hand this morning.
If I have occasion I will wear the articles mentioned in it. . . .
I have had, as well as the President, a perfect levee all day, and
am so tired that I must go to bed to be in good condition for
a continuation to-morrow. You ought to hear all the compli-
ments that are *heaped* upon me. Of course I haven't changed
a *bit*, except to improve, etc., etc.

But the President is the great centre of attraction. Everybody
says he is looked to to save the Union. Mr. Crittenden told me
to-night that he had great hopes through him. Gov. Morehead[31]
went off in a strain of eloquence, while in conversation with me,
upon the immortality he would achieve for himself if he (the
President) could bring all the discordant elements together.
They met to-day, but only to appoint committees for the organ-
ization of the Convention, and then adjourned.

The President has received a most important dispatch this
evening from Montgomery, Ala. The Convention there has
adjourned over to await the action and result of *this* meeting.
This shows a desire to conciliate and do what is right up to the
last moment.

[31] Charles Slaughter Morehead, of Kentucky. He was arrested in September 1861 and imprisoned without trial at Fort Lafayette in New York
Harbor.

. . . Mrs. Yulee and Mrs. Evans have been with me this evening, also many others whom you would not know. . . . Mrs. Clay, of Alabama, described to me the withdrawing scene in the Senate to-day of the Louisiana senators. She says Mr. Benjamin's speech was perfectly *thrilling*—full of feeling and eloquence. . . . How I wish you were here. . . .

In haste. Good night. With love to all.

The President is quite bright, bearing up wonderfully and looking remarkably well.

12. EMILY MASON

"Soldiers in Every Ward"

> Before joining her sister, Mrs. I. S. Rowland, in Alexandria, Virginia, Miss Mason takes a worried last look at Washington.

Washington, Feb. 4th, 1861

. . . The city looks very belligerent. The light artillery with big guns are daily dragged up and down the Avenue to strike terror to the hearts of the evil-planners. Soldiers are quartered in every ward. In one large building before which a sentinel tramps with fixed bayonet, and where soldiers' heads peer from door and window was a sign on the door "Collegiate Institute for Young Ladies." Gen'l Scott goes round with a body-guard, afraid of assassination.

13. JULIA GARDINER TYLER

"All Is Suspense"

> On February 18, while President Davis was being inaugurated in Montgomery, Letitia Tyler, daughter of John Tyler's son, Colonel Robert Tyler, hoisted the Confederate flag.
> Mr. Tyler still hoped for peace, but when the resolutions of the Convention were presented to Congress on February 27,

they were rejected. He returned to Richmond. Mrs. Tyler, in
a whirl of excitement, wrote a last letter to her mother before
leaving the Federal capital.

Brown's Hotel, Washington, February 13, 1861

I have a moment to myself just before tea, and I may have
time to write you in haste something of the doings here. Since I
last wrote, I have not been allowed a moment's leisure. When
within the hotel it has been an incessant stream of company, and
then I have had visits to return, the Capitol to visit, etc., etc.

Last night I attended, with the President, the party of Senator
Douglas, and I met in the throng my old friend, Mrs. Dixon,
who, by the way, looked so well that the President thought her
the handsomest person in the room. She had early called, but
I was out, as was the case with her when I called. She was,
of course, charmed to meet me again. We were all the time surrounded, and had greetings from old, and introductions to
new acquaintances without number. People turned up, and
recalled themselves to me that I certainly never expected to have
met again. I saw and shook hands with two Messrs. Griswold.
Mr. Bancroft[32] (the historian) claimed relationship with me
through the Chandlers, who married a Miss Gardiner, of Gardiner's Island. I paraded the rooms with the handsomest man
here, Governor Morehead, of Kentucky—one of the best like-
nesses of Papa you ever saw in appearance, voice, laugh, and
manner. I suppose I may conclude that I looked quite well.

No attempts at entertainments have succeeded before, I was
told, this winter, and to the hopes that are placed upon the
efforts of this Peace Convention is to be attributed the success
of this. People are catching at straws as a relief to their pressing
anxieties, and look to the Peace Commissioners as if they possessed some divine power to restore order and harmony. Here
you can realize more than any where else the distracted state
of the country. In the Peace Conference a committee are en-

---

[32] George Bancroft, who had been U. S. Minister to Great Britain.

gaged (one from each State) in the preparation of a plan of adjustment, and when they report, which will be on Friday, the end I suppose can be foreseen. In the meantime all is suspense, from the President down. The New York and Massachusetts delegation will no doubt perform all the mischief they can, and, it may be, will defeat this patriotic effort at pacification. But whether it succeeds or not, Virginia will have sustained her reputation, and in the latter event will retire with dignity from the field to join without loss of time her more Southern sisters; the rest of the slave Border States will follow her lead, and very likely she will be able to draw off, which would be glorious, a couple of Northern States. It is to be hoped that this state of suspense, which is bringing disaster to trade everywhere, will soon be removed in one way or another.

The President has hundreds of letters. . . .

Mr. Buchanan (the President) spent the evening in our parlor evening before last. I suppose it is the first visit he has paid since being the nation's chief. He first wrote the President a letter of gratitude for the relief he had afforded him in probably preventing, through his influence at Charleston, the attack on Fort Sumter. Miss Lane and Miss Ellis called upon me yesterday. If the President is detained here indefinitely, I shall run home. I want to be with my children. Probably I shall go on Friday, unless I hear from home in the meantime to my satisfaction. . . . I must conclude. I have so much to say of persons and events, and no time to say it in. . . . With love to all.

14. MARGARET SUMNER McLEAN

"Abraham Lincoln Is Here"

The McLeans had moved to Willard's Hotel in January and were still guests there when the President-elect arrived before daylight on February 23. Mrs. Lincoln and her three sons arrived on the following day. Of course, everyone in the hotel was curious about the new guests.

February 23, 1861.   All Washington in a ferment about the unexpected arrival of the President-elect—Abraham Lincoln. His movements since leaving his home in Springfield, Illinois, have been regularly reported, and by last advice he was in Baltimore to remain for the night, and arrive here to-morrow; but early this morning it was whispered that he was in the house, and by midday all kinds of stories were afloat. Infernal machines with Southern sympathies, plug-uglies, etc., etc.—altogether a state of affairs which, if we may believe Dame Rumor with her hundred tongues, rendered a Scotch cap and military cloak necessary disguises. Be that as it may, he is here and I have seen him! A tall, thin man with black hair and earnest eyes, not at all a handsome face, but one that inspires confidence and justifies the sobriquet of "Honest Old Abe." . . . I have heard a mob was feared in Baltimore, and the advisors of Mr. Lincoln, or those whose advice he took, deemed it wiser to avoid all occasion for trouble before he should be fairly inaugurated. . . .

[*February 25.*] Mrs. Lincoln arrived yesterday—one day after her husband—and again we have rumors of some disgraceful scenes during her stay in Baltimore. It is said she found it difficult to get to the depot, and again it is said she expressed her determination to go there at all hazards. If war on women is inaugurated at this early stage, what is to become of us? One of the large parlors with a suite of rooms adjoining has been appropriated to the use of Mr. Lincoln and family, and already a stream of people meander thither at all hours of the day. About eight in the evening it becomes a rushing torrent carrying everything before it. In other words, Mr. and Mrs. Lincoln receive every evening from eight to ten, and during those hours it is impossible to pass through the main hall; accordingly, the knowing ones take a cup of tea in order to secure good seats, favorable as well for making observations as for hearing those of others. . . .

15. VIRGINIA TUNSTALL CLAY
"The End Has Come"

> Many years after the war, Jefferson Davis said of the Peace
> Conference, "The plan was treated by the majority with the
> contemptuous indifference shown to every other movement
> for conciliation." The Convention adjourned on February 27,
> and John Tyler left Washington. Soon the Clays were on their
> way home to Alabama.

My husband was exceedingly depressed at the futility of the
Peace Commission, for he foresaw that the impending conflict
would be bloody and ruinous. One incident that followed the
dissolution of that body impressed itself ineradicably upon my
mind. Just after its close ex-President Tyler came to our home.
He was now an old man and very attenuated. He was completely undone at the failure of the Peace men, and tears
trickled down his cheeks as he said to Senator Clay, with in-
describable sadness, "Clay, the end has come!"

16. MARGARET SUMNER McLEAN
"We Leave for Richmond"

> Mrs. McLean closes her Washington diary with an account
> of Lincoln's inauguration and the weeks following.
> After nineteen years as an officer in the United States Army,
> her husband was about to resign. Her father would remain in
> the Army; so would two of her brothers. A brother-in-law,
> Armistead Long, of Virginia, would serve in the Confederate
> forces.
> On April 22, the McLeans left Washington, their home since
> 1850. They traveled south toward Richmond. "I have not
> dared to think of those nearer and dearer ones I am leaving
> behind," Mrs. McLean wrote.

The fourth of March, 1861, has seen Mr. Lincoln successfully installed as President of the United States, despite all predictions to the contrary. For the first time in the history of the United States it has been found necessary to conduct the President-elect to the Capitol surrounded by bayonets, and with loaded cannon at different points on the route. . . . From early in the morning the tramp of the troops could be heard, and dashing aids in showy uniforms seen urging horses almost to full speed and looking as if the fate . . . of the universe depended on their individual efforts. By nine the street in front of Willard's Hotel was lined with troops as far as the eye could see, and there they remained under arms until Mr. Lincoln appeared, leaning on the arm of Mr. Buchanan, who had previously driven down the avenue in his own carriage unattended. As soon as Mr. Lincoln stepped into the carriage that was to convey him to the Capitol, the troops presented arms, the band struck up "Dixie," and the sun which had been under a light cloud all the morning, shone with undiminished splendor, as if nothing should be wanting to give effect to the moment. It was a scene never to be forgotten. . . . As the carriage which might be said to contain the destiny of the United States, disappeared, the troops filed after it, followed by an immense throng of people of all ages and both sexes eagerly hurrying to the Capitol, where a platform had been erected outside of the building, from which Mr. Lincoln, after taking the oath of office as President of the United States, addressed them. I was not near enough to hear what he said, but on that sea of faces turned toward him I could read every variety of expression from exultation to despair, and felt long before I knew positively that there was no hope for the South. . . .

The Inauguration Ball. The dullest of all balls—scarcely a familiar face to be seen. The *haut ton* did not come out, because "the Lincolns are not yet the fashion." The strangers who patronized the affair tried to make the most of it, but the room, or tent, was arranged with so little taste and was so badly lighted that it required a brilliant imagination to fancy enjoyment in such a scene. Mr. Douglas opened the ball with Mrs. Lincoln, who looked extremely well in a light-blue "moiré," but did not seem to be in good spirits—it is said she remarked that it had been the most unhappy day of her life.

The Cabinet has been appointed, and the extreme radicals carry the day, which means war, say the prophets. Our prophets look gloomy enough; in the meanwhile we laugh and jest as if Rome were not burning. . . . It is well we can laugh if it is only to save our tears, which are ready to flow, as each hour develops the new policy. . . .

April 14. Fort Sumter has surrendered after three days' continued firing, and no one killed. War loses its horrors upon a nearer view, and we can read the heroic incidents of the attack and defense with minds at ease as to the fate of our friends on both sides.

Mr. Lincoln calls out seventy-five thousand troops to crush the rebellion. . . . Strange, strange, strange how we have accustomed ourselves to the thought, and accept the dissolution of the Union as a natural consequence! Whom have we to blame for bringing us to this state of discipline? Wherever the fault lies, I do not envy them their feelings in this hour, and fear both sections will atone in mourning and ashes for the crime.

It is difficult to realize all this, is it not? And to believe that our native land has been sacrificed on the altar of faction—does it not seem as if the whole country was an insane asylum for the exclusive benefit of the two classes of monomaniacs, abolitionists and secessionists? However, as my lot is cast with the latter, it will be wise in me to follow the stream without asking whence it cometh or whither it goeth.

Eugene resigned from the United States Army on Monday last, with many regrets, but his feelings are with the South, and, now that the difficulties have passed beyond State limits and assumed a sectional character in which the whole South is arrayed against the whole North, he is determined to act upon their dictates, deeming it dishonorable to remain in a service to which he could not give a cordial support. I believe he sacrifices his interests, but I can entirely sympathize in this sort of self-immolation, and, indeed, after all I have seen and heard this past winter it is refreshing to meet now and then a man capable of a generous sacrifice, and I must do the officers of the Army who have resigned this justice. They all believe they are leaving the stronger for the weaker side, and speak of old associations and broken ties with regret and sadness that will never be appreciated by those who forced this issue upon them—and, without having had anything to do with bringing about this state of affairs; it is very evident they will be the first victims.

April 22. We left Washington this afternoon, and, though I did not trust myself to bid some of my oldest friends farewell, it has been a most trying day to me, while I have not dared to think of those nearer and dearer ones I am leaving behind. As for the present, imagine me in a small room at the Mansion House, Alexandria, having passed the evening in the parlor and in Mrs. Johnston's room.[33] The General resigned to-day. The parlor was filled with officers of the navy and their families, all in a high state of excitement, evidently put on to cover deeper feelings. One poor little woman with five children could not conceal her apprehensions and anxiety for the future, and was rallied by the others upon a want of proper spirit. I sympathized with her, but was prudent enough to forbear any expression of it, feeling that in strict justice I ought to expend all that sort of sentiment on

---

[33] Mrs. Joseph E. Johnston, who was born Lydia McLane, of Delaware. Her father was Louis McLane, who had served in both houses of Congress, as minister to England, and as Secretary of State in Jackson's Cabinet. In 1834 he had brought his family to Baltimore when he became president of the Baltimore and Ohio Railroad.

General Joseph E. Johnston was a Virginian and 1829 graduate of West Point.

myself, as I fear my antecedents will not procure me a great deal of consideration—in Confederate circles.

Mrs. Johnston is sick and in low spirits; she feels the parting from old friends and, I imagine, does not look on the future with a very bright eye, though she is too politic to say so; but we sometimes instinctively feel what others think. At all events, her quiet room was a relief after the noisy parlor, and I remained there until a few minutes since.

To-morrow we leave for Richmond.

I

GAY CAPITAL

May—December 1861

On April 24, Virginia entered into a military alliance with the Confederate States, and, on April 27, she invited the Provisional Government, about to meet in Montgomery, to make Richmond the seat of government.

While the newspapers of the Confederate States hailed the selection of Richmond as the new capital, the Northern press began to urge its capture. Said the New York *Tribune*, "If the men in Washington are ready to do their duty, let them see to it that the Stars and Stripes fly over Richmond before the twentieth of July. The Nation's war cry is 'Forward to Richmond. Forward to Richmond!' The Rebel Congress must not be allowed to meet there on the twentieth of July."

General Winfield Scott, a native of Virginia, and chief of the Northern army, promised "himself and friends" to dine in Richmond on July 4.

Soon, ancient and quiet Richmond was a changed city. Its population of 37,000 was doubled. "When the high price of every necessary is considered, it appears strange that the city should be so crowded," an anonymous visitor commented. "The city, however, knew no interruption to the stream of its floating population, and balls, parties and theatres made a merry world of it; and Frenchmen say, it was Paris in miniature."

The social life of the Confederate capital centered around Mrs. Jefferson Davis, the First Lady. Also playing an important part were the ladies of the Provisional Cabinet: Mrs. Angela Moreno Mallory, of Florida, wife of the Secretary of the Navy; Mary Wilkinson Memminger, of Charleston, South Carolina, wife of Christopher Gustavus Memminger, Secretary of the Treasury; Eliza Dickson Pickett Walker, of Alabama, wife of Leroy Pope Walker, Secretary of War; Mrs. Toombs, of Georgia, wife of the Secretary of State; and Edwina Moss Helms Reagan, of Texas, wife of John Henninger Reagan, Postmaster-General. Natalie de St. Martin Benjamin, of Louisiana, wife of the Attorney General, was in Paris. Mary Evelina Dandridge Hunter, of Virginia, joined the ladies of the Cabinet when her husband succeeded Toombs as Secretary of State on July 24, 1861. When Thomas Bragg, of North Carolina, became Attorney General in November 1861, his wife, Isabella Cuthbert Bragg, accompanied him to the new capital.

Hospitable old Richmond welcomed the wives, mothers and daughters of the military and government officials, and all the volunteer nurses, office workers, and refugees who thronged the city.

These women speak from Richmond as war arrives—the war that "was to change all our lives," as Mrs. Pryor would write.

1. VARINA HOWELL DAVIS

"Richmond Was One Great Camp"

From the "flowery kingdom" of Montgomery, Mrs. Davis arrived in Richmond on a pleasant day in May. With her were her three little children and her young sister, Margaret Howell, who became a great favorite in official circles.

Naturally, everyone was interested in the President's wife; she was the subject of many encomiums. "She is a lady of great good sense and of much more than ordinary cultivation," said General Josiah Gorgas, Chief of Ordnance. "In society she was bright and witty," said Midshipman James Morris Morgan, of Louisiana. "She was politician and diplomat in one, where necessity demanded. She was naturally a frank though not a blunt woman, and her bent was to kindliness and charity," commented Thomas Cooper de Leon, the journalist. Her hus-

band, the President, once remarked, "She is a lady who comforts crying boys."

From her Virginia-born mother, Margaret Louise Kempe
Howell, Mrs. Davis had inherited a love and respect for the
traditions and charms of the state. The Kempes had owned
plantations where the First Battle of Manassas would soon be
fought.

On May 20, 1861, the Congress resolved that the seat of Government of the Confederate States should be transferred from
Montgomery to Richmond, and that it should adjourn to meet
there on July 20th. It had already become evident that Virginia
would be the battle-ground of the coming struggle, and it was
desirable, therefore, that the Confederate Government should
have its headquarters in that State.

Anxiety and unremitting labor had prostrated President
Davis; and, when he left Montgomery, it was upon his bed. His
mails were heavy with warnings of an attempt at assassination;
therefore it was a source of relief to us to know he had gone to
Virginia. A few days before he had seen a man heavily armed
peering into his room at our residence; he accosted him, but the
man jumped over a fence and ran out of sight. He went on, accompanied only by his cabinet and staff, and in advance of the
rest of the family. . .

Within a week, the family followed by the ordinary train. The
country was alive with soldiers—men in butternut trousers with
gray homespun coats and epaulets of yellow cotton fringe. Several companies of soldiers waiting for transportation gave us
very sweet serenades at the different stations.

We reached Richmond in the morning, and the President met
us in a carriage and four, sent down for our use by the citizens
until our own carriage and horses came. This equipage was a
trial to us, and as soon as possible we reduced our establishment
to a carriage and pair. We were conducted to the Spotswood
Hotel as guests of the city, until the house intended for the resi-

dence of the Chief Executive could be finished. In the hotel we were domiciled with the cabinet and the aids, besides a number of ladies and gentlemen. . . .

Richmond was one great camp—men hurried to and fro and without uniforms and arms, with that fixed look upon their faces that they acquire when confronted with danger and the necessity for supreme effort.

Upon the President's arrival in Richmond he found General R. E. Lee in command of the army of Virginia, with the rank of Major-General.

Many troops had been sent from other States of the Confederacy to the aid of Virginia, and the forces there assembled were divided into three armies: one, under command of General J. E. Johnston, at Harper's Ferry, covering the valley of the Shenandoah; another under General P. G. T. Beauregard, at Manassas, covering the direct approach from Washington to Richmond; and the third, under Generals Huger[1] and Magruder,[2] at Norfolk and in the Peninsula between the James and York Rivers, covering the approach from the seaboard.

Each of the three were confronted by forces greatly superior to their own, and it was doubtful which would first be the object of attack.

2. CHARLOTTE CROSS WIGFALL

"I Can Scarcely Realize That We Are at War"

Charlotte Maria Cross Wigfall was the wife of the former United States Senator from Texas. The Wigfalls had resided in South Carolina before they settled in Marshall, Texas. When they left Washington earlier in the year, their two daughters—Louise, fourteen, and Fanny, eight—were sent to their maternal grandmother, a native of Charleston then living in Longwood, a suburb of Boston. Their son, Francis Halsey, was at the University of Virginia Military School.

---

[1] Benjamin Huger, of South Carolina.
[2] John Bankhead Magruder, of Virginia.

In the meantime, Mrs. Wigfall accompanied her husband to Charleston, and later to Montgomery, where he represented Texas as a delegate. During the bombardment of Fort Sumter, he served as an aide to General Beauregard. His heroic trip to the fort in an open rowboat to demand its surrender won him wide acclaim. A Charleston newspaper called the exploit "as gallant and chivalrous as any deed of modern times."

The older Wigfalls were in Richmond. Mrs. Wigfall sends the following letters to her daughters.

Richmond, May 30th [*1861*]

After a terribly fatiguing journey we arrived here safely yesterday morning. We left Montgomery on Sunday night, at 8 o'clock, and travelled night and day, until yesterday morning.

The President was everywhere most rapturously received. . . . I was all packed to start for Texas, when your father found that the President was so unwilling for him to go back at that time, that he determined to accept the position of Aide and at least act in that capacity until the opening of Congress, which will be on the 20th July. So here we are. These Virginians seem likely to overwhelm your father with their attentions and kill him with kindness—for yesterday he had to make no less than four speeches.

The whole country as we came through was like a military camp. The cars crowded with troops, and all as jubilant as if they were going to a frolic, instead of to fight. The President is to take the field; but I don't know the exact programme, and if I did it would not be safe to write it—for there is no telling who may read our letters now-a-days. Your father of course will go with him. It seems strange to me that I don't feel more frightened.

June 11th and 14th

We are still at the Spotswood Hotel but I don't know whether we shall continue very long. The President and his family will move next week to the place selected for them. I hear it is very handsome and the City Council has bought and put it at the disposal of the Government. They have also given Mrs. Davis the use of a nice carriage and horses and seem disposed to do all they can to show their joy at the exchange from Montgomery. . . . So far all is quiet here and I can scarcely realize that we are at war, actually.

. . . I drove out with Mrs. Davis yesterday to one of the Camp grounds and it was really a beautiful, though rather sad sight to me, to see them drill and go through with their manoeuvres. Poor fellows! how many will never return to their homes! . . . There are several camp grounds in the neighborhood, and people throng them every afternoon and unless you engage a carriage in the morning, it is very hard to procure one.

3. JULIA GARDINER TYLER

"It Makes the Heart Beat and the Eyes Fill"

Since last hearing from Mrs. Tyler in Washington, ex-President Tyler, as a member of the Virginia State Convention, had cast his vote on April 17 in favor of secession. "Submission or resistance is only left us," he said. Soon afterward, he was elected to a seat in the Provisional Congress of the Confederacy.

Mrs. Tyler joined her husband in Richmond with her fifteen-year-old son, Gardiner. She placed twelve-year-old daughter Julia in Miss Pegram's boarding school in the city. The younger children were left behind at Sherwood Forest. Also at Sherwood was Mrs. Robert Tyler, the wife of Mrs. John Tyler's stepson, who was practicing law in Philadelphia and was threatened with mob violence before he could leave. Soon he would become Registrar of the Confederate Treasury in Richmond.

Fearing for the safety of her daughter and the children, Mrs. David Gardiner had urged them to come to her home on Staten Island. John Tyler assured her that there was no danger. "The whole state is clad in steel," he wrote.

Mrs. Tyler further reassured her mother in the following letter:

Richmond, June 16, 1861

I rejoice in an opportunity to write you through the kindness of a gentleman who has some means of communication with Baltimore. The Convention met again on the 12th, and I accompanied the President up. . . . In the meantime the children left behind are in good hands. Mrs. R. Tyler and family of four children are at Sherwood. Gardie is with me here enjoying the military excitement, and Julia is at Mrs. Pegram's. All are well.

You have heard of the battle in the vicinity of Hampton and Bethel (that is around the location of Bethel *Church*).[3] The fight on the Southern side was more wonderful than the taking of Sumter—only 1,100 troops were there, eight hundred of whom were engaged against a force of Northern troops amounting to four or five thousand; but *one* killed and four slightly wounded on the Southern side; loss larger on the other. How can it be otherwise than that? The hand of Providence should assist the holy Southern cause. The Northern papers give garbled accounts, but *this* is the true statement.

Hampton and the vicinity have suffered all sorts of depredation from Lincoln's army—unoffensive people, and their private residences have been disturbed in every possible way; but the Villa I hear has been treated with more respect as yet.[4]

More and more we have the realization of war; from day to day the people, the entire people, are making up their minds to it, until every family of high and low degree are seeing their male members don the soldier's dress and shoulder their musket to go forth for the protection of their invaded firesides. It makes the heart beat and the eyes fill to witness such noble resolution and bravery on the part of all, but in particular on the part of those who, bred in ease and luxury, still cheerfully accept every and any hardship that comes with a soldier's life, whether as

---

[3] The Battle of Big Bethel, Virginia, was fought on June 10, 1861. It was a Confederate victory.

[4] "Villa Margaret" was the summer home of the Tylers at Hampton. Two months later, it was reported to be "despoiled in a barbarous manner" by Union soldiers.

officers or in the ranks, for the latter are thick with accomplished gentlemen, [rather] than permit the unresisted invasion of their dearest right. The men have become heroes—*all,* from youths of seventeen to those far advanced in years; but one common feeling swells their bosoms, deep indignation against those who should have been their best friends, and not their worst enemies. An unlawful war has been waged against them, and if the possession of every warrior trait will enable them to "conquer a peace," there will soon be one for us.

Every way I turn I see an acquaintance and friend, either in the flannel shirt of a private, or in the braided jacket of the *zouave,* or the plumed cap of the cavalry's officer. It is women and children only that are not in arms *all ready* for a moment's notice. A large body of noble, brave Marylanders have found it impossible to *wait,* and have resigned with a feeling of relief their homes to *fight* side by side with their Southern brethren. By all sorts of stratagems they are slipping over fully armed, and joining their companions without delay.

Subjugate or *bring to terms* such a people! Little do you dream at the North of what stuff they are made. Why, even Gardie and Alex. mourn that they cannot at once be of them: they are *fired* up with enthusiasm for what they consider such a sacred cause as the defense of their soil from the wicked and cruel invader.[5]

It is a thrilling, melting sight to see the entrances into the city of troops by the trains from all parts of the Southern country, as they appear to feel, to the *rescue of old Virginia.* The fatigue of travel makes no impression upon them, and they joyfully march off to their encampments, apparently congratulating themselves they are so near the scene of action. "Still they come."

At church today Gen. Davis was introduced to me. He men-

---

[5] David Gardiner ("Gardie") and John Alexander ("Alex") Tyler enlisted in the Confederate Army as privates at the ages of 16 and 15 respectively.

tioned that Mrs. D. and himself would be to see me to-morrow.
He is a splendid man, fine manners, and the bearing of one good
and great. Gen. Lee called upon us after church; rather grayer
than when I last met him some years ago, but still the elegant
officer, looking animated and full of vigor. He spoke very calmly
and indifferently of the desecration of his home at Arlington, and
the flight of his invalid wife. She was moved out of the way of
the enemy twice, and now she says *they will have to take* her—
she will move no more. The General laughed, as he repeated
what she said, but added, as her health was much affected by
rheumatism, it was quite a trial to her to be deprived of her
home.[6]

And now adieu, dear Mamma. Continue perfectly at ease
about me. All I ask, take care of yourself, and don't get sick.

Your affectionate daughter,
JULIA

4. MARY BOYKIN CHESNUT

"I Am in Richmond"

Mary Boykin was born on March 31, 1823, at Statesburg,
South Carolina. She was the daughter of Stephen Decatur and
Mary Boykin Miller. Her father, whose motto had been "to
wear out, not rust out," had served his state as United States
Congressman, as Senator, and as Governor. He went to Missis-
sippi in 1835, to engage in extensive cotton planting, and died
there in 1838, two years before the marriage of his daughter to
James Chesnut, Jr., of Mulberry plantation, near Camden,
South Carolina.

---

6 From Arlington, Mary Custis Lee proceeded to Ravensworth, the home
of her aunt, Maria Fitzhugh, near Alexandria. Just before Union troops
occupied Alexandria on May 24, she fled to Chantilly, home of the Stuarts,
near Fairfax Court House. She stopped briefly with her relatives, the Randolphs, at Eastern View, and with her cousin, Edward Turner, at Kinloch
in Fauquier County.

Recently, James Chesnut had been a delegate to the Confederate Congress at Montgomery. Mrs. Chesnut was with him there and in Charleston, where he had been a staff officer at the fall of Fort Sumter. When she followed him to Richmond, she was accompanied by a young cousin, Mary Hammy, of Columbia, who had a fiancé in the war.

Mrs. Preston, introduced in the following account, was born Caroline Hampton, sister of General Wade Hampton. Her husband, John S. Preston, of Columbia, had made a fortune on his sugar and cotton plantations in Louisiana. He was serving as a volunteer aide to General Beauregard. Later he would command the conscript camp in Columbia before becoming head of the conscript service in Richmond. The two Preston daughters were Sally Buchanan, called "Buck," and Mary.

Mrs. Preston was described by a lady of Richmond as "handsome and aristocratic." Her daughters were "like goddesses upon a heaven-kissing hill, tall and stately, with brilliant fresh complexions."

June 27, 1861. I am in Richmond. . . .

At the depot in Richmond, Mr. Mallory, with Wigfall and Garnett,[7] met us. We had no cause to complain of the warmth of our reception. They had a carriage for us, and our rooms were taken at the Spotswood. But then the people who were in the rooms engaged for us had not departed at the time they said they were going. They lingered among the delights of Richmond, and we knew of no law to make them keep their words and go. Mrs. Preston had gone for a few days to Manassas. So we took her room. Mrs. Davis is as kind as ever. She met us in one of the corridors accidentally, and asked us to join her party and to take our meals at her table. Mr. Preston came, and we moved into a room so small there was only space for a bed, wash-stand, and glass over it. My things were hung up out of the way on nails behind the door.

As soon as my husband heard we had arrived, he came, too.

---

[7] Muscoe Russell Hunter Garnett, former U.S. Congressman from Virginia and now a member of the Confederate Congress.

After dinner he sat smoking, the solitary chair of the apartment tilted against the door as he smoked, and my poor dresses were fumigated. I remonstrated feebly. "War times," said he; "nobody is fussy now. When I go back to Manassas to-morrow you will be awfully sorry you snubbed me about those trumpery things up there." So he smoked the pipe of peace, for I knew that his remarks were painfully true. As soon as he was once more under the enemy's guns, I would repent in sackcloth and ashes.

Captain Ingraham[8] came with Colonel Lamar. The latter said he could only stay five minutes; he was obliged to go back at once to his camp. That was a little before eight. However, at twelve he was still talking to us on that sofa. We taunted him with his fine words to the F.F.V. crowd before the Spotswood; "Virginia has no grievance. She raises her strong arm to catch the blow aimed at her weaker sisters." He liked it well, however, that we knew his speech by heart.

This Spotswood is a miniature world. The war topic is not so much avoided, as that everybody has some personal dignity to take care of and everybody else is indifferent to it. I mean the "personal dignity of *autrui*." In this wild confusion everything likely is told you, and then everything is as flatly contradicted. At any rate, it is safest not to talk of the war. . . .

In Mrs. Davis's drawing-room last night, the President took a seat by me on the sofa where I sat. He talked for nearly an hour. He laughed at our faith in our own powers. We are like the British. We think every Southerner equal to three Yankees at least. We will have to be equivalent to a dozen now. After his experience of the fighting qualities of Southerners in Mexico, he believes that we will do all that can be done by pluck and muscle, endurance, and dogged courage, dash, and red-hot patriotism. And yet his tone was not sanguine. There was a sad refrain running through it all. For one thing, either way, he thinks it will be a long war. That floored me at once. It has been too long

---

[8] Duncan Nathaniel Ingraham.

for me already. Then he said, before the end came we would have many a bitter experience. He said only fools doubted the courage of the Yankees, or their willingness to fight when they saw fit. And now that we have stung their pride, we have roused them till they will fight like devils. . . .

Mrs. Bradley Johnson[9] is here, a regular heroine. She out-generaled the Governor of North Carolina in some way and has got arms and clothes and ammunition for her husband's regiment. There was some joke. The regimental breeches were all wrong, but a tailor righted that—hind part before, or something odd. . . .

Mr. Lamar says, the young men are light-hearted because there is a fight on hand, but those few who look ahead, the clear-heads, they see all the risk, the loss of land, limb, and life, home, wife, and children. As in "the brave days of old," they take to it for their country's sake. They are ready and willing, come what may. But not so light-hearted as the *jeunesse dorée*.

June 29th. Mrs. Preston, Mrs. Wigfall, Mary Hammy and I drove in a fine open carriage to see the *Champ de Mars*. It was a grand tableau out there. Mr. Davis rode a beautiful gray horse, the Arab Edwin de Leon[10] brought him from Egypt. His worst enemy will allow that he is a consummate rider, graceful and easy in the saddle, and Mr. Chesnut, who has talked horse with his father ever since he was born, owns that Mr. Davis knows more about horses than any man he has met yet. General Lee was there with him; also Joe Davis[11] and Wigfall acting as his aides. . . .

It is pleasant at the President's table. My seat is next to Joe

---

[9] Born Jane Claudia Saunders, of North Carolina. Her husband was major of the 1st Maryland Regiment.

[10] Author and diplomat in Egypt, and the older brother of Thomas Cooper De Leon.

[11] Joseph Robert Davis, the President's nephew.

Davis, with Mr. Browne[12] on the other side, and Mr. Mallory opposite. . . .

Read the story of Soulouque,[13] the Haytian man: he has wonderful interest just now. Slavery has to go, of course, and joy go with it. These Yankees may kill us and lay waste our land for a while, but conquer us—never!

July 4th. . . . Noise of drums, tramp of marching regiments all day long; rattling of artillery wagons, bands of music, friends from every quarter coming in. We ought to be miserable and anxious, and yet these are pleasant days. Perhaps we are unnaturally exhilarated and excited.

Heard some people in the drawing-room say: "Mrs. Davis's ladies are not young, are not pretty," and I am one of them. The truthfulness of the remark did not tend to alleviate its bitterness. We must put Maggie Howell and Mary Hammy in the foreground, as youth and beauty are in request. At least they are young things—bright spots in a somber-tinted picture. . . .

5. CHARLOTTE CROSS WIGFALL

"Our Glorious Victory"

At Manassas, twenty-five miles southwest of Washington, Major General Irvin McDowell and approximately 35,000 men were decisively defeated by Generals Beauregard and Joseph E. Johnston with less than 31,000.

"Why did we not follow the flying foe across the Potomac?" was the topic of conversation in Richmond drawing rooms.

Rose Greenhow, the Confederate spy, sent message after message from Washington: "Why don't you come on?" she

---

12 The reference is apparently to R. M. ("Constitution") Browne, who had been editor of the Atlanta Constitution and *ad interim* Secretary of State and Assistant Secretary of State of the Confederacy.

13 Soulouque, a Negro slave of Haiti, who took part in the insurrection against the French in 1803 and became the Emperor Faustin I.

pleaded. She reported the wildest disorder in the Northern capital, where the streets were filled with stragglers, each with a doleful tale to relate.

Mr. Wigfall believed that "nothing could have stopped us getting to Washington"—an opinion that was commonly shared.

The handcuffs exhibited at the Spotswood Hotel were brought from the "debacle of the Yankee army." It was the general opinion in Richmond that they had been meant for Jefferson Davis and his officers.

"Don't repeat anything I may say to you," Mrs. Wigfall cautioned her daughter Louise, then living in Massachusetts.

Richmond, July 21st [1861]

No news except that Genl. Johnston has joined Beauregard with a large force. A part of his troops are left still at Winchester, but the greater part are with him. The President went down to-day, but I don't know exactly in what capacity, whether he will command or not. . . . The troops are pouring in, and a general battle at Manassas is expected very soon. We brought up by one train upwards of 50 prisoners from Winchester, and crowds gathered on the way, at every roadside station, to see "the Yankees." I was almost sorry for them.

9 o'clock. You will have heard that we have gained a second victory, and a "glorious though a dear bought one," Mr. Davis telegraphs, at Manassas. Only some of the deaths are known as yet: Colonel Johnson of the Hampton Legion and poor Col. Bartow[14] they say are killed; Wade Hampton slightly wounded. All Beauregard's staff are safe. Poor Mrs. Bartow is here, but does not yet know the sad tidings. The enemy they say were in full retreat. All is excitement here and the people seem almost wild.

---

[14] Colonel Francis S. Bartow had once been Mayor of Savannah. Soon after his death, Mrs. Bartow held a post in the branch of the Confederate Treasury Department at Columbia, South Carolina.

23rd. We have been in the greatest excitement over our glorious victory. I am curious to know what the effect will be at the North—whether they will be panic stricken or exasperated to frenzy at such a defeat. Poor old Scott! If he had only died after the Mexican War, how much better it would have been for his military fame.[15] They say that the trunks of some of the men were actually directed to Richmond! In the next fight I suppose of course the President will take the field. He got down too late this time—just as they had begun to retreat. . . .

The fact is the fight took place sooner than he had expected, and he had made no preparations for engaging in it. Don't however repeat anything I may say to you on such subjects.

29th. I send you the *Examiner* of to-day, which has full extracts from the Northern papers—about the battle. Some of the handcuffs were shown at the Hotel, yesterday, but I did not happen to see them. 'Tis however a fact—how many exactly I don't know—but there are certainly a great many taken.

6. SALLY TOMPKINS

"Cheers and Shouts Rent the Air"

Sally, daughter of Christopher and Maria Booth Patterson Tompkins, was born in Poplar Grove, Mathews County, Virginia, on November 9, 1833. She was in Richmond when the First Battle of Manassas was fought. Ten days later, she opened at her own expense the "Robertson Hospital" in Richmond. The property had been the home of Judge John Robertson, who tendered it to her for that purpose. She oper-

---

[15] On July 4, 1861, Mrs. Judith Brockenbrough McGuire wrote in her diary as follows: "This day General Scott promised himself and his Northern friends to dine in Richmond. Poor old renegade, I trust he has eaten his last dinner in Richmond, the place of his marriage, the birthplace of his children, the home of his early friendships, and so near the place of his nativity and early years. How can he wish to enter Richmond but as a friend?"

ated it until July 13, 1865. In that interval, more than 1,300 soldiers were cared for by Miss Tompkins and her many volunteer helpers. When all private hospitals were ordered closed, President Davis gave her a commission as Captain, so that "Robertson Hospital" might be under formal government supervision. "Captain Sally" refused the salary that went with the commission.

Ellen Tompkins Bowen, addressed in this letter, would soon join the volunteer assistants in "Robertson Hospital," as would four of Sally's slaves.

Miss Tompkins was writing from the Arlington House, one of Richmond's popular hotels.

Arlington House, [Richmond] July 22, 1861

Dear Sister Ellen

It is now nearly 2 o'clock Sunday night but I am so excited by the news of the glorious victory that I cannot sleep. You have heard by this time of the battle at Manassas on Thursday the 18th. We gained it and since all have constantly expected another and a more *serious* one. It took place today and *thank God we have gained it.* Surely there were fervent prayers offered today and blessed be God he has answered them. Oh, may His goodness humble and make us live nearer to Him.

Gen. Cooper lives just opposite here and Mrs. Lee[16] his sister-in-law and his son Cooper live here so we always have the latest news. This afternoon Mrs. Lee told me the battle had begun at 4 o'clock and oh the intense anxiety we all felt for it must be a struggle, bloody and terrible. The enemy have two to one of ours. At ten we heard that the left wing under General Johnston was awfully pressed. Pres. Davis went up there this morning and took command and Gen. Beauregard had command of the right wing.

I felt constrained to go to church tonight to join my poor prayers with the people for victory and surely we all prayed from our inmost souls. I thought of br. C. and of you all and felt such

---

[16] Mrs. Sidney Smith Lee, also sister-in-law of General Robert E. Lee.

comfort in commending you to God. The prayer for the President and for deliverance from our enemy was responded to earnestly and touchingly. Mr. P.'s text was Ephesians VI:2, and at the close he offered a most beautiful prayer for victory. You may imagine that the excitement was great for all knew the battle was going on, all knew how much depended on the issue and all have friends in it. As we left church we heard that we had won the day. As we neared Broad St. cheers and shouts rent the air and we saw a large Regiment going off in double quick to the cars for Manassas. They seemed to pant and chaff to be there.

When I got to the Arlington I saw the dispatch which Gen. Cooper received. It read thus: "Night is closing in—we have won a glorious but *dearly* bought victory. The day and field are ours— the enemy are in full flight—all my force in close pursuit. Jefferson Davis." I felt that we could indeed say "thy right hand, O Lord, is become glorious in power; thy right hand, O Lord, hath dashed in pieces the enemy." Read the lesson of today, the 8th Sunday of the Trinity, and see how applicable they are to us now. . . .

You have heard ere this of the defeat of Gen. Garnett's[17] command and of his death—it was indeed distressing, discouraging, heartbreaking but we must still trust in the Lord and submit to His will. He was a brave noble man. . . .

I must close now, it is too late, long past 2 o'clock. God bless and keep you all.

SALLY

7. MARGARET SUMNER McLEAN

"The Trains Began to Bring in the Wounded"

Although many of his friends advised him to take an appointment under "the tyrant's heel," Eugene McLean

[17] General Robert S. Garnett was killed at Rich Mountain early in July when General G. B. McClellan directed Union operations in western Virginia.

offered his services to the Confederacy. "If one must be in a revolution," said Mrs. McLean, "I think myself that the center is more desirable than the circumference." After he was mustered into service at Montgomery, Eugene returned to Virginia in time to take part in the battle of Manassas. Mrs. McLean was staying with many of her old friends at the Spotswood Hotel.

How shall I describe the events of the last ten days, or give you any idea of the feeling by which I have been agitated? It seems as if ten years had rolled over my head, and that the scenes of suffering I have witnessed had burned themselves into my heart, withering every association of the past and every hope of the future. We have talked of battles, and said that they were fought here and there, or would be, but the 21st of July, 1861, made us realize for the first time what war means.

The day dawned quietly, calmly, beautifully. Although we knew Mr. Davis had gone to Manassas Junction, we never suspected the object, but enjoyed the day as one of rest, few of us even going to church. Nor was there anything to disturb the calm, except the sad duty of attending the funeral of a friends' child at five o'clock in the afternoon.[18] I remarked to Mrs. Davis and Mrs. Johnston,[19] who were in the carriage, that the people in the streets looked excited and I thought there must be some news, but they laughed at my nervous fancies, and I was somewhat reassured by Mrs. Davis saying that we would certainly know if there was any news of importance. However, upon our return, I again remarked the same anxious expression on every countenance, and, more to convince me of my error than anything else, Mrs. Davis asked a gentleman who was passing if there was any news. "Yes, madam," he replied, "they have been fighting at Manassas since six o'clock this morning."

I do not know how we got into the hotel, but when there we were met by the ladies, who had just received the same informa-

---

[18] The infant child of Captain and Mrs. John Withers.

[19] Mrs. Joseph E. Johnston.

tion, and were perfectly beside themselves with terror and anxiety. There were ten of us whose husbands were known to be on that field, while all the others had sons, brothers, or some near relation, and one poor lady's family was represented by her husband, two sons, a brother, and a brother-in-law.

Three hours passed in this suspense before we received a private telegram from Mr. Davis with a list of officers killed and wounded, which, while it relieved most of us, brought a crowning sorrow to Mrs. Bartow. Fortunately she was not in the room when it was read, and we were enabled to defer until the next day a communication which no one felt willing to convey. So we retired to our rooms with grateful hearts, though death came too near for us to feel any elation at Mr. Davis' other telegrams, which announced to the people victory. . . .

The next day was one of clouds and darkness, with pouring rain which disturbed the working of the wires. For nearly twenty-four hours we were without another word from Manassas, and no one would have imagined Richmond to be the capital of a victorious people. It seemed as if a pall had fallen on every house, and people spoke low to each other as they waited to learn with what price victory was bought. Every family had its representative with the army, and the women who talked so freely of their willingness to sacrifice them were bowed down to the dust, fearing they might be called upon. Among ourselves with that poor stricken woman in the midst of us, there could be nothing like rejoicing, and one of our number, coming out of her room, said, "God help us if this is what we have prayed for!"

The day wore on, and it was not until late at night that telegrams began coming in, each one bearing its message of joy or sorrow; but by the morning of Tuesday, which opened brightly, the Richmond people began to look up. There was more of good news than bad for them, and by the time Mr. Davis had returned and had addressed them in one of his stirring speeches they were almost wild with enthusiasm. To me, one of the saddest moments in all that time was when everything appeared the brightest—when Mr. Davis had returned, and the parlors were illuminated, and friends were congratulating one another, and the street in front of the house was crowded with a multitude cheering for "the President," "the Confederacy," "the Generals," and "the Army"; while like a passage in the minor key in some brilliant piece of music, I heard at a distance the "Dead March," and knew that the bodies of Gen. Bartow and Gen. Bee[20] were being escorted to the State Capitol. I left the parlor feeling that, let war bring what it would, I should always hear the accompaniment of that sad note.

The next day the bodies lay in state in the Senate Room, where they were visited by hundreds. Eloquent eulogies were pronounced by their personal friends, and the determination to avenge them recorded on high. The trains also began to bring in the wounded.

Richmond threw open the doors of its private houses, and ladies who would have shrunk a few days before from the sight of blood devoted all their time to dressing wounds and caring for the sick.

On the fourth day after the battle Mrs. Johnston and I, hearing of a good opportunity to go to Manassas, procured the necessary permission from the Secretary of War, and without listening to any remonstrances, took the early morning train. . . .

8. ANITA DWYER WITHERS

"The Day the Grand Battle Was Fought"

> Anita Dwyer Withers was twenty-two when she accompanied her husband, Captain John Withers, to Richmond. Their home was in San Antonio, Texas. Captain Withers (U.S. Military Academy, 1844) had resigned his commission

---

[20] Brigadier-General Barnard W. Bee, of South Carolina.

in the U.S. Army on March 1, 1861. On June 27, he accepted the position of Assistant Adjutant General in Richmond.

After several days' sojourn at the Spotswood Hotel, the Captain and his wife and baby moved to the boardinghouse kept by a Mrs. Duval, "home" for a number of other families of military and government officials.

Anita, a devout Catholic, began a diary on May 4, 1860. She continued it faithfully during her four years in Richmond. While others may have rejoiced in the victory of Manassas, the anniversary of the battle would forever be a day of sad recollections for Captain and Mrs. Withers.

[*Richmond*] *Saturday 20th July* [*1861*]. My own babe was gradually & quietly fading away, like a little Angel that he was, travelling to his Heavenly Home, where no pain, sickness, or sorrow will ever reach him.

Bishop McGill[21] came just a few moments before my babe departed, which was about 3 o'clock in the afternoon. The Bishop tried to comfort & console us, but it was difficult at that time of intense grief & anguish of heart. I felt as if they were tearing my soul from my body. He was layed out in the little room. The next day he was put in the coffin, buried on Sunday afternoon, the day the grand battle at Manassas was fought. The Bishop read the Funeral Service in the parlour, & made a beautiful address. I did not go down but the ladies told me. The parlour was crowded with ladies and gentlemen, Mrs. President Davis, Mrs. Johnston, Mrs. Wigfall, and Mrs. McLean[22] had the politeness to attend. My own was layed in the Bishop's Vault, so as to take him home with us when we return. . . .

Sunday the 28th [*July*]. We went to late Mass. I was in deep black. The bishop gave a beautiful Sermon.

---

21 John McGill, Bishop of Richmond.

22 *Née* Margaret Sumner, one of the delightful women in Mrs. Davis' coterie.

The Southern Congress met here the day that my own darling died. . . .

Saturday 31st [August]. I got up with a headache. Mrs. Brewer & myself went to Market & bought some peaches. I was knitting nearly all day, making socks for the soldiers. . . .

Friday 6th [September]. General Sidney Johnson[23] arrived here, with Major Howard. . . . I went around to the Office in the evening with the Captain.

Saturday 7th. All day at home. In the evening Captain Myers took his wife, Mrs. Brewer & myself to Pizzini's[24] to get some ice cream.

My Husband did not come until after eleven. He was kept on business with Gen. Johnson. . . .

Thursday 19th. I went shopping and bought me a Poplin dress to wear in the morning to breakfast. . . .

Saturday morning I walked all over town to purchase a wedding ring for Gen. K. Smith,[25] finally the Captain got one at Mr. Myers. In the evening we went up to Mrs. Williams to Tea. . . .

Sunday Sept. 22nd. My babe would have been one year & half old today. The Captain and myself went to Church at ten o'clock. Bishop McGill preached a beautiful sermon on the "Forgiveness of sin" or Confession. In the Afternoon I went to Vespers and to see Mrs. Stewart. My Husband walked back home with me. . . .

---

[23] General Albert Sidney Johnson.

[24] A popular Italian confectioner.

[25] General Edmund Kirby Smith and Cassie Selden were married on September 24, 1861.

9. FANNIE A. BEERS

"The Lovely, Joyous, Hopeful Days of Summer"

> Fannie lived in New Orleans with her husband and young
> son. When war came, he enlisted in the Dreaux Battalion and
> was sent to Virginia, while she joined her parents in the North.
> After First Manassas, she came down to Richmond to be near
> her husband. An old family friend was Commodore Matthew
> F. Maury, who had dedicated his book, *Geography of the Sea,*
> to her uncle, George Manning, of New York. Through his
> introduction, she made many dear friends among the ladies of
> Richmond.

Who that witnessed and shared the wild excitement which,
upon the days immediately following the victory at Manassas,
throbbed and pulsated throughout the crowded capital of the
Southern Confederacy can ever forget?

Men were beside themselves with joy and pride,—drunk with
glory.

By night the city blazed with illuminations, even the most
humble home setting up its beacon-light,—a sure guide to where
loyal, devoted hearts were throbbing with patriotism. . . .

Ah! the lovely, joyous, hopeful, patriotic days of that summer.
The Confederate gray was then a thing of beauty,—the outer
garb of true and loyal souls. Every man who wore it became en-
nobled in the eyes of every woman. These boys in gray were
strangers to none. Their uniform was a passport to every heart
and every home. Broad Street was thronged with them all day
long.

Officers of all grades rode hither and thither, or congregated
on the steps of the hotels. Squads of soldiers promenaded, gayly
chatting with acquaintances whom they chanced to meet. Occasionally the sound of drum and fife or the fuller music of a
brass band would herald the appearance of a company or regiment, perhaps just arrived from some distant State, eager to

reach the front. On more retired streets, at their homes, humble or luxurious, sweet young girls welcomed with kindly words and sunny smiles officers and private soldiers, extending equal courtesy to both. The elegant mansions on Clay Street and elsewhere were never without soldier guests. Impromptu meals were served whenever needed. In elegant dining-rooms stately servants supplied the wants of soldiers. No one asked who they were, whence they came. They were Confederate soldiers—that was quite enough.

In the cool drawing-rooms pleasant chat beguiled the summer hours, sweet songs floated out upon the air, or the more stirring notes of "Dixie" or "The Bonnie Blue Flag," played with a spirit and vim which electrified every listener.

If these warriors who lingered here could have chosen for themselves, they would never have thus quietly rested upon the laurels won at Manassas. Contrary to their wishes, they had been recalled from the pursuit of the flying foe and consigned to temporary inactivity.

As the new companies or regiments came in they were marched into camp in the suburbs or temporarily provided for in the immense tobacco warehouses which were numerous all over the city. Passing one of these, at every window appeared laughing or discontented faces of soldiers newly arrived, full of ardor, ready and expecting to perform prodigies of valor, yet ignominiously shut up within four brick walls, with a sentinel guarding every door.

The evening drills at the camp-grounds were attended by hundreds of ladies. So enthusiastic were these, so full of pride and admiration for the braves who had come to defend their homes and themselves, so entirely in accord with the patriotic spirit which burned in every manly heart, that not a soldier, no matter how humble, came near or passed before a group of these animated beauties who was not literally bathed in the radiance of kindly smiles—transformed into a demigod by the light of gloriously flashing eyes. . . .

Meanwhile, the summer sun still brightened the unharmed capitol. The summer wind still bore aloft on the dome in Capitol Square the flag of the new Confederacy, the "stars and bars." Here, after sunset and in the moonlight, came young men and maidens, matrons and children. Old men, too, who, baring their silvery heads to the cool breeze, gazed upward at the bonnie flag, with a look half triumphant, half sad. . . .

One moonlight evening I stood before the statue of that grand patriot and statesman, Patrick Henry. My companions were Mrs. Frances Gawthmey, of Richmond, and Commodore Matthew F. Maury. . . . Mrs. Gawthmey remarked, "If Patrick Henry had been living, I reckon Virginia would have stepped out of the Union side by side with South Carolina." "Well," replied Commodore Maury, "he would have acted as he thought. There would have been no 'pros and cons,' and his irresistible eloquence would have carried all before it." Then baring his head, he repeated a portion of that grand oration of Mr. Henry ending, "Give me liberty or give me death." After a moment we walked on very quietly, until, passing out of the mellow moonlight, we entered the brilliantly-lighted parlors of the Spotswood Hotel.

The hum of conversation, the sound of careless, happy laughter, the music of a band playing outside, soon brought us down from the heights of enthusiasm to the delightful realities of the present. For, spite of battle and death and perplexities, even certain trouble ahead, Richmond was gay, hopeful, and "all went merry as a marriage bell." Here in one corner laughing girls bewitched and held in thrall young soldier boys,—willing captives. Thrilling tales of the late battle were poured into credulous ears: "We were *here*. We were *there*. We were everywhere. *Our* company accomplished wonderful deeds of valor;" and if Beauty's smile be indeed a fit reward, truly these young heroes received it. . . .

On the corner of Clay and Twelfth Streets stood the pleasant and commodious residence of Mr. and Mrs. Booker. This model

Virginia household was so true a type of the homes of Richmond as they were at that time, that its description will present to the reader *all*, for the same spirit pervaded every one. As in almost every case, the young men of the family were in the Confederate service (the sons of this household were of the Richmond Howitzers). The father, in feeble health, yet lavished his means and his little strength upon every patriotic duty which arose. The mother, far more youthful, active, and energetic, full of enthusiasm for the cause, exceeding proud of the brave boys she had freely sent to battle, loving and serving all soldiers with heart and hand, was seconded with equal ardor and wonderful ability by her sweet young daughters. The spare sleeping-rooms were always daintily prepared, and at the service of any *soldier* who needed care and rest. Soldiers feeble from recent illness were encouraged to recline in restful arm-chairs in the cool flower-scented parlors, while the girls often entertained them with music or pleasant conversation.

Not a meal was set in that house unshared by one or more soldiers. The table was always as attractive as finest linen damask, elegant china and glass, and handsome silver could make it. The meals were abundant and nourishing, but plain. Delicacies of all kinds were prepared constantly in that "Virginia kitchen," and daintily arranged in the pantry by the ladies' own hands, but only to be sent to the sick and wounded strangers lying in the numerous hospitals.

Opposite to the house just described arose the spacious but unpretentious residence of President Davis. The main entrance was on Clay Street. On one side the windows opened on Twelfth Street, on the other lay a beautiful garden. . . .[26]

Within the Presidential mansion was no magnificence of furniture or appointments,—nothing in the style of living cal-

[26] The Confederate White House was built in 1816-1818 by Dr. John Brockenbrough, a leading citizen of his day. It had been designed by Robert Mills, of South Carolina, whom President Andrew Jackson later appointed the first Federal Architect and Engineer.

culated to create dissatisfaction or a sense of injustice in the
minds of those who, equally with their chosen leader, had already sacrificed much, and were willing to give their *all* to the
cause. No pomp and circumstance chilled loyal hearts. . . .

Jefferson Davis, the chosen exponent of undying principles,
was yet in his own house simply a Southern gentleman,—a kindly,
genial host, extending genuine hospitality to all.

Of Mrs. Davis my recollections are very pleasant. Always meeting from her a cordial reception, admiring the unaffected courtesy which put her visitors at their ease, I yet became distinctly
conscious that in her the feelings of wife and mother were
stronger than any other; that no matter into what station of life
it should please God to call her, devotion to these womanly
duties would be paramount.

10. LOUISE WIGFALL

"Drums Beating . . . Banners Flying"

> When Senator and Mrs. Wigfall were comfortably settled
> in Richmond, they summoned Louise (Louly) and Fanny
> from Massachusetts. The trip south was filled with exciting
> adventures. "Now suppose," said Mrs. Chesnut, "Seward had
> held them as hostages for Louis Wigfall's good behavior."
> Louly tells of the journey's end on August 1, 1861:

. . . Arrived in Richmond in the afternoon. We drove at once
to the Spotswood Hotel, to join my mother. Not knowing the
hour we would arrive, she had gone out to the Camp of the
1st Texas Regiment, which my father was commanding, to witness the presentation by the President of a beautiful Texas
State flag, which she had made for the Regiment. Nothing must
do but we must follow, as soon as possible. When we reached the
camp the ceremony was over, and my father was reviewing his
Regiment.

As the carriage stopped, word was carried forward of our arrival—and we immediately were surrounded by numbers of friends, eager to greet the little travellers; and my father, hurriedly dismounting from his horse, and leaving the regiment in charge of another officer, rushed forward to meet us. He returned with us to Richmond, and there, as we reached the Spotswood, coming down the stairs, we saw my mother, her beautiful face lit up with joy, and her fair arms held out to welcome us. She was clad in a lilac-colored gown, of some soft material, made in the fashion of the day, with the long angel sleeves falling away at the shoulder, leaving the throat bare. As I remember her that day, I love to think of her. Then we were feted and caressed to our heart's content; took tea with the President and his party that night, where our heads were completely turned by the attention shown us, and where we gave, to appreciative auditors, a full account of all our adventures "coming through the lines"—and the one query from all our eager audience was, "What do they think of the battle of Manassas?"

My sister and myself had been entered at Miss Pegram's[27] on Franklin Street, which was then the fashionable school in Richmond. With all the distractions of the time it was hard work to keep the girls at their books. It was difficult to fasten one's attention on ancient history and "belles lettres," when such very modern history was being made in our midst, and such "beaux Soldats," were marching, with drums beating, and banners flying, by our very doors.

11. CATHERINE COOPER HOPLEY

"No One Was Singular in Being Homeless"

Catherine Hopley was a British subject who was traveling in Virginia when the state seceded. From her room at the Ballard House, she wrote the following account of her experiences in

---

[27] Mary Pegram lived in the house of her mother, Mrs. James West Pegram.

Richmond in the fall of 1861, shortly before leaving for Rome.
After her return to England, a book of her experiences was
published in London in 1863 under the title *Life in the South,
by a Blockaded British Subject.*

By this time my Richmond acquaintances were increasing
fast, and among quite a different circle. It was interesting, though
painful, to hear about the battles, and blockade, and the determination of the people; and to watch the changes that were
taking place in their habits and customs. Instead of lounging
in their rocking-chairs, in dreamy listlessness, the ladies were
plying their crochet and knitting needles in such good earnest—
that soon I heard them say not another skein of wool or ball of
yarn was to be procured in the city. They had "bought up" all
that was to be found, and even made excursions to Petersburg
to do more shopping. They were preparing for the soldiers'
winter comforts. Then Mrs. Henningsen[28] brought home dozens
and dozens of yards of cotton sheeting, which she set every one
to work to prepare for a new hospital recently established. By
this time many stores were emptied of goods, and closed; and
what articles remained increased in value daily, so that it became
quite a matter of importance to the public to ascertain where
such or such things could be procured, and the papers were full
of advertisements to say that at such a place a cargo of this or
that had just "run the blockade;" or otherwise been smuggled
over from Maryland or through Kentucky. In order to stop the
intercourse between North and South, nothing less than a Chi-
nese wall from the Atlantic to the Pacific—and not even that—
would prove effectual, while diving-bells beneath the waves, and
balloons above, could be available; and where . . . the all-power-
ful magnet of affection influenced the agents, they would find
means to communicate with each other. The more severe the

---

28 Mrs. Charles Frederick Henningsen was born in Georgia, a niece of
Senator John McPherson Berrien, Attorney General under President Jack-
son. Her husband, a native of Belgium, offered his services to the Confederate
Army.

proclamations of President Lincoln, the more inventive did the Southerners become in their plans to defeat his frail attempt. . . .

The corners of some of the principal streets in Richmond were guarded by posts formed of old revolutionary cannon, partially buried; these, among other cases of practical economy, were dug up and converted into use; pity as it was, to destroy such old relics; but the Southerners had not then fought battles enough to supply themselves by capture. . . .

To fully chronicle the occurrences during my sojourn at the hotel in Richmond, would wear out the reader's patience. There were refugees from all parts of the *ci-devant* United States, each relating something linked with the civil war and its horrors. One feature was remarkable. Persons who had forsaken their homes with merely the clothes they wore, those who had sacrificed all to the war, whatever at another time would have been pronounced a dire misfortune, was now not thought of. No one was singular in being homeless, and no one ashamed to own his losses. A mutual confidence engendered a mutual sympathy. One heart, one mind, one cause was apparent, and this union of sentiment continued to strengthen, and will continue to strengthen, as the Confederacy is sifted from its foreign population. It was common to hear persons who escaped from the invaded districts say of their desolated homes, "We had already devoted all we had to the war, and our property without liberty is valueless to me." . . .

Judge Wright was personally acquainted with President Davis, and used to relate instances of his domestic life and his affection for his children; and how they came into the dining-room when company was present, and climbed upon his knees for dessert, and all that sort of thing. He said I ought to go and call on the President before I left Richmond; but I had never felt disposed to appear at the weekly or the evening receptions; and thought unless I could enjoy an especial salutation, and exchange of cordialities, there would be very little gratification in looking at him in a crowd, which one had often done as he rode about, or in church. "What should the President care about a stranger who went all alone to the receptions?"

Judge Wright insisted that I should visit the Presidential Mansion, and wrote a note to Mrs. Davis to say that "he hoped to have the pleasure of introducing an English lady who," etc., etc.—using some very complimentary expression; and "would she mention an hour when the President and herself would be disposed to receive us."

That promised to be just as I desired, and a great deal of pleasure was anticipated; because . . . I felt great respect for President Davis. Unfortunately . . . the President was very ill at that time, so ill indeed for several weeks, that his life was despaired of, and the Northern newspapers even went so far as to bury him, write an obituary, quite flattering, for an enemy, and appoint his successor. He left the city, however, for change of air; and subsequently Mrs. Davis and Mrs. General Johnston were thrown from their carriage, the former hurting her arm quite seriously; then it was time for my departure; and I never shook hands with President Davis! . . .

12. VIRGINIA TUNSTALL CLAY

"There's Bound To Be Somethin' Goin' On"

Because of ill health, Mr. Clay declined the office of Secretary of War in President Davis' cabinet. After spending the summer at the Huntsville home, he felt so much better that he accepted a seat in the Senate of the Confederacy.

Soon Senator and Mrs. Clay were journeying toward Richmond, where Mrs. Clay would renew old Washington friendships and take her place in the social life of the capital.

Among the many Richmond hostesses was her friend Mrs. George Wythe Randolph, née Mary Elizabeth Adams, of Mississippi, whose first husband was a Pope of Mobile. "She had money, beauty and talent," said R. G. H. Kean, head of the

Bureau of War, whose wife was Randolph's niece. Besides
entertaining on a lavish scale, Mrs. Randolph was a volunteer
helper in the hospitals and served as President of the Ladies'
Association. On March 19, 1862, her husband was appointed
Secretary of War in the first cabinet of the permanent government.

Mrs. James Alexander Seddon, née Sarah Bruce, was also
a friend. The Seddons' home was Sabot Hill, in Goochland
County, Virginia. Mr. Seddon, a lawyer and planter, was
a member of the Confederate Congress; on November 22, 1862,
he was appointed Secretary of War, succeeding Randolph.

Richmond, as seen from the hill, with the James River flowing
by, its broad, level streets, full foliaged trees, and spacious
homes, is a beautiful city. Rich in historic association, never
did it appear more attractive to Southern eyes than when, arriving in the late autumn of '61, we found our Confederate Government established there, and the air full of activity.

To accommodate the influx of Congressional and military
folk, the houses of the patriotic residents were thrown open, until
the capacity of every residence, hotel and lodging-house was
tested to the fullest. By the time Senator Clay and I arrived,
there was scarcely an extra bed to be had in the city, and though
everywhere it was apparent that an unsettled feeling existed,
there was nothing either indeterminate or volatile in the zeal
with which the dense community was fired. As the new-comers,
for the greater part, represented families which a season before
had been conspicuous in Washington, society was in the most
buoyant of spirits.

For a few months we revelled in canvas-backs and green-
backs, undisturbed by forewarnings of coming draw-backs. To
furnish the tables of Richmond nearly all the ducks in Chesa-
peake Bay fell victim. We feasted on oysters and terrapin of the
finest, and unmeasured hospitality was the order of the day on
every side. Never had I looked upon so great an activity, whether
military, political, or social. I had demurred when, as we were

about to start for the capital, my maid packed an evening dress or two.

"We are going to war, Emily," I said; "we shall have no need for velvet or jewels. We are going to nurse the sick; not to dress and dance."

But Emily's ardour on my behalf led her to rebel. "There's bound to be somethin' goin' on, Miss 'Ginnie," she declared, "an' I ain't goin' to let my Mistis be outshined by Mis' —— an' dem other ladies!"

There were many occasions afterward when I blessed the thoughtfulness of my little maid; for there were heroes to dine and to cheer in Richmond, both civil and military, and sombre garments are a sorry garb in which to greet or brighten the thoughts of men tired with the strain of building or fighting for a government.

A sororal spirit actuated our women, and while our greatest entertainment missed some of the mere display which had marked the social events in the Federal City, they were happier gatherings, for we were a people united in interest and in heart. Some of the brightest memories I carry of that first session are of informal evenings where neighbours gathered *sans cérémonie*. . . .

During our first winter in Richmond my husband and I made our home with Mrs. DuVal, near to the Exchange Hotel, a terrifically over-crowded hostelry at all Confederate times, and within a short walk of the Executive Mansion. It was a commodious and stately structure, in which our President, now domiciled, lived with an admirable disdain of display. Statesmen passing through the halls on their way to the discussion of weighty things were likely to hear the ringing laughter of the care-free and happy Davis children issuing from somewhere above stairs or the gardens. The circle of Mrs. DuVal's, our headquarters, as it came and went, comprised some of our former Washington mess-mates, and others newly called into public service. Among the favourites was General J. E. B. Stuart, a rollicking fellow, who loved music, and himself could sing a most pleasing ballad. He was wont to dash up to the gate on his horse, his plumes waving, and he appearing to our hopeful eyes a veritable Murat. . . . When the exigencies of the service brought him again and again to the capital, he entered heartily into its social relaxations. . . .

We were in gay spirits during that first session of the Confederate Congress. Our editors, filled with patriotism and alert, kept us informed of the stirring events of the field. . . . Scarcely a triumph, nevertheless, in which was not borne down some friend who was dear to us, so that all news of victory gained might be matched with the story of fearful loss. . . . Moreover, always before us was the stimulus of the presence of fearless men and the unceasing energy of our President.

I remember on one occasion seeing President Davis passing down the street, beside him on the left, General Buckner;[29] on the right, General Breckinridge[30]—three stalwart and gallant men as ever walked abreast; and as I watched them the thought came involuntarily, "Can a cause fail with such men at the head?"

Among the most active hostesses were Mrs. Randolph . . . and Mrs. Ives,[31] who put on some charming private theatricals in their parlours; there were the Lees and Harrisons; the Ritchies and Pegrams and Welfords; the Masons and Warwicks, MacFarlanes, Seddons, Leighs (near relatives, these, of Patrick Henry); besides the Branders, West Robinsons, Walkers, Scotts, Coxes, Cabells, Semmes,[32] and other hostesses of renown and long pedigree, whose homes dispensed the friendliest hospitality. . . .

---

[29] General Simón Bolivar Buckner.

[30] General John C. Breckinridge.

[31] Mrs. Joseph C. Ives, *née* Cora Semmes, was the sister of Senator Semmes of Louisiana. Her husband was a colonel on President Davis' staff.

[32] Mrs. Thomas Jenkins Semmes, *née* Myra Eulalie Knox, of Montgomery, was the wife of the Louisiana Senator, who lived opposite the Confederate White House; and Mrs. Raphael Semmes, born Anne Elizabeth Spencer, was the wife of the great raider.

13. CONSTANCE CARY

"Hospitable Old Town"

>   Constance Cary, daughter of Archibald and Monimia Fair-
> fax Cary, spent her girlhood at "Vaucluse," the family estate
> near Alexandria. She had a French governess before she went
> to boarding school in Richmond.
>   When she arrived in Richmond as a refugee in the winter of
> 1861, "Vaucluse" was in enemy hands and the site of an army
> camp. Her fifteen-year-old brother Clarence was a midship-
> man aboard the Confederate steamer *Nashville*. The family
> in Richmond included her uncle and aunt, Dr. and Mrs. Fair-
> fax, and her cousins, Jennie Fairfax and Hetty and Jennie
> Cary. The home soon became the gathering place for a wide
> circle of friends and acquaintances.

My first vivid impression of war-days was during a ramble in
the woods around our place one Sunday afternoon in spring,
when the young people in a happy band set out in search of
wild flowers. Suddenly the shrill whistle of a locomotive struck
the ear, an unwonted sound on Sunday. "Do you know what
that means?" said one of the older cousins who accompanied the
party. "It is the special train carrying Alexandria volunteers to
Manassas, and to-morrow I shall follow with my company." . . .

Before the week was over, the scattering of our household,
which no one then believed to be more than temporary, had
begun. Living as we did upon ground likely to be in the track
of armies gathering to confront each other, it was deemed advis-
able to send the children and young girls into a place more
remote from chances of danger. Some weeks later the heads of
the household, two widowed sisters, whose sons were at Manassas, drove in their carriage at early morning away from their
home, having spent the previous night in company with a half-
grown lad digging in the cellar hasty graves for the interment
of two boxes of old English silver-ware, heir-looms in the family,
for which there was no time to provide otherwise. . . .

The point at which our family reunited within Confederate lines was Bristoe, the station next beyond Manassas, a cheerless railway inn; a part of the premises was used as a country grocery; and there quarters were secured for us with a view to being near the army, a few miles distant. By this time all our kith and kin of fighting age had joined the volunteers. . . .

With August heat and lack of water, Bristoe was forsaken for quarters near Culpeper, where my mother went into the soldiers' barracks, sharing soldiers' accommodations, to nurse the wounded. . . .

The first winter of the war was spent by our family in Richmond, where we found lodgings in a dismal rookery familiarly dubbed by its new occupants "The Castle of Otranto." It was the old-time Clifton Hotel, honeycombed by subterranean passages, and crowded to its limits by refugees like ourselves from country houses within or near the enemy's lines—or "fugees," as we were called. For want of any common sitting-room, we took possession of what had been a doctor's office, a few steps distant down the hilly street, fitting it up to the best of our ability, and there we received our friends, passing many merry hours. . . .

Already the pinch of war was felt in the commissariat; and we had recourse occasionally to a contribution supper, or "Dutch treat," where the guests brought brandied peaches, boxes of sardines, French prunes, and bags of biscuit, while the hosts contributed only a roast turkey or a ham, with knives and forks. Democratic feasts those were, where major-generals and "high privates" met on an equal footing.

The hospitable old town was crowded with the families of officers and members of the Government. One house was made to do the work of several, many of the wealthy citizens generously giving up their superfluous space to receive the new-comers. . . .

Confederate White House at Richmond. Reprinted from Jefferson Davis, *The Rise and Fall of the Confederate Government*. D. Appleton & Company, 1881.

Mrs. Jefferson Davis. Reprinted from Virginia Clay-Clopton, *A Belle of the Fifties*. Doubleday, Page & Company, 1904.

Mrs. Clement C. Clay. Reprinted from Virginia Clay-Clopton, *A Belle of the Fifties*. Doubleday, Page & Company, 1904.

Mrs. James Chesnut. Reprinted from Virginia Clay-Clopton, *A Belle of the Fifties*. Doubleday, Page & Company, 1904.

Mrs. Robert E. Lee. Reprinted from R. A. Brock, ed., *General Robert Edward Lee.*
Richmond, Virginia, Royal Publishing Company, 1897.

Mrs. Lee's bedroom at 707 East Franklin Street, Richmond. Reprinted from R. A. Brock, ed., *General Robert Edward Lee*. Richmond, Virginia, Royal Publishing Company, 1897.

Sally Buchanan Campbell Preston. Reprinted from Mary Boykin Chesnut, *A Diary from Dixie*. D. Appleton, 1905.

II

SOUND THE ALARM

January—August 1862

At the slightest premonition of danger, the bell in the tower on Capitol Square would sound the alarm in Richmond. It rang often in the spring and early summer of 1862.

Early in November 1861, another grand campaign to capture the Confederate capital was planned in Washington. The Federal army would dine in Richmond on July 4, 1862—or so it was said. Jefferson Davis was inaugurated on Washington's birthday, and the permanent government of the Confederacy was established in Richmond. Martial law was proclaimed in March.

General McClellan and his army reached Fort Monroe on April 2. On May 15, a naval squadron came up the James River to Drury's Bluff, eight miles below the city. Five ships attacked the Confederate fort there and were repulsed.

After a sharp fight at Williamsburg on May 5, McClellan marched to White House Landing on the Pamunkey River, twenty miles east of Richmond. Meanwhile, General Joe Johnston had brought up his forces. At White House Landing, McClellan found this note attached to a mansion door: "Northern soldiers who profess to reverence Washington, forbear to desecrate the home of his first married life, the property of his wife, now owned by her descendants." It was signed, "A granddaughter of Mrs. Washington." The granddaughter was Mrs. Robert E. Lee.

In late May, McClellan, moving slowly toward his goal, reached the swamps of the Chickahominy River, within eleven miles of the city. On the way, Northern soldiers had camped

for two days on the grounds of Sherwood Forest, the home of
the Tylers.

On May 31 and June 1, General Johnston attacked Mc-
Clellan at Seven Pines, near Fair Oaks Station. On the second
day, Johnston was wounded, and General R. E. Lee was placed
in command of the Army of Northern Virginia. Along roads
where dogwood and Judas trees blossomed, the dead and
wounded were borne from the battlefield to Richmond.

Stonewall Jackson's Shenandoah Valley campaign had prevented McDowell from joining McClellan. Richmond children were soon singing a song about the great Stonewall and
this campaign:

> Go it, Stonewall Jackson,
> You're a terror to the Yanks;
> You've whipped out Frémont,
> And also Shields and Banks.

For seven long days of battle, the armies strove—from June
26 at Mechanicsville to July 1 at bloody Malvern Hill. The
Confederate victory was a costly one; more than 20,000 were
killed or wounded. On the last night, McClellan retreated to
Harrison's Landing on the James, twenty-five miles distant.

Soon after the Seven Days battles, "The Ladies of Richmond" was contributed by an anonymous poet to the Charleston *Courier*. These are the first two stanzas:

> Fold away all your bright-tinted dresses,
>   Turn the key on your jewels to-day,
> And the wealth of your tendril-like tresses
>   Braid back, in a serious way.
> No more trifling in boudoir or bower,
>   But come with your souls in your faces—
> To meet the stern needs of the hour!

> Look around! By the torch-light unsteady,
>   The dead and the dying seem one,
> What! paling and trembling already,
>   Before your dear mission's begun?
> These wounds are more precious than ghastly,
>   Time presses her lips to each scar,
> As she chants of a glory which vastly
>   Transcends all the horrors of war.

1. JULIA GARDINER TYLER

"The Death of a Confederate Congressman"

Early in the New Year of 1862, all Richmond mourned the death of John Tyler, Confederate Congressman and tenth President of the United States. For two days, the body lay in state. Funeral services were held at Saint Paul's Church; and afterward, the President, the Vice-President, the Cabinet, members of the Confederate Congress and other notables escorted his casket to Hollywood Cemetery.

Several days later, Julia Gardiner Tyler returned to Sherwood Forest.

"Mr. Tyler was greatly esteemed and admired by me," said President Davis. But no word of tribute came from the White House in Washington.

It was through a singular dream I had that I came to Richmond in time to be with Mr. Tyler during all his illness, which ended with his death, January 18, 1862. He had gone on before, in his usual health, and I was to follow with the baby, Pearl, for a stay of a few weeks, after visiting my friends at Brandon and Shirley on the river, which I intended should consume at least a week; but I awoke the morning I had proposed to leave with a troublesome dream. I thought I had risen to dress, but on looking back to the bed, observed Mr. Tyler lying there, looking pale and ill. . . .

Nancy, the maidservant, entered the room, and warned me it was time to dress for the boat. I surprised her by saying that I intended going right on to Richmond, without stopping anywhere on the river, and narrated my dream. . . .

None of the family could dissuade me from going direct to Richmond; and so, with old nurse, Fanny, and the baby, I arrived at the Exchange Hotel on Friday, January 10th, after dark, and entirely unexpected. On alighting from the carriage, I was recognized by Col. Edward C. Cabell, who assisted me. My first enquiry was in regard to the President [Mr. Tyler], and my anxiety was allayed on hearing he was quite well. He said I was taking my husband by surprise, as he had just left his room, and heard from him that I would not be in Richmond for some time. He proposed to go in search of him, as they had left his room together, and had parted at the reading-room. I knew the location of his room, and said we would await him there.

In a few moments I heard his hurried steps on the bridge, which, you know, joins the Exchange to the Ballard House. . . . He wanted to know what all this change in my plans, since my letter of the day before, meant. I told the dream, which quite amused him. The next day, the parlor was filled with our visitors, and all were remarking on the health and cheerfulness of the President. . . .

That night (Saturday) I awoke . . . suffering from headache. The President placed his hand on my head and said, "your forehead is so cold; shan't I send for the doctor? You see your dream is out; it is *your* head that I am holding, and not you mine." I asked for morphine. He arose, weighed some, and gave it to me, and very soon I was entirely relieved.

The next morning when I awoke, quite early, I observed him standing before the fire nearly dressed. Then he said, ". . . I believe I have had a chill, and I have determined to go down to the breakfast table and take a cup of hot tea." . . .

I was aroused by the entrance of the President returning. . . .

He exclaimed, "I would not have had it happen for a great deal; it will be all around the town!" and then went on to tell me he had risen to leave the table, staggered and fell. He was lifted and carried to the parlor, where, lying on the sofa, he recovered consciousness, and then insisted upon coming alone to his room, lest I should be alarmed.

His friends began surging into the room before I could rise to attend him. They were very solicitous, and extended him on the sofa; but he assured them he was better, and would send for his doctor, and then he could not help relating my dream, saying, "her dream is a true one, and I leave my wife and her children to God and my country." The gentlemen left the room,

expressing wishes soon to hear from him, and to be of service. . . .

His physician insisted he should go home and have perfect
quiet for a few days, for his mind was constantly exercised over
the situation of the country, and he could talk of little else. . . .

Mr. Rives had an interview with him on Thursday (the 16th)
in regard to his son residing in New York, whose property he
feared might be in danger of confiscation. He took occasion to
request that Mr. Rives would ask permission of Congress to
his absence for a few days, according to the wish of his physician.
He was always so scrupulous in his obedience to rules. He said
he would go to Sherwood on Saturday; but alas! on Friday night,
just after he had retired to bed, . . . he suddenly awoke with a
feeling of suffocation. Robert Tyler,[1] who had determined to
spend the night, and be of any assistance if needed, and had
arranged himself to sleep upon the sofa, hastened for Dr. Brown,
whose room was upon the same floor. . . .

The bedstead on which he died was exactly like the one I saw
him upon in my dream, and unlike any of our own. . . .

2. FANNIE A. BEERS

"I Am Called to the Work"

> Mrs. Beers, whom we have met, tells of her work at the
> Soldiers' Rest and the Third Alabama Hospital. She left Rich-
> mond in early spring after her husband was transferred to the
> Army of Tennessee. Bidding her farewell, her old friend Com-
> modore Maury said, "You bear the heart of a true and tender
> woman, in the breast of a noble patriot."
>
> Mrs. Beers served as a hospital matron until the end of the
> war at Gainsville, Alabama; Ringgold, Georgia; Newman,
> Georgia; and Fort Valley, Georgia.

Finding that my desultory wanderings among the larger
hospitals were likely to result in little real usefulness, and that

---

[1] The President's son had been his private secretary in Washington.

the ladies attached to the Soldiers' Rest would be glad of my
help, I became a regular attendant there. This delightful place
of refuge for the sick and wounded was situated high up on Clay
Street, not very far from one of the camps and parade-grounds.
A rough little school-house, it had been transformed into a
bower of beauty and comfort by loving hands. The walls, freshly
whitewashed, were adorned with attractive pictures. The windows were draped with snowy curtains tastefully looped back
to admit the summer breeze or carefully drawn to shade the
patient, as circumstances required. The beds were miracles of
whiteness, and clean linen sheets, in almost every case, draped
and covered them. By the side of each cot stood a small table.
Upon these were spread fine napkins. Fruit, drinks, etc., were set
upon them, not in coarse, common crockery, but in delicate
china and glass. *Nothing was too good for 'the soldiers.* The
school-house contained three rooms. The school-room proper
was quite large, and here were ranged about thirty beds. One
of the recitation-rooms was set apart for patients who might
need special attention or seclusion. The other was occupied by
the ladies whose duty it was to receive and distribute the delicate
and nutritious supplies of food which unfailingly arrived at
stated hours, borne by colored servants, on silver waiters or in
baskets covered with snowy damask. During every hour of the
day, gentle women ministered untiringly to the sick. All hearts
yearned over them, all hands were ready to serve them.

A few steps below, between Ninth and Tenth Streets, was
another private hospital, similar in almost every respect to the
one just described, organized and presided over by Mrs. Caroline
Mayo.[2] She also was assisted by several ladies, but had entire
direction, and threw herself into the work with all her soul. . . .

One morning, just as I had arrived there and was preparing
to begin my daily duties, a carriage stopped at the door, from

---

[2] She belonged to an old Virginia family that included Dr. William H.
Mayo, a Colonel Joseph Mayo, and the Joseph Mayo who was mayor of Richmond during the war.

which Mrs. Judge Hopkins[3] descended, and, hastily entering the hospital, announced to the ladies that she had "come for Mrs. Beers." They strongly demurred, and I felt at first great hesitation in obeying so hasty a summons. But Mrs. Hopkins was very much in earnest. "Indeed, you must come," said she, "for I have great need of you. A large number of sick and wounded Alabamians will arrive this morning. I have found a place to put them, but some one must be there to prepare for their accommodation, to receive hospital supplies, and direct their arrangement, while I make purchases and attend to other matters. Come, no hireling can fill the place. Come, now, with me; we have no time to lose." I hesitated no longer, but entered the carriage. We were at once driven down-town, stopping to order cots, mattresses, etc., then to an immense tobacco factory, owned by Messrs. Turpin & Yarborough.

Arrived there, a pitiful sight met our eyes. Perhaps fifty sick men had arrived unexpectedly, and were sitting or lying about in every conceivable position expressive of feebleness, extreme illness, utter exhaustion.

The men were soon under shelter, but no beds had yet arrived. Mrs. Hopkins led me into the factory, introduced me to Dr. Clark, who had come to take charge as surgeon, and placed me under him at the head of affairs as her deputy.

Meantime immense boxes arrived from the depot, sent by the people of Alabama. These contained pillows, comforts, sheets, as well as wines, cordials, and every delicacy for the sick, also quantities of shirts, drawers, and socks, old and new. The boxes were wrenched open, pillows placed quickly under the heads of

[3] Born Juliet Ann Opie, daughter of the Honorable H. L. Opie, of Jefferson County, Virginia. After the death of her first husband, Captain Alexander G. Gordon, U.S.N., she married Chief Justice Arthur Francis Hopkins of Alabama and lived in Mobile. Early in the war she organized and managed the Alabama Hospital in Richmond. She was twice wounded on the battlefield of Seven Pines while lifting the wounded, and as a result limped slightly until her death in Washington in 1890. General Joe Johnston said that the Alabama Hospital "was more useful to my army than a new brigade." He called Mrs. Hopkins "the angel of the South."

the sickest, and cordials administered. As the beds came in they were placed, made up, and the worst cases first, others afterward were transferred to them, until all were lying comfortably between clean sheets. . . .

Four of our sick died that night. I had never in my life witnessed a death-scene before, and had to fight hard to keep down the emotion which would have greatly impaired my usefulness. . . .

At the end of a long, large wing of the factory were two excellent rooms, formerly the offices of the owners. These were comfortably fitted up, the one as a bedroom for myself, and the other as a sitting-room and private office. As soon as matters were somewhat settled, my little son joined me in my new quarters, and thus the Third Alabama Hospital became our home. The little fellow spent very little time there, however. My Richmond friends never lost sight of me for one day during my service in that city. Nearly every day my little boy was sent for to play among happy children, far away from the impure atmosphere of the hospital.

As the demand for more room became pressing, the three stories of the main building were successively utilized, as well as a large storage-room in the yard. . . .

I loved very dearly these heroes whom I served, and felt that I was as well beloved. Every hour of toil brought its own rich reward. These were Confederate soldiers. God had permitted me to work for the holy cause. This was enough to flood my whole being with content and deepest gratitude. . . .

3. JUDITH BROCKENBROUGH McGUIRE

"They Shan't Get to Richmond"

> Judith Brockenbrough McGuire was the wife of the Reverend John P. McGuire, principal for many years of the Episcopal High School, near Alexandria, Virginia. She had

been born in Richmond in 1813, the daughter of Judge William Brockenbrough, of the Virginia Supreme Court.

When Federal troops moved into Alexandria, the McGuires were compelled to leave their home as refugees. "It makes my blood boil," Judith noted in her diary, "when I remember that our private rooms, our chamber, our very sanctums, are thrown open to a ruthless soldiery." In the weary months that followed, they sojourned in Chantilly, Danville, Lynchburg, and Charlottesville. When Mr. McGuire was appointed a clerk in the Post Office Department, they moved to Richmond. Two sons and many relatives were in the Confederate Army; the young daughters stayed with friends in Mecklenburg County.

Shortly after arriving in the city of her youth, Mrs. McGuire offered her services to the Captain Sally Tompkins Hospital.

Richmond, February 5, 1862. . . . Mr. [McGuire]received a letter, announcing his appointment to a clerkship in the Post-Office Department. The pleasure and gratitude with which it is received is only commensurate with the necessity which made him apply for it. It seems a strange state of things which induces a man, who has ministered and served the altar for thirty-six years, to accept joyfully a situation purely secular, for the sole purpose of making his living; but no chaplaincy could be obtained except on the field, which would neither suit his health, his age, nor his circumstances. His salary will pay his board and mine in Richmond. . . . We are spending a few days with our niece, Mrs. H. A. C.[laiborne], until we can find board. Mr. [McGuire] has entered upon the duties of his office, which he finds confining, but not very arduous. To-morrow I shall go in pursuit of quarters.

The city is overrun with members of Congress, Government officers, office-seekers, and strangers generally. Main Street is as crowded as Broadway, N. Y.; it is said that every boarding-house is full.

February 6. Spent this day in walking from one boarding-house to another, and have returned fatigued and hopeless. I do not believe there is a vacant spot in the city. A friend, who considers herself *nicely* fixed, is in an uncarpeted room, and so poorly furnished, that, besides her trunk, she has only her wash-stand drawer in which to deposit her goods and chattels; and yet she amuses herself at it, and seems never to regret her handsomely furnished chamber in Alexandria.

7th. Walking all day, with no better success. "No vacant room" is the universal answer. I returned at dinner-time, wearied in mind and body. . . .

13th. . . . Notwithstanding the rain this morning, I renewed my pursuit after lodgings. With over-shoes, cloak and umbrella, I defied the storm, and went up to Grace Street, to an old friend who sometimes takes boarders. Her house was full, but with much interest she entered into my feelings, and advised me to go to Mr. Lefevre, who, his large school having declined, was filling his rooms with boarders. His wife was the daughter of a friend, and might find a nook for us. I thought of the "Hare and many friends," and bent my steps through the storm to the desired haven. To my surprise, Mrs. L. said we could get a room; it is small, suits our limited means, and we will go as soon as they let us know that they are ready for us.

We have just been drawn to the window by sad strains of martial music. The bodies of Captains Wise[4] and Coles were brought by the cars, under special escort. The military met them, and in the dark, cold night, it was melancholy to see the procession by lamplight, as it passed slowly down the street. Captain Wise has been carried to the Capitol, and Captain

---

[4] O. Jennings Wise was the son of former Governor Henry A. Wise, who later became a Major General in the Confederate Army. Captain Wise was killed on Roanoke Island when his father's forces were defeated by General Burnside.

Coles to the Central Depot, thence to be carried to-morrow to the family burying-ground at Enniscorthy, in Albemarle County. Thus are the bright, glorious young men of the Confederacy passing away. Can their places be supplied in the army? In the hearts and homes of families there must ever be a bleeding blank.

Sunday, 16th. This morning we left home early, to be present at the funeral of Capt. Wise, but we could not even approach the door of St. James Church, where it took place. The church was filled at an early hour, and the street around the door was densely crowded. The procession approached as I stood there, presenting a most melancholy cortège. The military, together with civil officers of every grade, were there, and every countenance was marked with sorrow. As they bore his coffin into the church, with sword, cap, and cloak resting upon it, I turned away in sickness of heart, and thought of his father and family, and of his bleeding country, which could not spare him. . . .

February 22. To-day I had hoped to see our President inaugurated, but the rain falls in torrents, and I cannot go. So many persons are disappointed, but we are comforted by knowing that the inauguration will take place, and that the reins of our government will continue to be in strong hands. His term of six years must be eventful, and to him, and all others, so full of anxiety! What may we not experience during those six years! . . .

23d. . . . Last night was the first levee. The rooms were crowded. The President looked weary and grave, but was all suavity and cordiality, and Mrs. Davis won all hearts by her usual unpretending kindness. I feel proud to have those dear old rooms, arousing as they do so many associations of my childhood and youth, filled with the great, the noble, the *fair* of our land, every heart beating in unison, with one great object in view, and no wish beyond its accomplishment, as far as this world is concerned.[5]

But to-day is Saturday, and I must go to the hospital to take care of our sick. . . .

February 24. Just returned from the hospital. Several severe cases of typhoid fever require constant attention. . . . Some of them are very fond of hearing the Bible read; and I am yet to see the first soldier who has not received with apparent interest my proposition of being read to from the Bible. . . .

I met a very plain-looking woman in a store the other day. She was buying Confederate gray cloth, at what seemed a high price.

I asked her why she did not apply to the quartermaster, and get it cheaper.

"Well," she replied, "I *knows* all about that, for my three sons is in the army; they gets their clothes *thar;* but you see this is for my old man, and I don't think it would be fair to get his clothes from thar, because he ain't never done nothing for the country as yet—he's just gwine in the army."

"Is he not very old to go into the army?"

"Well, he's fifty-four years old, but he's well and hearty like, and ought to do something for his country. So he says to me, says he, 'The country wants men; I wonder if I could stand marching; I've a great mind to try.' Says I, 'Old man, I don't think you could, you would break down; but I tell you what you can do—you can drive a wagon in the place of a young man that's driving, and the young man can fight.' Says he, 'So I will'— and he's gwine just as soon as I gets these clothes ready and that won't be long."

"But won't you be uneasy about him?" said I.

---

[5] Dr. John Brockenbrough, who had built and long occupied this house, was Mrs. McGuire's cousin.

"Yes, indeed; but you know he ought to go—them wretches must be drove away."

"Did you want your sons to go?"

"Want 'em to go!" she exclaimed. "Yes; if they hadn't agone, they shouldn't a-staid whar I was. But they wanted to go, *my* sons did."

Two days ago, I met her again in a baker's shop; she was filling her basket with cakes and pies.

"Well," said I, "has your husband gone?"

"No, but he's gwine to-morrow, and I'm getting something for him now."

"Don't you feel sorry as the time approaches for him to go?"

"Oh, yes, I shall miss him mightily; but I ain't cried about it; I never shed a tear for the old man, for the boys neither, and I ain't gwine to. Them Yankees must not come a-nigh to Richmond; if they does I will fight them myself. The women must fight, for they *shan't* cross Mayo's Bridge; they shan't get to Richmond. . . ."

March 11. . . . Yesterday we heard good news from the mouth of James River. The ship "Virginia," formerly the "Merrimac," having been completely incased with iron, steamed out into Hampton Roads, ran into the Federal vessel "Cumberland," and then destroyed the "Congress," and ran the "Minnesota" ashore. Others were damaged. We have heard nothing further; but this is glory enough for one day, for which we will thank God and take courage. . . .

March 24. . . . Troops are passing through Richmond on their way to Goldsboro, N. C., where it is said that Burnside is expected to meet them. Everybody is busy in supplying wants as they pass through. On Sunday, just as the girls of one of the large seminaries were about to seat themselves at table, the principal of the school came in: "Young ladies," said he, "several extra

trains have arrived, unexpectedly, filled with troops. The committee appointed to attend them are totally unprepared. What
can we do to help our hungry soldiers?" "Give them our dinner,"
cried every young voice at once. In five minutes baskets were
filled and the table cleared. When the girls reached the cars, the
street was thronged with ladies, gentlemen, children, servants,
bearing waiters, dishes, trays, baskets, filled with meats, bread,
vegetables, etc. Every table in Richmond seemed to have sent
its dinner to Broad Street, and our dear, dirty, hungry graycoats
dined to their hearts' content, filled their haversacks, shouted
"Richmond forever" and went on their way rejoicing. . . .

April 10. Spent yesterday in the hospital by the bedside of
Nathan Newton, our little Alabamian. I closed his eyes last
night at ten o'clock, after an illness of six weeks. His body, at his
own request, will be sent to his mother. Poor little boy! He was
but fifteen, and should never have left his home. It was sad to
pack his knapsack, with his little gray suit, and colored shirts,
so neatly stitched by his poor mother, of whom he so often spoke,
calling to us in delirium, "Mother, mother." . . .

April 11. . . . Soldiers are constantly passing through town.
Everything seems to be in preparation for the great battle which
is anticipated on the Peninsula. . . .

April 15. A panic prevails lest the enemy should get to Richmond. Many persons are leaving town. I can't believe that they
will get here though it seems to be their end and aim. My mind
is much perturbed; we can only go on doing our duty, as quietly
as we can.

April 20. On Wednesday we saw eight thousand troops pass
through town. We were anxious to see many who were among

them. The sidewalks were thronged with ladies, many of them in tears. General C[orse][6] passed with his brigade, containing the 17th, with its familiar faces. . . . I knew the cavalry would pass through Franklin Street, and hurried there to see my dear W. B. N.[7] The order "Halt" was given just as he, at the head of his troops, was passing. I called him aloud. Amid the din and tumult of course he could not hear, but as he raised his cap to salute the ladies near him, his quick eyes met mine; in an instant he was at my side. "My dear aunt, what are you doing here?"

"I came to look for you; where are you going?"

"Our orders extend to the steamers at the wharf," he replied; "but don't be uneasy, we are going to the right place."

His face glowed with animation, and I meant to appear cheerful to him, but I found, after he was gone, that my face was bathed in tears. They all looked as if the world were bright before them, and we were feeling the appalling uncertainty of all things. A mother stood by, straining her weeping eyes for the parting glance at her first-born; and so many others turned their sad, weary steps homewards, as their dear ones passed from their sight.

April 21. The ladies are now engaged making sand-bags for the fortification at Yorktown; every lecture-room in town crowded with them, sewing busily, hopefully, prayerfully. Thousands are wanted. . . . Troops pass through. . . . What does it all portend? We are intensely anxious; our conversation, while busily sewing at St. Paul's Lecture-Room, is only of war. We hear of so many horrors committed by the enemy in the Valley— houses searched and robbed, horses taken, sheep, cattle, etc., killed and carried off, servants deserting their homes, *churches desecrated!* . . .

---

[6] Brigadier-General Montgomery D. Corse.

[7] Mrs. McGuire's nephew, Captain William B. Newton.

4. CLARA MINOR LYNN

"Richmond Went Dinnerless"

> Clara Lynn, who was in Richmond "for educational pur-
> poses," was a member of an old Virginia family whose home
> was near Norfolk. Her numerous kin included members of
> the Maury and Blackford families.
> On countless occasions Richmond played host to the con-
> stant stream of soldiers. Clara tells of one of the days when
> the city went without its dinner that the boys might be fed.

One Sunday of that sad Spring, a trooper clanked up the aisle
of each church in the city, and handed the minister an order
which he read to his trembling congregation. Announcements
that were important for the people to know at once, on Sunday,
or requests for their aid in some emergency of the government,
were often made in this way. Thus a soldier coming on an errand
to the minister set many an anxious heart quaking.

Now prompt help was wanted, for a large portion of the army
which for days had been fighting in the Valley of Virginia were
to pass through the city, on their way to meet the enemy below
Richmond. Every one was asked to go home, collect and cook
what they could on such short notice and take it to the trains.
The soldiers had been fighting on half rations for days, and now
could be delayed but two hours.

In an incredibly short time, strange processions were seen
on the streets—old men and children, officers in full uniform,
and ladies in their Sunday best, protected by big aprons, but
all alike bearing, with an absorbing anxiety, dishes, trays, pans
and buckets.

Our family party was headed by a grey-haired professor, who
had spent his life handling Greek roots, carrying with elaborate
care a dish of bacon and cabbage; for all dinners were taken and
Richmond went dinnerless that day. My Mother, a strong tem-

JUDITH BROCKENBROUGH McGUIRE 109

perance woman, was armed with a suspicious looking brown jug, but it contained only vinegar and water. Behind the leaders came a string of girls, children and Negroes, each carrying dishes, trays of corn pones, buckets and pitchers of sorghum or vinegar and water, the "Confederate lemonade."

As we approached the long trains—flats, freight and stock cars, all loaded with their precious freight—the laughter produced by the street processions was turned to weeping over the poor hungry, dirty fellows. I shall never forget the eagerness with which they seized upon the drinks of vinegar or sorghum— but of course no ice. Mothers found sons, and sisters, brothers, of whose fate they had for days been uncertain. But alas, some were not found and oh, the bitter woe of it!

Many were slightly wounded, their ragged uniforms bespattered with blood, their own or that of comrades who had fallen at their side. But they were full of fight, saying "Mars Bob (their pet name for General Lee) did not have half as many soldiers as the Yankees and could not spare one of them."

Thus did they go to the fearful scenes that awaited them— our dearly loved boys.

5. JUDITH BROCKENBROUGH McGUIRE

"Heavy Firing on the River"

Thaddeus S. C. Lowe, who made daily flights over Richmond in his balloon, reported to McClellan that the city was being evacuated. The Confederate government did discuss such a possibility and many families were moved from Richmond.

Despite the dangers of those May days, Mrs. McGuire did not neglect her hospital; nor did she ever lose hope.

Rocketts was just below Libby Hill in the oldest settled part of Richmond.

May 3d, 1862. It is distressing to see how many persons are leaving Richmond, apprehending that it is in danger; but it will not—I know it will not fail. It is said that the President does not fear; he will send his family away, because he thinks it is better for men, on whom the country's weal is so dependent, to be free from private anxiety. . . .

May 5. Yesterday we had a blessed Sabbath, undisturbed by rumours; it is generally a day of startling reports set afloat by idlers. The Bishop preached and administered confirmation at St. Paul's. The President was a candidate for confirmation, but was detained by business. . . .

May 7. Our "peaceful" Sabbath here was one of fearful strife at Williamsburg. We met and whipped the enemy. Oh, that we could drive them from our land forever! Much blood spilt on both sides; our dear W. B. N. is reported "missing"—oh, that heart-sinking word! . . . Richmond, or the *croakers* of Richmond, have been in a panic for two days, because of the appearance of gun-boats on James River. I believe they will not get nearer than they are now. I sat up last night at the hospital with D. L., who is desperately ill. My companion during the night was Colonel N., of Maryland. While listening to the ravings of delirium, two gentlemen came in, announcing heavy firing on the river. We had been painfully conscious of the firing before, but remembering that Drury's Bluff was considered impregnable, I felt much more anxious about the patient than about the enemy. The gentlemen, however, were panic-stricken, and one of them seemed to think that "sunrise would find gunboats at Rocketts." Not believing it possible, I felt no alarm, but the apprehension of others made me nervous and unhappy. At daybreak I saw loads of furniture passing by, showing that people were taking off their valuables. . . .

6. VARINA HOWELL DAVIS

"The Enemy's Gun-Boats Are Ascending the River"

"The troubles and thorns innumerable" which President Davis had foreseen on the day he was inaugurated at Montgomery, became a reality as spring came to Richmond.

Mrs. Davis and the children were hurried out of the threatened city. "My ease, my health, my property, my life I can give to the cause of my country. The heroism which could lay my wife and children on any sacrificial altar is not mine," the President wrote on June 13. "Spare us, good Lord."

When Mrs. Davis returned to Richmond many weeks later, "the odors of the battle-field were distinctly perceptible all over the city."

About May 9th, Mr. Davis insisted that we should leave Richmond, and relieve him from unnecessary anxiety. On the eve of the 9th there was a reception, and we were to go in three days. A courier came to the President with despatches, and as he passed me on his return to the drawing-room I looked a question and he responded, in a whisper, "The enemy's gun-boats are ascending the river." Our guests remained quite late, and there was no opportunity for further conversation.

As soon as they were gone my husband told me he hoped the obstructions would prevent the gun-boats reaching the river, but that he preferred we should go the next morning. Always averse to flight, I entreated him to grant a little delay, but he was firm, and I communicated the news to the family. Dr. William M. Gwin and his daughter were visiting us, and a friend from the next corner had tarried beyond the rest. As soon as our dear little neighbor was told the news, she dropped on her knees and raising her hands to heaven, ejaculated, "Lord Jesus, save and help us." Notwithstanding the crucial period through which we were passing, we all laughed heartily, except our friend. She was a woman of rare attainments and keen wit, and had written a journal which extended over a long period of intercourse with the greatest men of their day at home and abroad. Such a record of the passing show would have been almost as valuable an addition to the history of the time as Madame Junot's or Madame de Rémusat's diaries, but she burnt it at once for fear of its being taken from her by the enemy.

We left for Raleigh, N. C., on the morning of May 10th; the panic began some days later, and it was pitiable to see our friends coming in without anything except the clothes they had on, and mourning the loss of their trunks in a piteous jumble of pain and merriment.

The Sunday before our departure, Mr. Davis was baptized at home by Mr. Minnegerode,[8] in the presence of the Right Rev. Bishop Johns,[9] and a peace which passed understanding seemed to settle in his heart, after the ceremony. . . .

7. JUDITH BROCKENBROUGH McGUIRE

"God Help Us"

As Mrs. McGuire noted in her diary, the Legislature of Virginia was in constant session. On May 14 it adopted a resolution which concluded:

"That the General Assembly hereby expresses its desire that the capital of the State be *defended to the last extremity,* if such defense is in accordance with the views of the President of the Confederate States, and that the President be assured that whatever destruction and loss of property of the State or individuals shall thereby result, will be cheerfully submitted to."

---

[8] Charles G. Minnegerode, Rector of St. Paul's (Episcopal) Church.
[9] Bishop John Johns.

On May 15, when enemy gunboats were driven back at Drury's Bluff, Mrs. McGuire received distressing news of Captain Newton.

As May ended and June began, she and the ladies of the city prepared to receive the wounded and dead from the battlefield of Seven Pines, or Fair Oaks.

May 14. The anxiety of all classes for the safety of Richmond is now intense, though a strong faith in the goodness of God and the valour of our troops keeps us calm and hopeful. Others, as is too frequently the case in times of trouble, attribute all our disasters to the incompetency and faithlessness of those intrusted with the administration.of public affairs. Even General Lee does not escape animadversions. I have been shocked to hear that a counter-revolution, if not openly advocated, has been distinctly foreshadowed, as the only remedy for our ills.

The Legislature is in almost constant session during these dark days. The whole body is as true as steel, and its constant effort is to uphold the hands of the President, to fire the popular heart, and to bring out all the resources of Virginia in defense of the liberty and independence of the South. . . .

May 15. It is now ascertained beyond doubt that my nephew, W. B. N., reported "missing," at Williamsburg, is a prisoner in the enemy's hands. . . .

May 18. The 16th was the day appointed by the President for fasting and prayer. The churches here were filled, as I trust they were all over the land. . . .

May 29. No official accounts from "Stonewall" and his glorious army, but private accounts are most cheering. In the meantime, the hospitals in and around Richmond are being cleaned,

aired, etc. preparatory to the anticipated battles. Oh, it is sickening to know that these preparations are necessary! Every man
who is able has gone to his regiment. . . .

May 31. . . . The booming of cannon, at no very distant point,
thrills us with apprehension. We know that a battle is going on.
God help us!

Evening. General J. E. Johnston brought in wounded, not
mortally, but painfully, in the shoulder. Other wounded are
being brought in. The fight progressing; but we are driving
them.

Night. We have possession of the camp—the enemy's camp.
The place is seven miles from Richmond. . . .

June 1. The loss yesterday comparatively small. General
Johnston had managed his command with great success and
ability until he received his wound. What a pity that he should
have exposed himself! but we are a blessed people to have such
men as General Lee to take his place. He (Gen. J.) is at the
house of a gentleman on Church Hill, where he will have the
kindest attention, and is free from the heat and dust of the city.

June 2d. The battle continued yesterday near the field of the
day before. We gained the day. The enemy were repulsed with
fearful loss; but our loss was great. The wounded were brought
until a late hour last night, and to-day the hospitals have been
crowded with ladies, offering their services to nurse, and the
streets are filled with servants darting about, with waiters covered with snowy napkins, carrying refreshments of all kinds to
the wounded. Many of the sick, wounded, and weary are in
private houses. The roar of the cannon has ceased. Can we hope
that the enemy will now retire? . . . Oh, Lord, how long! How
long are we to be a prey to the most heartless of foes? Thousands
are slain, and yet we are no nearer the end than when we began!

8. ROSE O'NEAL GREENHOW

"Our President Did Me the Honor"

Rose O'Neal Greenhow, a native of Maryland, was the widow of Robert Greenhow, a prominent Washingtonian. In 1861, she was forty-four years old and the mother of four children. It was then that she became a leading figure in the Confederate espionage system. From Washington, she sent messages in code to General Beauregard, and on this information, he based his defense at First Manassas.

She was arrested on August 21, 1861, and confined first in her own home at 308 16th Street, and later in the Old Capitol Prison, where the record book listed her as "a dangerous, skillful spy." On May 31, 1862, she was sent under guard to Baltimore.

"Sir," Mrs. Greenhow said to her chief escort, "ere I advance further, I ask you, not as Lincoln's officer, but as a man of honour and a gentleman, are your orders from Baltimore to conduct me to a Northern prison, or to some point in the Confederacy?"

"To Fortress Monroe, and thence to the Southern Confederacy," she was assured.

At this point Mrs. Greenhow tells her own story.

At five o'clock on the afternoon of Sunday, June 1, [1862] the officer of the guard announced that all was in readiness to depart for the boat, which had been detained for the purpose of conveying me to Fortress Monroe. A large number of persons had by this assembled to offer congratulations. The good news had reached *our friends* that a battle had been fought, and that skirmishing was still going on at Seven Pines, near Richmond, in which we had defeated the Yankees with heavy loss. This, of course was the brightest augury that could have greeted me.

The "good-bye" was spoken, and many friends followed to the boat. Upon reaching it a guard was stationed around, who, with bayonet in hand, repulsed every attempt of any but the prisoners to go on board, such being the orders. General Dix[10] and suite being expected, the boat was detained for them several hours. . . .

General Dix arriving about eight o'clock, the signal was given to weigh anchor, and I was fairly en route for the capital of the Confederacy. . . .

The boat reached the wharf at Fortress Monroe at an early hour on the morning of June 2. . . .

No orders had been given to provide refreshments, but the captain of the boat, who was a most gentlemanly person, prepared at his own cost a most ample luncheon, together with some iced champagne; and I had the pleasure of proposing the health of President Davis and the success of the Confederate cause under the bristling guns of the enemy, and my toast drunk by all present, several visitors having been added to the number on board. . . .

Meantime an aide-de-camp of General Wood, accompanied by the Provost-Marshal, Colonel Jones, came on board to make arrangements for forwarding me on my journey. Colonel Jones asked me where I wished to go. I replied, "To the capital of the Confederacy, wherever that might be." He told me that it was still Richmond—asserting that that city had not fallen, as had been published at the North, but that it would be in their hands before I got there. I said I would take the chances, and only asked that no time might be lost. . . .

About four o'clock in the afternoon I was called upon to be in readiness to go on board of the boat which had been chartered to take me to City Point, and marched through the broiling sun to the place where she lay. Some time after, the boat got under way, but made no great progress. Night coming on, and the James River being difficult of navigation, the buoys having all been taken up by our people, the Captain was afraid of running aground, so lay to until daylight.

---

[10] General John Adams Dix, former Secretary of the Treasury, then in command of the Union Department of the East.

On the morning of the 3rd, about seven o'clock, we came in sight of the glorious achievements of the *Virginia,* the wrecks of the *Congress* and other vessels destroyed by her. The *Monitor* lay down the stream at a short distance, and I had a good view of the low black ugly thing. At this point the Captain again anchored, and an officer went off in a small boat to get instructions from the commander of the *Monitor* for landing me. After an absence which seemed endless, a large-sized boat put off from her, in which I, with the other prisoners, embarked, and were taken alongside of the *Monitor,* an officer from that boat coming on board, in command of the party to go to City Point.

I was under intense excitement, for, after nearly ten weary months of imprisonment, I was in sight of the promised land. In a short time we reached the shore, and my foot pressed the sacred soil. I had worn on my shoulders from Fortress Monroe, in the folds of a shawl, a large battle-flag, which had been made by myself and other prisoners whilst in prison for General Beauregard. I felt strongly tempted to unfold it and cast it to the breeze, as a parting defiance to the Yankees; but I remembered that the same means might be useful again.

I was received by Colonel Ash and other Confederate officers, whose bold and soldierly bearing contrasted most strikingly with the Vandal race whom I had seen, I hope, for the last time.

I was conducted under escort of those gentlemen to Petersburg, where I was received with every demonstration of kindness and respect. General Ransom,[11] the Commander of the Department, came to call upon me, and took charge of the arrangements for my departure to Richmond, and sent Colonel Ash to escort me.

I arrived in Richmond, on the morning of the 4th, and was taken to the best hotel in the place, the Ballard House, where rooms had been prepared for me. General Winder,[12] the Commandant of Richmond, came immediately to call upon me, so

---

[11] General Matt Whitaker Ransom, of North Carolina.
[12] General John H. Winder, of Maryland, was Provost Marshall.

as to dispense with the usual formality of my reporting to him.

On the evening after my arrival our President did me the honour of calling upon me, and his words of greeting, "But for you there would have been no battle of Bull Run," repaid me for all that I had endured, even though it had been magnified tenfold. And I shall ever remember that as the proudest moment of my whole life, to have received the tribute of praise from him who stands as the apostle of our country's liberty in the eyes of the civilized world.

It would swell these pages far beyond my prescribed limits if I were to enter upon a description of the exciting scenes which met my eye on my arrival at Richmond. All was warlike preparation and stern defiance and resistance to the invader. . . .

9. ELIZABETH L. VAN LEW

"The Roar of the Guns Grew Louder and Louder"

Elizabeth Van Lew and her mother lived in a handsome house on Grace Street in Richmond. Elizabeth was a spy for the Federal government in Washington.

She was born in New York in 1818, the daughter of John Van Lew and the granddaughter of Hillary Baker, who was once mayor of Philadelphia. The family moved to Richmond, where her father prospered as a hardware merchant. Mr. Van Lew, a slaveholder, was described as an "excellent man and an old Whig." Visitors from the United States and Europe admired the stately residence and its terraced gardens.

Elizabeth attended school in Philadelphia and became an avowed Abolitionist. Upon her father's death, early in 1860, she and her mother freed their slaves. When war began, she became an active and efficient spy for the Union. She sent valuable military information to the North, ministered to Federal prisoners confined in Richmond, and, on several occasions, placed one of her freed slaves in the Confederate White House as a maid to the Davis children.

Miss Van Lew kept a journal, but "keeping a complete journal," she sensed, "was an impossibility and a risk too fearful to take. Keeping one's house in order for Government inspection with Salisburg prison in prospective, necessitated this. I always went to bed at night with anything dangerous on paper beside me so as to be able to destroy it in a moment."

As summer began, Elizabeth waited impatiently to welcome General McClellan to her home.

Friday, June 20, 1862. How long is this to last? We are in hourly expectation of a battle. It will come when Gen. McClellan gets ready. It is said that the two armies have been drawn up in line of battle for two days. We have hatched eight chickens today, and have a prospect of serving and eating them under our "dear young government;" and so we go, mixing peace and war. . . .

Mother had a charming chamber with new matting and pretty curtains all prepared for Gen. McClellan—and for a long time we called it Gen. McClellan's room.

Saturday, June 21, 1862. The newspapers say that Beauregard and Halleck are both expected. Captain Alexander, in charge of Castle Thunder,[13] told me I had been reported several times. Thursday, the same young man called upon me who was here last winter and made the mysterious appointment—told which works interested me greatly and the government, etc. etc. He came now, insisting—urging us to board him—let him sleep anywhere—in the library on the floor—and move him for any one. "He wished to come for the surroundings." Yes, our surroundings. We were kind and polite. We have to be wonderful and circumspect—wise as serpents and harmless as doves, for truly the lions are seeking to devour us.

---

[13] Castle Thunder in Richmond was a jail for political prisoners and deserters from the Federal army. Libby Prison, a former tobacco warehouse, was converted into an officers' prison. Belle Isle, in the James River, was still another prison.

Thursday, June 26. There has been skirmishing for several
days. This afternoon I rode out with Miss C. . . . The cannonading was heard more loudly as we progressed. The excitement on
the Mechanicsville turnpike was more thrilling than I could
conceive—men riding and leading horses at full speed—the rattling of their gear, their canteens and arms—the rush of the poor
beasts into and out of the pond at which they were watered—the
dust, the commotion . . . the ambulances—the long lines of infantry awaiting orders. We inquired the news of the picket who
stopped us. He told us that we were whipping the Federals right,
left and in the center—had taken many prisoners. The roar of
the guns grew louder and louder. . . .

The rapid succession of the guns was wonderful. . . . No ball
could be as exciting as our ride this evening. . . .

10. CHARLOTTE CROSS WIGFALL

"Our Success Is Glorious"

On June 21, President Davis wrote to his wife, "We are
preparing and taking position for the struggle which must be
at hand." On June 25, he reported, "Skirmishing yesterday
and today." On the morrow, the first of the Seven Days battles was fought at Mechanicsville.

The young Wigfall daughters, along with many other
young Richmond girls, had been sent from the assailed city
in early spring. Their brother Halsey, home from the University of Virginia, had reported for duty. The Senator
posted back and forth from the scene of fighting.

Mrs. Wigfall sent Louly bulletins from Richmond.

Richmond, June 25th, 1862

. . . I am getting a great deal better, and went out this afternoon to take a drive with your father. We stopped at Genl.
Johnston's to see how he was, and Mrs. Johnston came out and
sat in the carriage with me. He is recovering rapidly, but will

not be in the fight, which has, in fact, begun. There has been very heavy firing all the afternoon, and there will be a regular attack made at daybreak tomorrow, if the present plan is followed out. I presume it will be, as Genl. Jackson is to move into position tonight, and of course, has to be supported. This was agreed upon last night. What has caused the fight this afternoon we do not know—but I trust it is all right. Jackson and his forces are to make the attack on the rear, and I trust it has all been so planned that McClellan will find himself glad enough to take the road away from, instead of *on* to Richmond.

Thursday 26th

I wrote you your father had acted as Aide to Genl. Longstreet. After we got home last evening, your father determined to go to Genl. Longstreet's Headquarters, to see if there had been any change in the programme since the night before. He did not get back till nearly twelve o'clock—and at that time, the original plan was to be carried out—and he accordingly was off at four o'clock this morning. Strange to say, however, there seems to be an impression in town, that there has been no fighting to-day; not a gun has been heard, and everyone has been on the lookout for tidings. Halsey came in just before dinner and he has heard nothing of it—so I am afraid (I was going to say) that something has disconcerted the plan and I feel quite impatient for your father's return. He said he would be back some time to-night.

Friday night, 27th

Yesterday afternoon I took a drive with Halsey and as soon as we got on Church Hill we heard the cannon and it seems the fight had begun at 3 o'clock in the afternoon instead of at daylight as it had been arranged. Your father got back after twelve last night. The news was all good, as you have seen, I suppose. We had driven them from Mechanicsville and taken several batteries, etc. The battle was to be renewed this morning at daylight, and accordingly, off went Papa, and I don't expect to see him again until midnight or maybe to-morrow. Robert Nicholas, however, told me about sundown that he had left him well an hour or two before and that the Yankees had been driven back six miles. All the accounts we have yet received, altho' meagre, yet agree that we are in hot pursuit and the enemy trying to get away. God grant that our victory may be complete! I will write more to-morrow when I can tell you what your father says. Good night.

Saturday, 28th

Your father did not come last night, dear L. I got a note from him early this morning. Thank God, he was unhurt! and remained to look up our wounded Texans. So far our victory has been brilliant, but oh! at what sacrifice of life! Poor Col. Marshall (1st Texas) is killed; so is Lieut. Col. Warwick. His poor mother's heart will be broken, I fear. (He was an only child.) The Major of the Regiment, too, is dangerously wounded. Genl. Hood is not hurt or was not when your father wrote. God grant your father may be safe now! He expected to be up all night collecting and caring for our wounded. We have heard no cannon to-day and I don't know whether the fighting has continued or not. Cousin Lewis has just been here and says he hears 1,500 prisoners have already arrived, and among them 2 generals. There are all sorts of reports, one, that we have taken eighty officers above the rank of major. Your father thought the battle would be over to-day. I am almost afraid to believe it. Halsey has not been at all in the direction of the fight. He is guarding the batteries on the extreme right, and the contest has all been on the left. He has got his commission for 2nd Lieutenant—or rather, I have got it here for him.

Sunday, 29th

Another note from your dear father this morning. It was written last night, the other side of the Chickahominy at Headquarters. He says they were still driving the enemy before them, and that operations would begin again at daybreak, and that he hoped it would be over to-day. I shall not expect him back until it is entirely concluded. He says the slaughter has been terrible, but our success glorious.

11. JUDITH BROCKENBROUGH McGUIRE

"Beautiful, yet Awful!"

While rumors were being circulated in Washington that Richmond had been captured, the ladies of the Confederate capital, from atop its tall buildings, witnessed "a scene terrifically grand."

Faithful to the diary which she kept "for the members of my family who are too young to remember these days," Mrs. McGuire continued her record during the Seven Days of critical combat.

June 27. Yesterday was a day of intense excitement in the city and its surroundings. Early in the morning it was whispered about that some great movement was on foot. Large numbers of troops were seen under arms, evidently waiting for orders to move against the enemy. A. P. Hill's Division occupied the range of hills near "Strawberry Hill," the cherished home of my childhood, overlooking the old "Meadow Bridges."

About three o'clock the order *to move,* so long expected, was given. The Division marched steadily and proudly to the attack. . . . The enemy's pickets were just across the river. . . . The gallant Fortieth, followed by Pegram's Battery, rushed across the bridge at double-quick, and with exultant shouts drove the enemy's pickets from their posts. The enemy was driven rapidly down the river to Mechanicsville, where the battle raged long and fiercely. At nine o'clock all was quiet; the bloody struggle over for the day. Our victory is said to be glorious, but not com-

plete. The fighting is even now renewed, for I hear the firing of
heavy artillery.

Last night our streets were thronged until a late hour to catch
the last accounts from couriers and spectators returning from the
field. . . . The President, and many others, were on the surround-
ing hills during the fight, deeply interested spectators. The
calmness of the people during the progress of the battle was
marvelous. The balloons of the enemy hovering over the battle-
field could be distinctly seen from the outskirts of the city, and
the sound of musketry as distinctly heard. All were anxious, but
none alarmed for the safety of the city. From the firing of the
first gun till the close of the battle every spot favorable for observation was crowded. The tops of the Exchange, the Ballard
House, the Capitol, and almost every other tall house were covered with human beings; and after nightfall the commanding
hills from the President's house to the Alms-House were covered, like a vast amphitheatre, with men, women and children,
witnessing the grand display of fireworks—beautiful, yet
awful. . . .

Ten o'clock at night. . . . Another day of great excitement in
our beleaguered city. From early dawn the cannon has been roaring around us. Our success has been glorious! The citizens—
gentlemen as well as ladies—have been fully occupied in the
hospitals.

Visions of the battle-field have haunted me all day. Our loved
ones, whether friends or strangers—all Southern soldiers are dear
to us—lying dead or dying; the wounded in the hot sun, the dead
being hastily buried. McClellan is said to be retreating. "Praise
the Lord, O my soul!"

28th. . . . The booming of cannon still heard distinctly, but
the sound is more distant.

June 30. McClellan certainly retreating. We begin to breathe
more freely; but he fights as he goes. . . .

The city is sad, because of the dead and dying; but our hearts are filled with gratitude and love. The end is not yet—oh that it were! . . .

July 2. . . . Richmond is disenthralled and the only Yankees there are in the Libby and other prisons. McClellan and his "Grand Army" are on James River near "Westover," enjoying mosquitoes and bilious fevers. . . .

12. SARA RICE PRYOR
"The Hospital Was Filled to Overflowing"

> After leaving Washington, Mrs. Pryor and her young children went to stay with her father, the Reverend Samuel Blair Rice, in Petersburg, while her husband continued on to Montgomery. Dr. Rice became a chaplain in the Confederate Army; Roger was made a colonel of the 3rd Virginia Infantry, and, after the battle of Williamsburg, a brigadier general. He fought at Fair Oaks and in the Seven Days.
> Early in the war, Mrs. Pryor was determined to follow her husband and his regiment. She was in Richmond during the Seven Days.

All the afternoon the dreadful guns shook the earth. I shut myself in my darkened room. At twilight I had a note from Governor Letcher,[14] telling me a fierce battle was raging, and inviting me to come to the Governor's mansion. From the roof one might see the flash of musket and artillery.

No! I did not wish to see the infernal fires. I preferred to watch and wait alone in my room.

The city was strangely quiet. Everybody had gone out to the hills to witness the aurora of death. As it grew dark a servant entered to light my candles, but I forbade her. Did I not mean

---

[14] John Letcher, of Lexington, a former U.S. Congressman who had been elected Governor of Virginia in 1859.

to go to supper? I would have coffee brought to me. God only knew what news I might hear before morning. I must keep up my strength.

The night was hot and close. I sat at an open window, watching for couriers on the street. The firing ceased about nine o'clock. Surely now somebody would remember us and come to us.

As I leaned on the window-sill with my head on my arms, I saw two young men walking slowly down the deserted street. They paused at a closed door opposite me and sat down upon the low step. Presently they chanted a mournful strain in a minor key—like one of the occasional interludes of Chopin which reveal so much of dignity in sorrow. I was powerfully affected—as I always am by such music—and found myself weeping, not for my own changed life, not for my own sorrows, but for the dear city; the dear, doomed city, so loved, so loved!

A full moon was rising behind the trees in the Capitol Square. Soon the city would be flooded with light; and then!—would the invading host come in to desecrate and destroy?

The night wore on and I waited and watched. Before dawn a hurried footstep brought a message from the battle-field to my door.

"The General,[15] Madam, is safe and well. Colonel Scott has been killed. The General has placed a guard around his body, and he will be sent here early to-morrow. The fight will be renewed, and will continue until the enemy is driven away."

My resolution was taken. My children were safe with their grandmother. I would write. I would ask that every particle of my household linen, except a change, should be rolled into bandages, all my fine linen be sent to me for compresses, and all forwarded as soon as possible.

I would enter the new hospital which had been improvised in Kent & Paine's warehouse, and would remain there as a nurse as long as the armies were fighting around Richmond.

---

[15] General Roger A. Pryor.

But the courier was passing on his rounds with news for others. Presently Fanny Poindexter, in tears, knocked at my door.

"She is bearing it like a brave, Christian woman."

"*She!* Who? Tell me quick."

"Mrs. Scott. I had to tell her. She simply said, 'I shall see him once more.' The General wrote to her from the battle-field and told her how nobly her husband died,—leading his men in the thick of the fight,—and how he had helped to save the city."

Alas, that the city should have needed saving! What had Mrs. Scott and her children done? Why should they suffer? Who was to blame for it all?

Kent & Paine's warehouse was a large, airy building, which had, I understood, been offered by the proprietors for a hospital immediately after the battle of Seven Pines. McClellan's advance upon Richmond had heavily taxed the capacity of the hospitals already established.

When I reached the warehouse, early on the morning after the fight at Mechanicsville, I found cots on the lower floor already occupied, and other cots in process of preparation. An aisle between the rows of narrow beds stretched to the rear of the building. Broad stairs led to a story above, where other cots were being laid.

The volunteer matron was a beautiful Baltimore woman, Mrs. Wilson. When I was presented to her as a candidate for admission, her serene eyes rested doubtfully upon me for a moment. She hesitated. Finally she said: "The work is very exacting. There are so few of us that our nurses must do anything and everything—make beds, wait upon anybody, and often a half a dozen at a time."

"I will engage to do all that," I declared, and she permitted me to go to a desk at the farther end of the room and enter my name.

As I passed by the rows of occupied cots, I saw a nurse kneeling beside one of them, holding a pan for a surgeon. The red stump of an amputated arm was held over it. The next thing I knew I was myself lying on a cot, and a spray of cold water was falling over my face. I had fainted. Opening my eyes, I found the matron standing beside me.

"You see it is as I thought. You are unfit for this work. One of the nurses will conduct you home."

The nurse's assistance was declined, however. I had given trouble enough for one day, and had only interrupted those who were really worth something.

A night's vigil had been poor preparation for hospital work. I resolved I would conquer my culpable weakness. . . .

I took myself well in hand. Why had I fainted? I thought it was because of the sickening, dead odor in the hospital, mingled with that of acids and disinfectants. Of course this would always be there—and worse, as wounded men filled the rooms. I provided myself with sal volatile and spirits of camphor,—we wore pockets in our gowns,—and thus armed I presented myself again to Mrs. Wilson.

She was as kind as she was refined and intelligent. "I will give you a place near the door," she said, "and you must run out into the air at the first hint of faintness. You will get over it, see if you don't."

Ambulances began to come in and unload at the door. I soon had occupation enough, and a few drops of camphor on my handkerchief tided me over the worst. The wounded men crowded in and sat patiently waiting their turn. One fine little fellow of fifteen unrolled a handkerchief from his wrist to show me his wound. "There's a bullet in there," he said proudly. "I'm going to have it cut out, and then go right back to the fight. Isn't it lucky it's my left hand?"

As the day wore on I became more and more absorbed in my work. I had, too, the stimulus of a reproof from Miss Deborah Couch,[16] a brisk, efficient middle-aged lady, who asked no quarter and gave none. She was standing beside me a moment, with a

---

[16] One of many volunteer nurses. We will meet her again at Camp Winders Hospital.

bright tin pan filled with pure water, into which I foolishly dipped a finger to see if it were warm; to learn if I would be expected to provide warm water when I should be called upon to assist the surgeon.

"This water, Madam, was prepared for a raw wound," said Miss Deborah, sternly. "I must now make the surgeon wait until I get more."

As she charged down the aisle with a pan of water in her hand, everybody made way. She had known of my "fine-lady faintness," as she termed it, and I could see she despised me for it. She had volunteered, as all the nurses had, and she meant business. She had no patience with nonsense, and truly she was worth more than all the rest of us.

"Where can I get a little ice?" I one day ventured of Miss Deborah.

"Find it," she rejoined, as she rapidly passed on; but find it I never did. Ice was an unknown luxury until brought to us later from private houses.

But I found myself thoroughly reinstated—with surgeons, matron, and Miss Deborah—when I appeared a few days later, accompanied by a man bearing a basket of clean, well-rolled bandages, with promise of more to come. The Petersburg women had gone to work with a will upon my table-cloths, sheets, and dimity counterpanes—and even the chintz furniture covers. My fine linen underwear and napkins were cut, by the sewing circle at the Spotswood, according to the surgeon's directions, into lengths two inches wide, then folded two inches, doubling back and forth in a smaller fold each time, until they formed pointed wedges for compresses. . . .

The bloody battle of Gaines's Mill soon followed—then Frazier's Farm, within the week, and at once the hospital was filled to overflowing. Every night a courier brought me tidings of my husband. When I saw him at the door my heart would die within me! One morning John came in for certain supplies.

After being reassured as to his master's safety, I asked, "Did he have a comfortable night, John?"

"He sholy did! Marse Roger cert'nly was comfortable las' night. He slep' on de field 'twixt two daid horses!"

The women who worked in Kent & Paine's hospital never seemed to weary. After a while the wise matron assigned us hours, and we went on duty with the regularity of trained nurses. My hours were from seven to seven during the day, with the promise of night service should I be needed.

Every morning the Richmond ladies brought for our patients such luxuries as could be procured. The city was in peril, and distant farmers feared to bring in their fruits and vegetables. One day a patient-looking middle-aged man said to me, "What would I not give for a bowl of chicken broth like my mother used to give me when I was a sick boy!" I perceived one of the angelic matrons of Richmond at a distance, stooping over the cots, and found my way to her and said: "Dear Mrs. Maben, have you a chicken? And could you send some broth to No. 39?" She promised, and I returned with her promise to the poor wounded fellow. He shook his head. "To-morrow will be too late," he said.

I had forgotten the circumstance next day, but at noon I happened to look toward cot No. 39, and there was Mrs. Maben herself. She had brought the chicken broth in a pretty china bowl, with napkin and silver spoon, and was feeding my doubting Thomas, to his great satisfaction.

It was at this hospital that the little story originated which was deemed good enough to be claimed by other hospitals, of the young girl who approached a sick man with a pan of water in her hand and a towel over her arm.

"Mayn't I wash your face?" said the girl, timidly.

"Well, lady, you may if you want to," said the man wearily. "It has been washed fourteen times this morning! It can stand another time, I reckon."

At the end of a week the matron had promoted me! Instead

of carving the fat bacon, to be dispensed with corn bread for the hospital dinner, or standing between two rough men to keep away the flies, or fetching water, or spreading sheets on cots, I was assigned to regular duty with one patient.

Each of the battles of those seven days brought a harvest of wounded to our hospital. I used to veil myself closely as I walked to and from my hotel, that I might shut out the dreadful sights in the street,—the squads of prisoners, and, worst of all, the open wagons in which the dead were piled. Once I *did* see one of these dreadful wagons! In it a stiff arm was raised, and shook as it was driven down the street, as though the dead owner appealed to Heaven for vengeance; a horrible sight never to be forgotten.

After one of the bloody battles . . . a splendid young officer, Colonel Brokenborough, was taken to our hospital, shot almost to pieces. He was borne up the stairs and placed in a cot—his broken limbs in supports swinging from the ceiling. The wife of General Mahone[17] and I were permitted to assist in nursing him. A young soldier from the camp was detailed to help us, and a clergyman was in constant attendance, coming at night that we might rest. Our patient held a court in his corner of the hospital. Such a dear, gallant, cheery fellow, handsome, and with a grand air even as he lay prostrate! Nobody ever heard him complain. He would welcome us in the morning with the brightest smile. His aide said, "He watches the head of the stairs and calls up that look for your benefit." "Oh," he said one day, "you can't guess what's going to happen! Some ladies have been here and left all these roses, and cologne, and such; and somebody has sent—champagne! We are going to have a party!"

Ah, but we knew he was very ill! We were bidden to watch him every minute and not be deceived by his own spirits. Mrs. Mahone spent her life hunting for ice. My constant care was to keep his canteen—to which he clung with affection—filled with

17 General William Mahone.

fresh water from a spring not far away, and I learned to give it to him so well that I allowed no one else to lift his head for his drink during my hours.

One day, when we were alone, I was fanning him, and thought he was asleep. He said gravely, "Mrs. Pryor, beyond that curtain they hung up yesterday poor young Mitchell is lying. They think I don't know! But I heard when they brought him in,—as I lie here, I listen to his breathing. I haven't heard it now for some time. Would you mind seeing if he is all right?"

I passed behind the curtain. The young soldier was dead. . . .

When I returned Colonel Brokenborough asked no questions and I knew his keen senses had already instructed him.

To be cheerful and uncomplaining was the unwritten law of our hospital. No bad news was ever mentioned, no foreboding or anxiety. Mrs. Mahone was one day standing beside Colonel Brokenborough when a messenger from the front suddenly announced that General Mahone had received a flesh-wound. Commanding herself instantly, she exclaimed merrily: "*Flesh*-wound! Now you all know that is *just impossible*." The General had no flesh! He was as thin and attenuated as he was brave. . . .

One night I was awakened from my first sleep by a knock at my door, and a summons to "come to Colonel Brokenborough." When I reached his bedside I found the surgeon, the clergyman, and the Colonel's aide. The patient was unconscious; the end was near. We sat in silence. Once, when he stirred, I slipped my hand under his head, and put his canteen once more to his lips. After a long time his breathing simply ceased, with no evidence of pain. We waited awhile, and then the young soldier who had been detailed to nurse him rose, crossed the room, and, stooping over, kissed me on my forehead, and went out to his duty in the ranks.

Two weeks later I was in my room, resting after a hard day, when a haggard officer, covered with mud and dust, entered. It was my husband.

"My men are all dead," he said with anguish and, falling across the bed, he gave vent to the passionate grief of his heart.

Thousands of Confederate soldiers were killed, thousands wounded.

Richmond was saved!

13. JENNIE D. HARROLD

"Give Me the Privates"

> At this time, Jennie was a little girl in Richmond. She cheerfully helped "The Cause" in any way she could, carrying food to the hospitals and fanning the sick. Her mother was "full of good deeds" for the Johnny Rebs.
>
> The city children played soldiers and sang songs about their idolized Confederate leaders. Jennie liked this one:

> > I want to be a soldier,
> > And with the soldiers stand,
> > A knapsack on my shoulder,
> > A musket in my hand;
> > And there beside Jeff Davis,
> > So glorious and so brave,
> > I'll whip the cussed Yankee
> > And drive him to his grave.

... My mother, who was born in Hanover Junction, Thomasia Christian Winston, reared at her uncle's Major Thomas Doswell's home, near Hanover Junction, was, like all other good Hanovarians, given to hospitality and full of good deeds. She became a widow at twenty-three years of age, and I, the eldest child, was made to do her bidding. . . .

My mother opened a room, which was given, from the beginning of the war until its close, to the private soldier, who was not as much sought after as the officers. On one occasion . . . an ambulance drove up to our next door neighbors' and the lady of the house was asked if she would take in some of the wounded.

She inquired, "Who have you there? I only take in the officers."
My mother stepped forward and said, "Give me the privates." So
we made it a rule to look for those unsought.

I was sent out every week day with what delicacies my mother
could provide, from one hospital to another, having certain days
for certain patients at certain hospitals. After distributing the
things, my duty was to fan the sick. . . .

I remember being at Seabrook's Warehouse hospital when two
Negro men came in to take out two dying soldiers (both side by
side with a leg off, and I was fanning them) to the dead house and
one of the men said, "What are you going to do with us?"

They answered, "We want to make room for those coming in."

One soldier said, "Can't you wait until we are dead?"

They said, "No."

And while they were taking them out, one dying man kept
repeating, "Retribution, retribution." . . .

One Sabbath afternoon, a battery arrived to camp on a vacant
lot at Fourth and Main Streets, next to our house. The men
seemed worn out, and being summer time and so warm and
they were preparing to get supper, when my mother sent an invitation for the company, about thirty in number, to come in
and have supper with us. Mr. William Henry Haxall,[18] our next-
door neighbor, invited the officers, so only the privates came to
our house. When the battery left next day, Colonel Ruffin, who
commanded the battery, thanked my Mother and said, "Mrs.
Harrold, if any of my men get sick, or wounded, I shall ship them
back to you." She agreed to this and in a few days two came back
sick. They soon recovered. . . . In a few days, two more were
sent and one of them died. A furniture wagon arrived filled with
coffins to the top, and he, a Mr. Presson, we placed on the others.
We, as a family, followed to Hollywood and looked after his
grave until it was leveled.

---

[18] The William Haxalls lived on Main Street. They had no children but
the whole Haxall connection was large and influential.

About that time the battles were raging around Richmond. A deaf-mute, a playmate, Willie Johnston, used to put his ear Indian-fashion to the ground and make wild gestures and we would listen and hear the firing.

On one Sunday morning, Miss Sarah Dabney, who attended Dr. Hoge's church,[19] came running past our house with her canton crepe shawl flying. The fringe caught in our front gate, which was iron, and she pulled to the utmost trying to get loose, crying, "The Pawnee war is coming." I did not know whether that was man or beast but it turned out to be a U.S.A. ship which was supposed to have passed Drewry's Bluff, our fort, and [be] making up the James River for Richmond. The old men and boys who were the guards of Richmond were rushed to Libby Hill, which was a natural fort. Cannon and side arms were provided and there they stood sentinel but no Pawnee War ever came.

On one occasion Miss K. W. came from near Ashland with a servant, bringing a basket of good Hanover provisions to take to a sick soldier friend who was at Camp Winder Hospital. When we arrived we found he had died and was buried that morning in beautiful Hollywood. We followed out the directions of those in charge and found upon a little wooden head board this inscription,

"I leave my boy at 5 A.M. for my North Carolina home.

His father."

---

[19] Dr. Moses Drury Hoge was pastor of the Presbyterian church in Richmond that General Stonewall Jackson attended.

III

THE SECOND AUTUMN
AND WINTER

October 1862—April 1863

Ambrose E. Burnside planned a winter campaign to capture Richmond. It called for a fast drive from Fredericksburg on to the Confederate capital; but when the Army of the Potomac reached Fredericksburg, they found General Lee and the Army of Northern Virginia posted in force and well-entrenched across the Rappahannock. Burnside ordered his men to "seize some strong point on the other side and keep your whole force in position for a move toward Richmond."

On December 13, the Battle of Fredericksburg was fought, and resulted in a disastrous defeat for Burnside. On January 26, 1863, Lincoln, with some misgivings, appointed swashbuckling Joe Hooker to replace Burnside. He would be the fourth commander to lead the Union army against General Lee.

1. SALLIE ANN BROCK PUTNAM

"The Radiant Image of Peace"

Sallie Ann Brock Putnam, a young Richmond lady, was the wife of Richard Putnam. She saw the first Confederate flag hoisted above the Capitol, and, for four years, the singular scenes occurring in the city formed a part of her daily experience. Shortly after the close of the war, the story of her personal experiences and observations were published under the title of *Richmond During the War*. The book was dedicated to "Her Southern sisters, who, in the cause of the late Southern Confederacy, for which their brethren yielded up their lives—'Did all that woman ever dares.'"

Little more than three months had passed since we had seen Richmond surrounded by the "Grand Army," our government quaking, and ready to give up the capital, our people discouraged and frantically flying in all directions for safety, all classes demoralized, save our trusty army—now, we had not only beheld the mighty host of the enemy driven from its strong position, at our very doors, but beaten back across the Potomac, and the country of our enemies inviting to invasion from the conquering armies of the "rebels."

It seemed almost impossible for us to realize the change. The clouds were breaking on all sides, they had been lifted from Richmond, and an incubus so heavy that it had well nigh crushed out the life of many of us, had been lifted from our hearts. . . .

The close of the summer found the soil of Virginia free from the hostile tread of the invader. . . .

The Confederate Congress, which had adjourned about the time that the gunboat panic took possession of so many of the people of Richmond, convened again in a "called session" in August. With unfeigned courtesy we welcomed back this illustrious body; but they were subjected to the most unmerciful twittings for the fleetness of foot they had exhibited when Richmond was so alarmingly threatened. These unpleasant allusions were received with laughable grace, the best they could summon to aid them in apology for so frantically *"skedaddling,"* when General McClellan had his army planted around the Confederate Capital.

To the pungent but not unamiable taunts that would sometimes assail these honorable gentlemen from their fair friends in

Richmond, they would reply in the golden aphorism (which the ladies claimed to have been captured from themselves) "Discretion is the better part of valor," or rather, the ladies would reform, "Selfpreservation is the first law of nature," with the added assurance that in case of another threatening demonstration, *they* would "keep guard" over the Congress while sitting.

That this illustrious body of Confederate legislators were not insensible to, nor unappreciative of the charms of the women of the capital, is proved by the fact that more than one was consoled in his lonely estate by having conferred on him the hand of a Richmond lady.

The hearts of our grave senators and representatives were not invulnerable, and Cupid kept up a lively business in the "Rebel Capital." . . .

In various offices under the government, and particularly in those of the Treasury Department, the services of females were found useful. Employment was given and a support secured to hundreds of intelligent and deserving women of the South, who, by the existence of the war, or other misfortunes, had been so reduced in the means of living as to be compelled to earn a support. The Treasury Note Bureau, in which the greatest number of women were employed, was under the supervision of experienced and gentlemanly clerks, and no place in the Confederate Capital was more interesting or attractive than that where these fair operatives were engaged in signing and numbering Mr. Memminger's Confederate bills. The duties were pleasant and profitable, and so much sought after by those in need, that hundreds of applications were placed on file by women to whom it was impossible to furnish employment.

It sometimes required considerable diplomacy and influence to secure an office under our Government, and their fair friends made ample use of the members of Congress, the clergy and the military, for reference as to social position, qualification, worth, and need for such assistance. . . .

From the Treasury Department, the employment of female clerks extended to various offices in the War Department, the Post Office Department, and indeed to every branch of business connected with the government. They were in all found efficient and useful. By this means many young men could be sent into the ranks, and by the testimony of the chiefs of Bureaus, the work left for the women was better done. . . .

When our Congress reassembled in August, very differently did our own political skies appear from what they did when it adjourned in the spring previous. They were now spanned by the rainbow-tinted arch of future prosperity. The heavy clouds of war seemed to be breaking up on all sides. The radiant image of Peace, obscured from our vision by only trifling impediments, was ready once more to shed her beams of brightness over our beautiful Southern land.

2. LORETA JANETA VELAZQUEZ

"In the Secret Corps"

Loreta was born of an affluent family near Havana, Cuba. In 1849, at the age of eleven, she was sent to school in New Orleans. On April 5, 1856, she married an army officer and planter named Roach and was living in St. James Parish, Louisiana, when the war began.

After her husband's early death in the Confederate cause, Loreta aspired to be "a second Joan of Arc." She raised a cavalry company, the "Arkansas Grays," and equipped it at her own expense. Disguised as a man, she passed as "Lieutenant Buford." Her company went to Virginia and took part in First Manassas. She then went west and fought under General Leonidas Polk in Kentucky and Tennessee, where she was twice wounded. She was in New Orleans when the Federals occupied it in the spring of 1862.

Still restless and dissatisfied with the small part she played, she traveled to Richmond in the early autumn of 1862 to undertake more important assignments. She had not been there since a visit following First Manassas.

Richmond was a very different place from what it was on my last visit to it, as I soon found to my cost. Martial law was in force in its most rigorous aspect, and General Winder, the chief of the secret service bureau, and his emissaries, were objects of terror to everybody, rich and poor. Beleaguered as Richmond was, every person was more or less an object of suspicion, and strangers, especially, were watched with a vigilance that left them few opportunities to do mischief, or were put under arrest, and placed in close confinement, without scruple, if Winder or his officers took it into their heads that this would be the most expeditious way of disposing of them.

It is not surprising, therefore, that almost immediately upon my arrival in Richmond I fell under the surveillance of Winder as a suspicious character, and was called upon to give an account of myself. My story was not accepted in the same spirit of credibility that some rather tough yarns I had manufactured in the course of my career, for the purpose of satisfying the curiosity of inquisitive people, had been. The fact that my secret had already been several times discovered, was against me to begin with; then my disguise was not in as good order as it had been when I first assumed it; and my papers were not of such a definite character as to inspire respect in the minds of the Richmond police authorities. There was, evidently, something suspicious and mysterious about me; and, suspicion having once been excited, some lynx-eyed detective was not long in noting certain feminine ways I had, and which even my long practice in figuring as a man had not enabled me to get rid of; and the result was, that I was arrested on the charge of being a woman in disguise, and supposedly a Federal spy, and was conducted to Castle Thunder, to reflect upon the mutabilities of fortune, until I could give a satisfactory account of myself.

I thought this was rather hard lines; but as good luck often comes to us in the guise of present tribulation, as matters turned out it was the very best thing that could have happened to me, for it compelled me to reveal myself and my plans to persons who were willing and able to aid me, and to tell my story to friendly and sympathetic ears.

The Commander of Castle Thunder was Major G. W. Alexander, a gentleman, who, ever since I made his acquaintance through being committed to his custody as a prisoner, I have always been proud to number among my best and most highly-esteemed friends. Major Alexander, and his lovely wife, both showed the greatest interest in me, and they treated me with such kindness and consideration that I was induced to tell them exactly who I was, what my purpose was in assuming the male garb, what adventures I had passed through, and what my aspirations were for the future. They not only believed my story, but thinking that my services to the Confederacy merited better treatment than I was receiving at the hands of the authorities, interested themselves greatly in my behalf.

Both the major and his wife—but the lady, especially—seemed to be shocked, however, at the idea of a woman dressing herself in the garb of the other sex, and attempting to play the part of a soldier; and they eagerly urged me to resume the proper costume of my sex again, assuring me that there would be plenty of work for me to do, if I were disposed still to devote myself to the service of the Confederacy. The major, however, was evidently impressed with the narrative I had given him of my exploits, and was convinced that if regularly enlisted in the secret service corps I would be able to render assistance of the first value. He, however, was urgent that I should abandon my disguise, and represented, in forcible terms, the dangers I ran in persisting in wearing it.

To these remonstrances I turned a deaf ear. I had passed through too many real trials to be frightened by imaginary ones, and I did not like to change my costume under compulsion. I accordingly refused positively to put on the garments of a woman, except as a means of gaining my liberty, and with the full intention of resuming male attire at the earliest opportunity.

Major Alexander, therefore, finding me fixed in my determination to have my own way, undertook to have matters arranged to my satisfaction without putting me to the necessity of discarding my disguise, in representing my case to General Winder, and inducing him to give me a trial in his corps.

General Winder ordered my release, and, assigning me to a position in the secret corps, . . . started me off with despatches for General Earl Van Dorn. . . .

3. MARY BOYKIN CHESNUT

"My Dear Friend"

> Mrs. Louisa Susanna McCord was the daughter of Langdon Cheves of South Carolina and the widow of David J. McCord, a lawyer of Columbia. Early in the war, she had raised a company for her only son, Cheves. She gave her time to her hospital in Columbia.
>
> When Captain McCord was wounded at Second Manassas, his mother went at once to Richmond. She tried to get a passport to Manassas Junction. After being told that it was impossible because the Government had seized all the trains, she chartered a special train and brought Cheves home. But in Columbia he was restless and insisted on returning to his regiment, with fatal result.
>
> The "dear friend" to whom Mrs. Chesnut writes is Mrs. Louis T. Wigfall.

[*Richmond, October 29, 1862*]

My dear friend,

My heart is heavier to-day than it has been since the murderous war began. I daresay I have told you, over and over, as I always talk of what is uppermost, that my *cronies* in Columbia, my bosom friends, were Mrs. Preston, Mrs. McCord and Mrs. Izard. Captain Cheves McCord, *only son* of my friend, lies dead at a Mr. Meyers' only a few doors below us. I did not know he was here. Mr. Chesnut had a letter from him *yesterday* dated Fredericksburg. He was wounded at the Second Manassas, two balls in his leg, and one in his head. Contrary to the advice of his doctors, he had rejoined his company, and this is *the end*. He died in convulsions from a pressure on the brain. His mother is expected by every train—poor thing—I could not sleep for thinking of her. She seemed to have but one thought in this world—"My Son." He is barely twenty-one—is married—his wife a beautiful girl—unfortunate and miserable and wretched is it all!

. . . I will try to see you as soon as possible, but I will not, as I had hoped, take the box with you. This unhappy boy, lying dead so near us, makes the thought of theatres hateful to me just now. . . . I feel you are too true-hearted a mother not to sympathize.

Your friend,
M. B. C.

4. LOUISE WIGFALL

"The Suffering Among the Poor Was Great."

> Louise Wigfall, still a schoolgirl, was for the time being with her parents in Richmond. Halsey was with the army, and Henry, one of the Wigfalls' Texas slaves, was his body servant.
>
> Here are her brief recollections of the fall and winter of 1862, and two November letters to her brother.

October 1862 found us delightfully situated in a comfortable house on Grace Street. General and Mrs. Joseph E. Johnston, ourselves, and Major Banks, composed our "Mess." The house stood back from the street with a large garden in front, now, in the fall, fragrant with the aromatic scent of that sweetest of all flowers, the white chrysanthemum, which grew in great profusion in the old-fashioned borders. General Johnston was still suffering from his wound and too unwell to report for duty for some weeks. One great trouble in Richmond during the winter of '62 was the want of fuel, and prices began to mount up fabulously, and the suffering among the poor was great.

November 9th, 1862

To Halsey Wigfall:
We had quite a snow-storm day before yesterday, and it is still very cold. I am afraid our poor soldiers will suffer dreadfully from the weather this winter, as I heard yesterday that we had upwards of 10,000 men without shoes. . . .

November 14th
. . . Mama sends you by Capt. Sellers the buffalo robe and blanket and also a cake of soap, which will be sufficient for *present emergencies*—and as soon as another occasion offers she will send some more. Mama says as soap is $1.25 a cake you must economize! Capt. Sellers will also take the flag that Mama has had made for the 1st Texas; the tassel on it is one taken by Col. Brewster,[1] from the field of Shiloh, just where Sidney Johnston fell, and of course therefore enhances the value of the flag.

We are expecting to leave Richmond next week for Amelia, to return in January when Congress meets. Genl. Johnston reported for duty yesterday and we suppose he will be given command of the Department of the West. They are expecting to leave by Wednesday of next week, so you see there will be a general breaking up of our nice little "Mess." I am really very

---
[1] Henry P. Brewster, aide to General Hood.

sorry; for Mrs. Johnston is a sweet lovely person. . . . Mama has promised to leave us with her next Summer when she and Papa go back to Texas.

There have been several distinguished visitors at our house last week—viz., Prince Polignac; an M.P.; and our Bishop-General Polk. Yesterday Major Daniel[2] and Col. Meyers dined here. Mrs. Elzey and the General were here evening before last; he is to have another operation performed on his jaw, poor fellow, and he looks miserably. . . .

5. KATE MASON ROWLAND

"The Bloody Battle-Field So Near"

Kate and Lizzie (abbreviated by Kate to "L.") were the daughters of Major Isaac S. and Catherine Armistead Mason Rowland. They were living in Alexandria, Virginia, when the enemy came on May 24, 1861. "We could not endure it," wrote Kate. Shortly afterward, the women of the family became refugees; brother Tommie ("T.") entered the Confederate Army; brother Mason ("M.") joined the Navy. Kate's mother and her aunt, Emily Mason, whom we have met in Washington, became volunteer nurses, the former at the springs near Warrenton, and the latter at White Sulphur Springs, Greenbrier County. In November of 1862, they were all gathered together in Richmond. Kate's wartime diary tells what happened.

Richmond, November 17th, 1862. L. and myself are boarding with a private family. Mother and Aunt E. are at Winder Hospital, a short walk from town. We find T. here sick at a private hospital. M. came up to see us with him. It is the first time we have seen them together in several years; our first glimpse of T. since the war commenced.

---

[2] John M. Daniel, editor of the Richmond *Examiner.*

November 21st. Yesterday morning we went out to the hospital in an ambulance to see Mother and Aunt E.

Nov. 23rd. The army is near Fredericksburg. The Yankees at Falmouth across the river. They demand the surrender of the city and the women and children are leaving. The enemy fire on the cars! Gen'l Lee has declared he will not give up the town.

Dec. 10th. T. has gone back to the army.

December 12th. We can hear the firing at Fredericksburg this evening—in low steady, muffled pulsations, distinct from the buzz and clamor of city sounds. The cars have been bringing in the wounded to-day and yesterday. The Yankees shelled the town killing several citizens. We walked to the Square again this evening, the gay crowd, the music and martial parade have a fascination for me; it brings a short oblivion, and the bloody battle-field so near! God preserve our dear boy!

Monday 15th. M. was up this evening. They have been in quarantine on account of the smallpox but came up to bring Commodore Barron.[3] The smallpox it is said has become epidemic, but so absorbed is the public mind with the battles, that it has hardly been realized. We went yesterday evening to the cars on Broad St. and saw them bringing in the wounded. The street was thronged, and ambulances, hacks and omnibuses were all in requisition to carry the brave unfortunates to the various hospitals. They fought the great battle Saturday and repulsed the enemy. Aunt E. received a letter from Uncle R.[4] He and T. both safe.

---

[3] Commodore Samuel Barron, of Virginia, who had been a captain in the United States Navy.

[4] Her uncle, Major Robert Mason.

Friday 26th December. We spent Christmas Eve with Mother at the Hospital, and the next morning, Christmas Day, helped to make good things for the soldiers, stewed oysters and made egg-nog and then superintended the preparation for the Christmas dinner for the Convalescents. It was delightful to see their enjoyment. Four hundred men were served with chickens, ducks, · pies and cider; and the wounded and sick in the wards had turkey, oysters etc. M. had forty-eight hours leave which expired to-day and he has left us. . . .

Tuesday January 6th, 1863. R.'s Division marched through the city this morning en route to Petersburg. T. rode on in advance, stopped at the Hospital to see Mother, then galloped in town to have a few minutes with us before the Division came up. We were on the street looking for the troops and came near missing him. Only time for a few hurried sentences and brief farewells when the staff came in sight and had to leave us to take his place beside the General. We watched them until the long line was out of sight. One soldier was barefooted and several without shoes marching in stocking feet. Such dusty travel-stained looking men, but they seemed in good spirits; many of them with loaves of bread under their arms or stuck on their bayonets, which they munched as they walked along. . . . What pleasure even that glimpse of T. unsatisfactory and tantalizing as it was, meeting as we did in the street, and for so short a time. But to see him after the hardships and battles of the past month safe and well. We should be very thankful. God be with him in the unknown future!

February 3rd. Went to Congress yesterday. Heard Mr. Henry[5] of Tennessee in the Senate. The debate was on the question of the Supreme Court. In the course of his speech Mr. Henry denied the right of secession and maintained that the constitution of

---

[5] Gustavus A. Henry.

the Confederate States made no provision for it. His colleague[6] rose in reply and stated that even Mr. Webster had declared of our union that were it a compact between Sovereign States and not a social compact (as he viewed it) the right of secession must logically follow. In this our new Government, the nature of the agreement is plainly stated to be a compact of states. Strange that such questions should be argued at this early age of the Confederacy. That principle denied in the legislative halls which our armies are maintaining with their life-blood in the field!

February 5th. The ground covered with snow, bitter cold. Went out to the hospital yesterday. A great many wounded and sick still there. . . .

We are trying to get an office at the Bureau for "gumming" stamps. . . .

February 11th. Went to a party last night at Mrs. Semmes.[7] Her husband is in the Senate from Louisiana. It was an elegant affair for war-times. The supper *malgré* the blockade very handsome, and the toilettes, some of them magnificent—velvet and diamonds, silks and point lace. There were four or five Generals present. Huger the handsomest man in the room. Toombs the politician and quondam soldier, Elzey, Williams, Sparrow, etc. Mr. Mallory and his wife with a host of lesser lights.

6. AGNES

"A Sort of Court Is Still Kept Up"

> When Mrs. Pryor included some of her letters in *Reminiscences of Peace and War,* she explained why her gifted, lifelong friend preferred the designation "Agnes": "Being a

---

[6] Landon C. Haynes.

[7] Mrs. Thomas Joseph Semmes. Their Richmond home was directly opposite the Confederate White House.

lady of the old school, she is averse from seeing her name in print." We do know that her husband had been a member of Congress in Washington at the same time as Mr. Pryor, and was at this time in the war a colonel on service with the Confederate Army near Richmond, while Agnes lived at the Spotswood Hotel.

Mrs. Pryor was with her husband at his camp on the Blackwater, near Suffolk. Despite Richmond gossip, Brigadier-General Pryor would not be promoted Major-General. Within a few weeks, his brigade was broken up, and he joined Fritz Lee's cavalry as a private in early April. "It was a bitter hour for me," Mrs. Pryor noted.

[February, 1863]

... In Richmond everybody says the General is to be promoted to Major-General. When he is, I shall attach myself permanently to his staff. The life of inglorious idleness here is perfectly awful. If you suppose I don't long for a rich experience, you are mistaken. Give me the *whole* of it—victory, defeat, glory and misfortune, praise and even censure (so it be *en plein-air*)—anything, everything, except stolid, purposeless, hopeless uselessness.

The worst effect of this inaction is felt in this city, where we can manufacture nothing for the soldiers, and only consume in idleness what they need. A sort of court is still kept up here—but the wives of our great generals are conspicuous for their absence. Mrs. Lee is never seen at receptions. She and her daughters spend their time knitting and sewing for the soldiers, just as her great-grandmother, Martha Washington, did in '76; and General Lee writes that these things are needed. People here, having abundant time to find fault, do not hesitate to say that our court ladies assume too much state for revolutionary times. They had better be careful! We won't guillotine them—at least not on the block (there are other guillotines), but it would be lovelier if they could realize their fine opportunities. Think of Florence Nightingale! Mrs. Davis is very chary of the time she allots us. If King Solomon were to call with the Queen of Sheba on his arm the fraction of a moment after the closing of her reception, he would not be admitted! I can just see you saying, in that superior manner you see fit to assume with me:

"But, Agnes dear! that is good form, you know, and belongs to the etiquette of polite life."

Of course I know it! Did I say that Mrs. Davis should admit King Solomon? *I* wouldn't! I only tell you what other folks think and say—but *ajew,* until I hear some more news and gossip.

Dearly again,

AGNES

7. JUDITH BROCKENBROUGH McGUIRE

"The Blockade"

> Shortly after the Seven Days battles, the McGuires were called from Richmond to the bedside of a daughter who was ill in Mecklenburg County. They spent the winter in Ashland in a small cottage with other refugees.
>
> Her nephew, Major Bowyer Brockenbrough, was wounded at Fredericksburg and carried to Richmond. "Of course," Mrs. McGuire determined, "I shall go down in the early cars, and devote my life to B. until his parents arrive." Her diary continues:

February 11, 1863. For ten days past I have been at the bedside of my patient in Richmond. The physicians for the third time despaired of his life; by the goodness of God he is again convalescent. Our wounded are suffering excessively for tonics, and I believe that many valuable lives are lost for the want of a few bottles of porter. One day a surgeon standing by B.'s bedside said to me, "He must sink in a day or two; he retains neither brandy nor milk, and his life is passing away for want of nourishment."

In a state bordering on despair, I went out to houses and stores, to beg or buy porter; not a bottle was in town. At last a lady told me that a blockade runner, it was said, had brought ale, and it was at the medical purveyor's. I went back to Mr. P.'s instantly, and told my brother (B.'s father) of the rumor. To get a surgeon's requisition and go off to the purveyor's was the work of a moment. In a short time he returned, with a dozen bottles of India ale. It was administered cautiously at first, and when I found that he retained it, and feebly asked for more, tears of joy and thankfulness ran down my cheeks. . . . Life seemed to return to his system; in twenty-four hours he had drunk four bottles; he began to take milk, and I never witnessed anything like the reanimation of the whole man, physical and mental.

The hospitals are now supplied with this life-giving beverage . . . though great care is taken of it, for the supply is limited. Oh, how cruel it is that the Northern Government should have made medicines and the necessaries of life to the sick and wounded, contraband articles!

March 5th. Spent last night in Richmond with my friend Mrs. R. This morning we attended Dr. Minnegerode's prayer meeting at seven o'clock. It is a blessed privilege enjoyed by people in town, that of attending religious services so often, particularly those social prayer-meetings, now that we feel our dependence on an Almighty arm, and need of prayer more than we ever did in our lives. The President has issued another proclamation, setting aside the 27th of this month for fasting and prayer.

Again I have applied for an office, which seems necessary to the support of the family. If I fail, I shall try to think that it is not right for me to have it. Mr. McGuire's salary is not much more than is necessary to pay our share of the expenses of the mess. Several of us are engaged in making soap, and selling it, to buy things which seem essential to our wardrobes. A lady who has been perfectly independent in her circumstances, finding it necessary to do something of the kind for her support, has been very successful in making pickles and catsups for the restaurants. Another rejoices in her success in making gooseberry wine, which sparkles like champagne, and is the best domestic wine I ever drank; this is designed for the highest bidder. The exercise of this kind of industry works two ways; it supplies our wants, and gives comfort to the public.

Almost every girl plaits her own hat, and that of her father, brother, and lover, if she has the bad taste to have a lover out of the army, which no girl of spirit would do unless he is incapacitated by sickness or wounds. But these hats are beautifully plaited of rye straw, and the ladies' hats are shaped so becomingly that though a Parisian milliner might pronounce them old-fashioned, and laugh them to scorn, yet our Confederate girls look fresh and lovely in them, with their gentle countenances and bright enthusiastic eyes; and what do we care for Parisian style, particularly as it would have to come to us through Yankeeland? The blockade has taught our people their own resources; but I often think that when the great veil is removed, and reveals us to the world, we will, in some respects, be a precious set of antiques.

March 15th. Richmond was greatly shocked on Friday, by the blowing up of the Laboratory, in which women, girls, and boys were employed making cartridges; ten women and girls killed on the spot, and many more will probably die from their wounds. May God have mercy upon them.[8]

---

[8] An accident in the Laboratory of the Ordnance Department left sixty-nine of the women and girls dead or wounded. General Josiah Gorgas, Chief of the Ordnance Department, noted in his diary shortly afterward, "Mama [his wife] has been untiring in aiding, visiting and relieving these poor sufferers and has fatigued herself very much."

8. MARY CUSTIS LEE

"Your Patriotic Labour"

In the winter of 1862 Mary Custis Lee was a guest of Mr. and Mrs. James Caskie of Richmond, while her daughter Mary visited Dr. and Mrs. Richard Stuart in King George County, and her daughter Mildred was at school in Raleigh, North Carolina. The three sons were in service—Fitzhugh in the cavalry; Custis on President Davis' staff; and Rob, who had left the University of Virginia, was a private with Stonewall Jackson.

The wife of General Lee dutifully and kindly responded to the many requests which came to her. Young Miss Jeanetta Emily Conrad of Harrisonburg had asked for help in making a wreath.

Richmond 17th Febry 1863

You must pardon my long delay my dear Miss Conrad in replying to your letter received long since with a request for the hair of some of our generals. I assure you I sent messages to them all or rather to *all* I knew but have only been able to procure a few specimens and will not wait longer to send them to you. Genl Lee's stock of hair is so small that I fear the small lock I send will be of little use. You will have to supply all deficiencies from the flowing locks of our very youthful Brigadiers. I hope you will succeed in your patriotic labour and that I shall have the pleasure of seeing it when completed.

Yrs very truly
M. C. LEE

I send you an autograph of Genl Lee which I thought you might like to have.

9. AGNES

"Our Starving Women and Children"

> The bread riot which Agnes describes for Mrs. Pryor took place on April 2. Mrs. Davis said that the riot was headed by "a tall, daring, Amazonian-looking woman, who had a white feather standing erect from her hat."

Richmond, April 4, 1863

My Dear: I hope you appreciate the fact that you are herewith honored with a letter written in royal-red ink upon sumptuous gilt-edged paper. There is not, at the present writing, one inch of paper for sale in the capital of the Confederacy, at all within the humble means of the wife of a Confederate officer. Well is it for her—and I hope for you—that her youthful admirers were few, and so her gorgeous cream-and-gold album was only half filled with tender effusions. Out come the blank leaves, to be divided between her friend and her Colonel. Don't be alarmed at the color of the writing. I have not yet dipped my goose-quill (there are no steel pens) in the "ruddy drops that visit my sad heart," nor yet into good orthodox red ink. There are fine oaks in the country, and that noble tree bears a gall-nut filled with crimson sap. One lies on my table, and into its sanguinary heart I plunge my pen.

Something very sad has just happened in Richmond—something that makes me ashamed of all my jeremiads over the loss of the petty comforts and conveniences of life—hats, bonnets, gowns, stationery, books, magazines, dainty food. Since the weather has been so pleasant, I have been in the habit of walking in the Capitol Square before breakfast every morning. Somehow nothing so sets me up after a restless night as a glimpse of the dandelions waking up from their dewy bed and the songs of the birds in the Park. Yesterday, upon arriving, I found within the gates a crowd of women and boys—several hundreds of them, standing quietly together. I sat on a bench near, and one of the number left the rest and took the seat beside me. She was a pale, emaciated girl, not more than eighteen, with a sunbonnet on her head, and dressed in a clean calico gown. "I could stand no longer," she explained. As I made room for her, I observed that she had delicate features and large eyes. Her hair and dress were neat. As she raised her hand to remove her sunbonnet and use it for a fan, her loose calico sleeve slipped up, and revealed the mere skeleton of an arm. She perceived my expression as I looked at it, and hastily pulled down her sleeve with a short laugh.

"This is all that's left of me!" she said. "It seems real funny, don't it?"

Evidently she had been a pretty girl—a dressmaker's apprentice, I judged from her chafed forefinger and a certain skill in the lines of her gown. I was encouraged to ask: "What is it? Is there some celebration?"

"There is," said the girl, solemnly; "we celebrate our right to live. We are starving. As soon as enough of us get together we are going to the bakeries and each of us will take a loaf of bread. That is little enough for the government to give us after it has taken all our men."

The girl turned to me with a wan smile, and as she rose to join the long line that had now formed and was moving, she said simply, "Good-by! I'm going to get something to eat!"

"And I devoutly hope you'll get it—and plenty of it," I told her.

The crowd now rapidly increased, and numbered, I am sure, more than a thousand women and children. It grew and grew until it reached the dignity of a mob—a bread riot. They impressed all the light carts they met, and marched along silently and in order. They marched through Cary Street and Main, visiting the stores of the speculators and emptying them of their contents. Governor Letcher sent the mayor to read the Riot Act, and as this had no effect he threatened to fire on the crowd. The city battalion then came up. The women fell back with frightened eyes, but did not obey the order to disperse. The President then appeared, ascended a dray, and addressed them. It is said he was received at first with hisses from the boys, but after he had spoken some little time with great kindness and sympathy, the women quietly moved on, taking their food with them. General Elzey[9] and General Winder wished to call troops from the camps to "suppress the women," but Mr. Seddon,[10] wise man, declined to issue the order. While I write women and children are still standing in the streets, demanding food, and the government is issuing to them rations of rice.

This is a frightful state of things. I am telling you of it because *not one word* has been said in the newspapers about it. All will be changed, Judge Campbell[11] tells me, if we can win a battle or two (but, oh, at what a price!), and regain the control of our railroads. Your General has been magnificent. He has fed Lee's army all winter—I wish he could feed our starving women and children.

Dearly,
Agnes

10. ANITA DWYER WITHERS

"My Bonnet Is Finished"

On January 5, 1863, Anita celebrated her twenty-fourth

---

[9] General Arnold Elzey, of Maryland, was seriously wounded in the Seven Days fighting. When partly recovered, he was commissioned Major-General and put in command of the Department of Richmond, where he organized the government clerks into a "Local Defense" brigade.

[10] James A. Seddon, Secretary of War, November 21, 1862-February 1865.

[11] John A. Campbell, of Alabama, had been an Associate Justice of the U.S. Supreme Court. He was at this time Assistant Secretary of War in the Confederacy.

birthday. Her husband, Captain Withers, gave her "a nice
large cake and apples."

The new Richmond Theatre was opened on February 9,
1863. *The Southern Illustrated News* called it "the new and
gorgeous temple of Thespis."

Belle Maury was the niece of Commodore Matthew Fontaine Maury. Mrs. Gorgas was Amelia Gayle Gorgas, daughter
of John Gayle, former Governor of Alabama. Her husband
was Josiah Gorgas, Chief of the Ordnance Bureau.

April 17th. Friday. We all went to the Theatre much to my
dislike. The house is much prettier than I expected to find—the
performance tolerably good. They played the *Carpenter of
Rouen.* . . .

Tuesday 21st. We went around to Mrs. Maury's to spend the
evening. Belle Maury made me some collars.

I bought me a straw hat and trimmed it prettily.

Wednesday 22nd. A pleasant day. In the afternoon my Husband and myself walked to see Mrs. Col. Gorgas. . . .

I received an English barege, shoes, corset and fine flannel
from Maryland. . . .

Tuesday 28th April 1863. It rained nearly all day. My bonnet
is finished, black lace, it cost $25. I furnished everything but
the frame. . . .

11. MRS. MARK VALENTINE

"The Girls Wore Homespun Dresses"

Many years after the war, Mrs. Mark Valentine wrote her
"recollections of a girl of the sixties in Richmond . . . little
realizing the horror of it all and only viewing it through the
roseate eyes of happy girlhood."

When the war was over, she married her Confederate soldier, and they made their home in Little Rock, Arkansas.

Several times the great Army of Northern Virginia, under General Lee, passed down Franklin Street, right by our house on their way to another field of action. As far as the eye could reach were seen old men and women, young maidens and children handing to the jaded soldiers everything available to wear and to eat. They would hang clothing on their bayonets and eat as they cheered us.

On one occasion when the army was passing and General Pickett's division came in view I ran out and gave a young officer a bunch of flowers. The soldiers of his company cheered so lustily that I flew to the house greatly embarrassed. My friend wrote me after he got back to camp that it was hard for him to decide which was the prettier, the flowers or my blushes.

The girls wore homespun dresses. We had an aunt who lived in the country, and she managed to raise a few sheep. From them she gathered wool and spun it into cloth and gave my sister and myself each a dress, which we made and wore with great pride over big hoop skirts, and were the envy of all our girl friends. I made a hat of the sleeve of an old broadcloth coat and put a feather in it that came from the waving plumes of a "chanticleer."

Very often when General Lee was in Richmond he would drop in to see us, as his home was only a few doors below us on Franklin Street. He was fond of us and the girls who generally gathered with us at our uncles', and he always urged us to make it as gay as possible for the soldiers, which we did. General Lee was grand in every way.

The War Department was just across the street from us and we often sat at the windows and watched the coming and going of the officers. We could see General J. E. B. Stuart with his waving plume on his wide-brimmed hat, his clanking spurs sounding loudly on the pavement as he dismounted from his fine horse. One time at the house of a friend we met the "Gallant Pelham."[12]

---

[12] Captain John Pelham, of the Virginia artillery.

I knew and admired so much President Davis. I several times attended his "Levees." He was a stately, elegant man. I can see him now on his superb charger riding the streets unattended and lifting his hat in response to greetings. On one occasion he went out to view the troops that were stationed at the Fair Grounds near the city. We were present and heard his speech. There was a vast audience. I stood very near Mr. Davis while he was speaking. After he had ended his speech and mounted, there was, of course, wild cheering, which so frightened his horse that he reared fearfully, and one of his fore feet grazed my shoulder, which alarmed me so I screamed as I jumped away. Mr. Davis alighted from his horse, came to me, and was much pleased when he found I was not hurt.

There was great diversity of styles in the sixties. At our gatherings there might be one belle attired in handsome velvet or satin, trimmed with point lace which had been worn by an ancestress; while others in the room would feel very elegant in a wash muslin or calico dress, costing perhaps, fifteen dollars a yard. On one occasion I wore an old tarleton dress that had been resurrected, though rumpled and worn. I had no trimming but rows of arborvitae which I plucked from the bush in the yard. The evergreen was put on flat like insertion all over the waist and skirt, and I thought it was the gem of the evening. I wore a green ribbon in my hair. My shoes, which were trimmed with green ribbon bows, were borrowed from some one in the house who had a smaller foot than I.

After the first two years of the war the storerooms became almost empty and our fare was very frugal. We often sat down at the table to bread, a dish of rice, and no butter. If we had more, it was reserved for the soldiers in camps and hospitals.

I can still hear the sound of bugle and drum, the tramp, tramp, tramp of the marching army, and I can see the soldiers, ragged, unkempt, sockless, and shoeless, yet always bright and brave. I can hear the moan of the widow for her loved one lost in battle.

I can see the bright faces and hear the gay laughter of our young friends as we walked and danced with the soldier boys. General Lee's voice is as clear to me now as when I heard him years ago. . . .

12. SARAH A. C. GIBSON

"Watch over Charley"

> Mrs. Gibson's "little boy Charley" may have been a drummer boy, or one of the many very young enlisted "men."
> She wrote this letter to Charley's lieutenant.

[no date]

Lieut. Sauntey

Dear Sir; I feel under obligations to you and Col. Richardson for sending my little boy to see [me] in the hour of trouble. I am glad to know that you simpathise with me so deeaply. I have one request to ask of you, that is to watch over Charley & take good care of him & if he gets sick pleas send him to me pleas do not let him suffer for any thing. I put my little boy under your protection, I will take [it] as a great favor for you to write to me when you can make it convenient to do so as he is small & cannot do as a grown person & if any of your men [are] wounded let me know & I will send bandages for them.

Yours respectfully.

IV

"HOPE ON, HOPE EVER"

May—December 1863

Hooker's "On to Richmond" movement was the fifth futile attempt. On April 27, he began his grand march up and across the Rappahannock in the hope of striking Lee in the rear and cutting his communications with Richmond. So confident was he of success, that he declared Lee's army "the property of the Army of the Potomac."

At Chancellorsville, in the first days of May, General Lee won a great victory over Hooker, but he lost Stonewall Jackson. More than 10,000 of his gallant soldiers fell, dead or wounded.

In early summer, the Confederacy once again took the offensive and invaded the North.

"On Wednesday, Thursday and Friday (1st, 2d and 3d of July) was fought the great battle of Gettysburg, in Pennsylvania, between the forces of Gen. Lee and the Yankee army under the command of Gen. Meade, who succeeds Hooker, superseded for incompetency," reported *The Southern Illustrated News* on July 25, 1863. "This was probably the most obstinate battle of the war. For the first two days our troops drove those of the enemy before them, and captured 4,000 prisoners. . . . On Friday Gen. Lee renewed the attack on the enemy. . . .

"The most astounding lies were telegraphed to the cities, and spread over the country by means of the press. Lee's army according to them, had been completely routed and disorganized. . . . In the meantime, a telegram announcing a great victory and the capture of 40,000 Yankees, had been received in Richmond, and the people were jubilant. Suddenly their joy was cut short by the arrival of the flag-of-truce boat with the Yankee papers. Something very like a panic succeeded. The people seemed to take the Yankee lies for gospel; and when news arrived of the surrender of Pemberton at Vicksburg, the public pulse ebbed lower than we have ever known it. . . ."

As the women in Richmond waited for the return of their loved ones, the death of a Cabinet lady—gentle, quiet Mrs. John H. Reagan—was announced. On a July day she was carried to Hollywood Cemetery. She left six young children, who remained in Richmond with their father.

Throughout the remainder of 1863, there was many a cavalry engagement in the Richmond area, but no decisive battle.

1. MARY BOYKIN CHESNUT

"They Are Within Three Miles of Richmond"

On Sunday morning, May 3, 1863, the bell in the tower on Capitol Square rang out a fresh alarm. Federal cavalry under General George Stoneman were at the very gates of Richmond. While the safety of the city was thus threatened, Generals Lee and Jackson were attacking the enemy at Chancellorsville.

Mrs. Chesnut admitted she lost her head and burned part of her journal. Her maid Molly had steadily warned, "Missis, listen to de guns. Burn up everything. . . . They are sure to come, and they'll put in their newspapers whatever you write here every day." And Mrs. Chesnut had to admit that "The guns did sound very near."

During Stoneman's raid, on a Sunday, I was in Mrs. Randolph's[1] pew. The battle of Chancellorsville was also raging. The rattling of ammunition wagons, the tramp of soldiers, the everlasting slamming of those iron gates of the Capitol Square just opposite the church, made it hard to attend to the service.

---

[1] President of the Ladies Association of Richmond.

Then began a scene calculated to make the stoutest heart quail. The sexton would walk quietly up the aisle to deliver messages to worshipers whose relatives had been brought in wounded, dying, or dead. Pale-faced people would then follow him out.

Finally, the Rev. Mr. Minnegerode bent across the chancel-rail to the sexton for a few minutes, whispered with the sexton, and then disappeared. The assistant clergyman resumed the communion which Mr. Minnegerode had been administering. At the church door stood Mrs. Minnegerode, as tragically wretched and as wild-looking as ever Mrs. Siddons was. She managed to say to her husband, "Your son is at the station, dead!" When these agonized parents reached the station, however, it proved to be someone else's son who was dead—but a son all the same. Pale and wan came Mr. Minnegerode back to his place within the altar rails.

After the sacred communion was over, someone asked him what it all meant, and he said: "Oh, it was not my son who was killed, but it came so near it aches me yet!"

At home I found L. Q. Washington,[2] who stayed to dinner. I saw that he and my husband were intently preoccupied by some event which they did not see fit to communicate to me. Immediately after dinner my husband lent Mr. Washington one of his horses and they rode off together. I betook myself to my kind neighbors, the Pattons, for information. There I found Colonel Patton had gone, too. Mrs. Patton, however, knew all about the trouble. She said there was a raiding party within forty miles of us and no troops were in Richmond! They asked me to stay to tea—those kind ladies—and in some way we might learn what was going on. After tea we went out to the Capitol Square, Lawrence and three men-servants going along to protect us.

They seemed to be mustering in citizens by the thousands.

---

[2] Lucius Quentin Washington, newspaper reporter, often mentioned by Mrs. Chesnut.

Company after company was being formed; then battalions, and then regiments. It was a wonderful sight to us, peering through the iron railing, watching them fall into ranks.

Then we went to the President's, finding the family at supper. We sat on the white marble steps, and General Elzey told me exactly how things stood and of our immediate danger. Pickets were coming in. Men were spurring to and from the door as fast as they could ride, bringing and carrying messages and orders. Calmly General Elzey discoursed upon our present weakness and our chances for aid.

After a while Mrs. Davis came out and embraced me silently. "It is dreadful," I said. "The enemy is within forty miles of us—only forty!"

"Who told you that tale?" said she. "They are within three miles of Richmond!" I went down on my knees like a stone.

"You had better be quiet," she said. "The President is ill. Women and children must not add to the trouble." She asked me to stay all night, which I was thankful to do.

We sat up. Officers were coming and going; and we gave them what refreshment we could from a side table, kept constantly replenished. Finally, in the excitement, the constant state of activity and change of persons, we forgot the danger. Officers told us jolly stories and seemed in fine spirits, so we gradually took heart. There was not a moment's rest for anyone. Mrs. Davis said something more amusing than ever: "We look like frightened women and children, don't we?"

Early next morning the President came down. He was still feeble and pale from illness. Custis Lee and my husband loaded their pistols, and the President drove off in Dr. Garnett's carriage, my husband and Custis Lee on horseback alongside him. By eight o'clock the troops from Petersburg came in, and the danger was over. The authorities will never strip Richmond of troops again. We had a narrow squeeze for it, but we escaped. It was a terrible night. . . .

2. KATE MASON ROWLAND

"The Sick and Wounded Are Pouring In"

> Unable to find employment in Richmond, Kate and Lizzie joined their mother and Aunt Emily at Winder Hospital outside the city. "Adieu to Richmond and warm houses; henceforth our home is a cabin," Kate wrote on April 5, 1863.
> There was no end of work to do at Winder Hospital when the sick and wounded from the battle at Chancellorsville began to arrive. More grievous news was still to come.

Camp. May 4th, [1863]. We had a great fright last night. The report was brought out in the evening that the Yankees were at Ashland, tearing up the railroad. A man had galloped in on horseback to tell the news; the cars had not made their appearance. We sat out at our door in the moonlight and discussed the probabilities of Richmond being captured.

A battle took place yesterday and Gen'l Lee drove the enemy back; this Mr. S. told us while we sat here. Finally about 10 P.M. an order was sent out directing all the men at Camp to form in companies and go in to help in the defense of the city. Dr. D. marched at the head of our squadron and every man that was able, black and white, left the place. Mr. E. limped round with a gun in his hand and told us not to be afraid. I had retired but Mrs. D. and L. were too excited and sat up by the window. . . . The men from the hospital amounted to 100 or 150. They went into town, were provided with arms at the armory and then marched out again. Dr. L. says the enemy were within five miles of Richmond. I am very anxious to go in town but we cannot get an ambulance; all the horses have been taken off.

12 o'clock, Midday. An officer has just come out from town to order our Regiment away. I stopped writing to fill haversacks.

Thursday 6. The excitement has somewhat subsided. A number of Yankees have been taken prisoners. Fifty men from here have been sent in to guard Libby Prison. Everybody in town is armed; even "B" I saw the other day shouldering his musket as if it had been an umbrella. All the old men, boys, clerks in Departments, Clergymen etc. have formed companies and drill in the Square. The Yankee cavalry came within three miles of the city, stealing horses and Negroes. It certainly was the most daring thing they have done.

Every soldier had been ordered away; the Defences left entirely without defenders; even the City Battalion which was always considered a *fixture,* had been sent off. The Yankees did a great deal of damage. . . . The railroad has been repaired partly and the trains are coming in full of the wounded from the late battle. It was a victory for us and the army of Hooker has recrossed the Potomac. General Jackson was wounded. . . . Our brave old Stonewall! I hope he will soon be able to lead our armies again. Troops are pouring in to Richmond now from Petersburg and elsewhere, Longstreet's Division. . . .

L. and myself move in town tomorrow. We have taken a room in some house with Aunt and will have a private mess. L. will teach a class of small children. I commence my duties at the Marine hospital—going twice a week.

9th May. Still at Camp. Cannot get an ambulance to carry our trunks or ourselves. The sick and wounded are pouring in. Our Division has about 250. Last night during the rain the ambulances were coming out until late in the night. We all went out to the wards with lanterns, tin buckets of water and sponges and wet the wounds, we carried a supply of lint and bandages, but with only two surgeons it was a long while before all could be attended to. Sounds of misery greeted our ears as we entered, some groaning, others crying like children, and some too weak and suffering to do anything but turn a grateful look upon us as we squeezed the cold water from the sponge over their stiffened and bandaged limbs. Our tears fell fast as we moved from bed to bed, such a sight as it was; the men black with dirt and powder, some barefooted, and every form of wound from the maimed hand and broken arm to the bandaged head with perhaps one or both eyes gone and the poor sufferer drawing slow and painful breath with the fatal ball in the chest. Oh, it was fearful. I had no words to say to them, only prayers and tears.

May 11th. My heart is oppressed to-day with the thought of *Jackson's death.* Our great hero, the idol of the people, "old Stonewall"! It comes so suddenly upon us, and seems such a grievous stroke to the Confederacy. But we must not question the wisdom of the Father who has called him, in the plenitude of his greatness and in the midst of his usefulness. . . .

Tuesday 12th. Stopped on my way to the Marine at the Capitol to see the last and the first of Stonewall Jackson. Such an immense crowd. Dr. D. met me and pushed me in with his party. I looked a moment, but only for a moment, when the eager silent multitude hurried me on. Only a thin glass lay between me and the grey lifeless features of him who was our country's boast. . . . The city is one house of mourning; the stores closed and crepe hanging from each door and window. Bells tolled mournfully as the body was brought in town; the soldiers, marching with arms reversed and downcast faces, the members of the old "Stonewall Brigade," all that were here, sick and disabled, came out to follow for the last time their beloved commander. Strong men as well as women weep for him. . . . Little children were brought to look at him so that they might say in after years, "I have seen Stonewall Jackson." He lay wrapped in the white flag of the Confederacy, with its cross of stars upon his breast. White flowers covered the coffin. I could not refrain from carrying away a small blossom as a fleeting memento of the great immortal chieftain. . . .

For two days the town has been full of sorrowful excitement. The streets crowded with people. The bells tolling and flags at half-mast. Yesterday he was brought from Guinea Station and laid in the Governor's house. Two sentinels had to keep watch at the gates to keep the people from coming in. All day long they stood in the square and on the pavement, soldiers, citizens, women and children gazing at the house which contained the sacred remains. All business was suspended and schools closed. To-day the procession formed early. . . . Cannon pealed forth from the foot of the monument and to the sound of sad music and the tramp of the sorrowful multitude he was carried and laid in state at the Capitol, where until late in the evening thousands flocked to gaze upon him for the last time. . . .

3. CHARLOTTE CROSS WIGFALL

"Now What?"

> The sad, sad news of General Stonewall Jackson's death was for days the most important topic of conversation in the capital. "One more year of Stonewall would have saved us," wrote Mrs. Chesnut, echoing the belief of the Confederacy.
>
> Mrs. Wigfall sends along the news to seventeen-year-old Halsey, who will soon be a major. The war must go on!

Richmond, May 11th, 1863

We are all saddened to the heart to-night by hearing the death of our hero Jackson. . . . It will cause mourning all over our land and each person seems to feel as if he had lost a relative. I feel more disheartened about the war now than I have ever felt before. It seems to me it is to be interminable, and what a wretched life of anxiety it is to look forward to! I suppose the death of Jackson has affected us all and I can't help thinking it will put new life into the enemy and give him courage to make another attempt very soon. You see by the papers they claim having taken almost as many prisoners as we have and I am sure the loss of Jackson has turned the last fight into a calamity, if not a curse. I expect you will think I am really blue—but you know Jackson has been my hero and favorite for a long time. We must, though, hope on, hope ever!

I have just come up from witnessing the funeral of dear "old Stonewall." I never saw a more solemn scene and hope never to see another such. This morning early I went to the Governor's and saw the body lying in state. He looks perfectly natural, more as if he were asleep than dead. No one seems to know who will succeed to his command.

Richmond, May 17th, 1863

I send you, with our letters, a pound of candy and a box of Guava jelly which was given me. I know you have no sugar, and I have no doubt that although you will laugh at the idea you will nevertheless enjoy the sweets.

Mrs. McLean (Genl. Sumner's daughter) has been staying with Mrs. Davis for three weeks, waiting for a passport from the Yankee Secretary of War, and Mrs. Chesnut told me the other day that it had been peremptorily refused—so I doubt if Rose will be able to get to Baltimore to her children. We are all very anxious to know the next move. I heard yesterday that Genl. Stuart was to go immediately on an extensive raid, but your father says it is not so. Genl. Lee is still here. Your father is talking of going up with Genl. Stuart in the morning.

4. LOUISE WIGFALL

"Hood's Division Passed Through"

"Louly Wigfall is a very handsome girl," Mrs. Chesnut observed. Evidently General John B. Hood agreed. Later on, Richmond gossip whispered that he was courting four girls, one of them Louly. Now in late May of '63 she was still in school, and the general and his brigade were on their way to Gettysburg.

The Wigfalls had received an account of Chancellorsville from Halsey. Louise answered his letter.

Richmond, May 15, 1863

. . . Lieut. J. called to see Mama and delivered both the letter and the overcoat. The letter was by far the most welcome of the two, as we had heard so little from you since the battle. . . .

Though your first letter written by moonlight on a limber chest was the most romantic, the last was by far the most satisfactory and interesting.

Hood's Division passed through several days ago and we girls had our usual fun, waving, &c., &c. . . . Quantities of prisoners, thousands at a time, have passed also. Three thousand went through on the day that General Jackson's funeral took place.

Quite a misfortune happened last night in the way of the Tredegar Iron Works taking fire—or being set on fire as some people believe by Yankee spies. Genl. Anderson[3] they say has lost an immense amount of money and it will seriously retard the making of arms.

Mama is thinking of leaving town Monday, for what destination *she does not know.* She and Papa both think it useless to wait in Richmond for information of a pleasant locality, so they have determined to get on the cars and travel till they come to some agreeable stopping place. They will then write me of their whereabouts and I will join them, as soon as my examinations will be over, which will be the end of June.

There is no news of any sort at present in Richmond. Everything jogs on as usual—and the devotees of the Capitol and

---

[3] General Joseph R. Anderson, president of the Tredegar Iron Works, one of the largest foundries in the United States. During the war some eleven hundred cannon for the Confederacy were made there.

Franklin St. take their usual promenades, and with the exception of a new face now and then, and a little variation in the way of stars and gold lace, all is the same as when you were here last winter. Richmond is looking beautiful just at present but in a few weeks the heat and dust will have become intolerable.

5. MARY CUSTIS LEE

"Wishing You Much Success"

> On June 9, at the Battle of Brandy Station, Mrs. Lee's son Fitzhugh was wounded; later he was captured and sent to Fortress Monroe. Her husband was on the way to Gettysburg. Mrs. Lee sorrowfully remarked to a friend in Richmond, "I, a poor lame mother, am useless to my children."
>
> Shortly after writing to her little friend, Miss Jeanetta Emily Conrad, Mrs. Lee went to the Hot Springs, in Alleghany County, for several months stay. (The wreath was successfully completed and is now in the Confederate Museum.)

Richmond 16 June 1863

My dear Miss Conrad

I have deferred replying to your letter a long time hoping to collect a few more locks for your wreath. But as I am now about to leave Richmond for the Hot Springs to alleviate a severe attack of rheumatism which has confined me to the House for several months, I will send you all I have, the hair and autograph of the President and a lock of Genl. John Pegram's now in the West. I do not know Mrs. Morgan's direction. I endeavoured to obtain for you some of the hair of our lamented hero Jackson but have not succeeded. You may now have an opportunity of seeing some of the young Genl's yourself and I hope may be more successful than I have been. Wishing you much success and a speedy deliverance from our unprincipled enemy I am yrs most truly

M. C. LEE

6. KATE MASON ROWLAND

"Remember New Orleans!"

While the armies were in Pennsylvania, Major General
John Adams Dix, in command of Federal troops down the
Peninsula, sent raiders to harass and threaten Richmond.

The broadside or handbill noted by Miss Rowland in her
diary on June 28, was signed by Joseph Mayo, Mayor of Richmond. It was dated Saturday afternoon, June 27, 1863, and
read:

"DEFENSE OF OUR CAPITAL

NO SURRENDER!

UNDER ANY CIRCUMSTANCES

"My fellow-citizens, to arms! I have just received a message
direct from the highest authority in the Confederacy, to call
upon the militia organizations to come forth and upon all
other citizens to organize companies for the defense of this
city, against immediate attack of the enemy. They are approaching, and you may have to meet them before Monday
morning. I can do no more than to give you this warning of
their approach. Remember New Orleans! Richmond is now in
your hands. Let it not fall under the rule of another Butler.
Rally, then, to your officers to-morrow morning at 10 o'clock,
on Broad Street, in front of the City Hall."

June 6th [1863]. I was waked up this morning by the sweet
music of the Band on Broad Street. They have been cheering
there too. I hope it is a token of good news from Vicksburg. . . .

June 28th. The Yankees are again threatening Richmond. . . .
The enemy is said to be from 18 to 20,000, within 20 miles of
Richmond. I went in to the Marine yesterday evening. As I
walked through the Square, the militia were assembling to drill;
the stores all closed for that purpose. Such a motley array, old
men and young, with and without arms. Handbills were pasted
on the street corners, "Remember New Orleans," etc., etc.

July 1st. "All quiet along the Potomac to-night." . . .

July 3rd. . . . The city yesterday was excited by many rumors. The militia were all out and stores closed at 11 A.M. Our army in the meantime is marching triumphantly through Pennsylvania. . . .

Sunday, July 5th. . . . Splendid news yesterday in the Extra. The Feds fortifying Philadelphia; our cavalry within five miles of Washington; General Early levying on the people for large amounts of provisions to maintain his army, giving them twenty-four hours to bring in the supplies. . . .

7. ANITA DWYER WITHERS

"On the Day Vicksburg Fell"

While the great fortunes and misfortunes of war kept the people of Richmond in a continual state of anxiety, Anita Withers was absorbed in personal matters. An important event was impending in her household.

Here are items that she noted in her diary starting in May:

Saturday 23rd May. I did not walk out all day until evening. I dressed up and we went around to call on Mrs. Davis. Mrs. Tom Semmes came to see us. . . .

Monday 15th June. We have been married four years today. . . . In the evening Capt. Myers[4] took Cousin Jeannie[5] and myself to Pizzinni's. . . .

Thursday 25th June. It rained all day long. I received some few things from Maryland today.

---

[4] Captain William Myers.
[5] Mrs. Clement C. Clay.

Friday 26th June. A gloomy day. General Lee's Army is in Maryland. In the morning I walked. In the afternoon I made one or two visits—spent the evening at Mrs. Grant's.[6] The Yankees have made another cavalry raid. . . .

Thursday 2 July. There has been a deal of excitement in the city about Yankees coming. The Militia has been ordered out. Mrs. John Purcell called on me. In the evening we walked out to Antonis and had some delicious ice cream.

The weather is intensely hot.

July 3rd. A very *hot* day. The Militia is out again today. I felt very badly all the evening, retired about ten o'clock.

July 4th. Last night I did not rest well, I felt uncomfortable all night long,—waked up very early, sent for Dr. Dean before breakfast, he said there was no doubt but that I was in labour. Aunt Sally, the nurse, Mrs. Duval and my Husband were with me—the baby was born about 15 minutes after eleven. Not a Doctor was near me. . . . Our dear little Johnny is a fine little fellow, weighed nearly eight lbs. My friends were *exceedingly kind* to me, sending me *nice* things, and coming to see me. I had company nearly every day until I left Mrs. Duval's.

The Semmes left whilst we were there. The house was exceedingly *noisy* & disagreeable during my confinement, if it had not been for Mrs. Duval's kindness we could not have stood it. We moved up to Mr. Starke's. . . .

August 15th. Saturday. I had my baby christened today by the Bishop, who stood by as god-father, and Miss Emily Mason god-mother. We returned home and had some champagne and cake. Mrs. Gen. Cooper came around.

Vicksburg fell on the day the baby was born. . . .

---

[6] Mrs. James Grant. Her husband owned large tobacco factories in Richmond.

8. EMMA MORDECAI

"Willy and John Are Safe"

Emma Mordecai was the daughter of Jacob and Judith Myers Mordecai. For many years her father had conducted a nonsectarian female seminary at Warrenton, Virginia. In 1819, the family moved to "Spring Farm" near Richmond and later to the city. Emma had several nephews in the Confederate service; three of them had recently marched into Pennsylvania with General Lee.

When news of Gettysburg and the boys reached Richmond, Emma passed it on to her sister Ellen, who was living in Mobile, Alabama.

Richmond, Tuesday morning, July 12, 1863

My dear Ellen

When I got your letter the other day I was in the depths of despondency at the bad news which reached Richmond that day of the fall of Vicksburg and that Lee's army was defeated and retreating rapidly to the Potomac which was so high that it was impossible for them to cross it. The fall of Vicksburg seemed like a drop in the bucket in comparison with the latter terrible calamity. You may depend upon it there was a long-faced and sadly depressed community in this capital on that day. People could scarcely credit the reports, yet were afraid to discredit them entirely.

George and Gusta were here spending the day. George was much cast down but yet he said he knew that army too well to believe that it could be whipped by any other army in the world. It was impossible for it to be whipped.

Later in the day came more encouraging news—still it seemed to be true that Lee had retreated and was pursued and this seemed to argue a decided reverse. News came in very slowly after this (particulars have not reached us yet), rumours of terrible loss of life on our side that made us almost afraid to hear more.

Some names of our killed have reached us, among them Colonel H. Carrington who married Charlotte Cullen. He was wounded in the hand very badly, and took shelter behind a rock. His men clustered around him and he told them to return to the fight—finding they still lingered, he rose and said he would lead them back himself, and had already proceeded twenty steps when he was shot dead. George W. is reported wounded and in the hands of the enemy.

Since I have been writing this Mr. Cohen has come up with excellent news. Lee telegraphed that the enemy was defeated at all points—that their loss was *immense* and ours not small. That, being much annoyed by the enemy's sharpshooters and artillery among the mountains, to save unnecessary loss of life, and also to secure and dispose of the large number of prisoners and the quantity of stores &c. captured, he deemed it best to withdraw from Hagerstown. An officer who came down last night told Mr. Cohen that the army was in fine condition and spirits, that not a straggler was to be seen and that the train of captured men, wagons, stores &c. was fifteen miles long. Lee says if there are reinforcements to spare they can be sent to him but he has plenty of men without them.

Mr. Cohen saw a person belonging to the Howitzers[7] who knows our boys and says they were neither of them wounded in the first three days' fight—altho' they were in the hottest of the action, the artillery suffered very little loss. We have also heard through Mr. McCarley whose sons are in the same company that both his boys and ours are entirely unhurt. Of William we have heard nothing. I trust he is safe.

A good many slightly wounded men came down on the Fredericksburg train last evening—some were put into ambulances,

---

[7] Richmond Howitzers, an artillery corps d'élite, was organized in the early days of secession.

but the greater number walked to the hospitals. I happened to be on Broad Street at the time. The poor fellows looked hot and uncomfortable enough—and went along like soldiers, as if nothing uncommon had taken place where they had been. So much for public matters. . . .

Willy and John are safe. . . .

9. MARY E. ROWLAND

"The Blood of the Bravest and Best"

Mary E. Rowland was a volunteer nurse at Chimborazo Hospital when word came that an old family friend, General J. Johnston Pettigrew, had been wounded while directing the advance on Pickett's left in the famous charge at Gettysburg. Despite his wound, he displayed conspicuous ability as a rear-guard commander during the withdrawal to the Potomac.

Mary Rowland's letters to his sister, Mary Pettigrew, of North Carolina, were at first hopeful of his recovery. But then the news trickled into Richmond that he had been mortally wounded near Falling Water.

[*Chimborazo Hospital*]
Richmond, July 13th [*1863*]

My dear Mary: I have just this moment learned thro kindnesses of Drs. Brown & Seabrook that a wounded man from your Brother's brigade has arrived. The man was not able to come to me & was not in a condition for me to see him. But I learned the following statement—a horse was shot under Gen. Pettigrew on Wednesday. Another man saw him on Thursday in perfect health but on Friday afternoon he was wounded in the left hand or arm & he is still with his command. The man gained this information from the servant in attendance on your brother. I give you this simple statement just as I heard it—it may be some comfort to you & the fact of his being with his command would leave us to infer that his wound is not dangerous. O, I trust not for your sake & that of the country. I will keep you informed of all that I may be able to gather. The soldier who gave this information is not in my division. I will see him as soon as is practicable. God bless you. I will write in a day or two.

Ever yrs.
M. E. R.

Richmond, July 20th

I wrote a few lines very hastily on Sat. my dear Mary to go with Dr. Gibson's[8] note to you. But later intelligence rendered that letter useless. I did not send it & what can I say to you now my dear friend? Of my sincere love, sympathy & prayers you are always assured & I feel that our Blessed Lord will comfort & support you & human sympathy is nothing compared with that. I am deeply grieved, the whole country mourns for your noble brother. O, it would seem as if we had suffered sufficiently, if as Bishop M.[9] said, the price of a nation's guilt was the blood of the bravest & best. . . .

Mrs. Baylor's son was graciously preserved through all that terrible battle—she heard from him yesterday therefore her anxiety for the time is relieved but her thankfulness only makes her feel more deeply the affliction of others. She has been very sad all day. I heard her say that you had scarcely been out of her thoughts.

Perhaps already you have received all the information from reliable sources. Major Gibson came to tell me this evening that a man from his Brigade was in the hospital. He did not see your brother after he was wounded but he was told by others that he lived but a short time afterwards & died on the battlefield. Capt. McCrerry too was killed but that was the first day at Gettysburg.

---

8 Dr. Charles Bell Gibson, of Maryland, Chief of the Officers' Hospital.

9 Bishop William Meade, of Virginia, died in Richmond in March 1862, and was accorded "a great funeral."

He was Inspector Gen. of his Brigade. I saw a lady who had seen a letter written by Gen. P. to the young man's mother telling all the circumstances.

Your letters came today. I have not the heart to reply now but I will answer your questions in my next. My hands & heart are full all the while, this hospital is filled & likely to be for some time to come. . . .

My head aches badly & it is very late. . . . May our Heavenly Father be with you to bless & comfort & enable you to say "thy will be done." O my darling friend I know how your heart must be bowed down with grief so intense & so bitter & I can do nothing for you. Good night. God bless you my dear Mary.

Most affect. yrs.

MARY R.

Richmond, July 23rd/63

My Dear, dear friend. You are in my thoughts all the while & I write not that there is anything of importance to tell, but simply from the deep interest I take in all that concerns you. . . . I have watched eagerly for some contradiction of the sad tidings. Hope is slow to believe & once before the premature announcement of his death led me to trust that it might not be true.[10] But he was placed in the Capitol last evening & carried to N.C. today. . . .

I had a letter today from Major Frank Huger[11] written at Bunker Hill. He tells . . . of the mortal wound of Gen. P., "brave & gallant soldier for whom the whole country will mourn." It is a comfort to you to know that one so dear was regarded with so

---

[10] General Pettigrew had been reported killed at the battle of Seven Pines, May 31, 1862. He had been severely wounded, bayoneted, and captured. Yet in two months he was exchanged, and took command at the defenses of Petersburg.

[11] Of South Carolina.

much admiration & honor; as some one said "he was blessed with more virtues than ordinarily fall to the lot of man."[12] . . .

This is a dark day truly & a time to try men's hearts. I often think with comfort of Joshua's charge to the people of Israel. "Be strong & of good courage. I will not fail thee nor forsake thee."

Mrs. Baylor heard from her son. He fainted on the march & went through the battle of Gettysburg with only one shoe & one sock—surely God never gave a people such an army as that of Northern Virginia. . . . God bless you.

Most affect. yrs.
M. E. R.

10. MARY CANTEY PRESTON
"My Mind Is So Full of One Thing"

Mary Preston, daughter of General John Preston, sends news of her engagement to Dr. John T. Darby, in the following letter to her friend Mrs. Chesnut. John, of Columbia, was at the Medical College in Philadelphia when war came. He became surgeon for the Hampton Legion and later chief surgeon for General Hood's division. At the time of this letter, he was on the way to Chickamauga. Before their wedding in September 1864 he would run the blockade to Europe for medicines and a wooden leg for General Hood.

Mary Preston refers to Dr. Darby as "the Straggler."

Richmond, September 18th, 1863

. . . On Sunday I went to see Mrs. Davis. She was ill, but I saw Miss Howell. I intended going there today but had a headache and was afraid of the walk. I am sorry I have not seen Mrs. Davis. . . . John Robinson has returned thoroughly anglicised in speech—manner and dress. He was here last evening. Ives too

---

[12] General Lee reported, "Brigadier-General Pettigrew . . . was a brave and accomplished officer and gentleman, and his loss will be deeply felt by the country and the army."

and Mrs. Ives, who came sociably in her morning dress. We like the Lawtons[13] very much. Mrs. Lawton is remarkably pleasant. . . . My mind is so full of one thing I can think of nothing else. Do write to the Straggler. He does not know yet what his address will be but means to send it to me from Columbia or Atlanta. He says he is coming back in December and Buck hopes everything will be over then. I doubt it. Beside my sister and my parents you are the only person I have told. Don't betray me, and send *him* either congratulations or condolences which ever you may think most appropriate.

J. B. Hood was to go to Columbia and stay one day with Uncle Wade. Hood is positively *not* engaged.[14]

September 19th

I went to Mrs. Davis' yesterday and spent an hour or so with her. I thought she seemed to be in bad spirits—perhaps it was only my imagination. . . .

So write soon.

M. C. P.

11. PHOEBE YATES PEMBER

"From Chimborazo Hospital"

Phoebe Pember was the daughter of Jacob Clavius and Fanny Yates Levy, of Charleston. A belle of South Carolina, she married Thomas Pember of Boston and was early left a widow. Her sister was Mrs. Philip Phillips, who was imprisoned near New Orleans by order of General Benjamin F. Butler. Phoebe made the journey to Richmond in the hope

---

[13] General Alexander Robert Lawton, of Savannah, was Quartermaster-General of the Confederacy. Mrs. Lawton was Sarah Gilbert Alexander, of Washington, Georgia.

[14] On the way to Chickamauga, Hood stopped briefly with General Wade Hampton in Columbia. Before leaving Richmond, he had proposed to Sally Preston, known as "Buck."

of helping the war wounded, and soon became superintend-
ent of one of the wings of the immense Chimborazo Hospital. From there, she wrote to her friend Louisa Frederika
Alexander Gilmer, wife of Major General Jeremy F. Gilmer,
Chief of the Engineering Bureau. He was then helping in the
construction of the defenses at Charleston, and his wife was
with him.

20 October 1863

I am divided dear Lou between the double duty and pleasure
of writing to you and testing coffee, as Candis is sick and Kate
Ball gone to Charlotte in search of another brother who is reported slightly wounded. Whatever I say or however stupid and
complicated my epistle is you will at least give me credit for my
intentions. . . .

I received a note from Lucy whom I did not see till a few
days ago telling me of your safe arrival and the adventurous
visit you and Sallie made to Fort Sumter. Wishing to hear more
of your warlike doings I paid a visit to sixth street. My first misfortune occurred then as the Ambulance as usual did not come
for me in time, and I walked long after dark to my lonely room
on Church Hill. . . .

I am preparing to go to my new room. Dr. McCaw[15] sent me
word to make use of the Ambulance as it had to go to market
every morning, and a few squares farther could make no difference. This makes me more comfortable as from the prices
charged me monthly I could not have afforded to engage the
little carriage of the next division. On paying a visit to Mrs.
Skinner I found that I was to have the third story front room, no
gas above the second story and no carpet in this bitter climate,
and without light, fuel, or carpet I was to pay sixty dollars a
month. She had told me that she did not want to make anything
from her lodgers, that she had twelve rooms and paid eighteen
hundred dollars a year, and I pledged myself under the circum-

---

[15] Dr. James B. McCaw, Surgeon-in-chief of Chimborazo Hospital.

stances to take one of the rooms. She asked me if I thought it was too much, and I said she was the best judge, and there the matter ended. I cannot say that I made much of a bargain.

I met Gen. Lawton on the street, looking much stronger and better, he was on horseback, so I only had a word with him. How did you find your "lord and master?" . . .

I have but little news to tell you. Dr. H. has forsworn the flesh pots of Egypt. . . . He comes early to his Hospital and returns late. His purpose is to devote himself to the future happiness of his children and by way of ensuring it he toots away at his flute all the leisure time he has, as when they attain the years of maturity he thinks they will stay at home to hear him play. . . .

Mrs. Randolph has gone into the country with her husband to recruit his health, he looks most miserably, pale and of the consistency of white paper. Unless she takes great care of him I do not think he will live long.[16] . . .

I really don't know what I am writing—it is one of my nervous days and a man in the next room has been bawling some information about a chicken that he got from Georgia that fought when "he cut off his wings and his spurs." I have heard that "chicken man" for an hour, and have not a thought beyond. . . .

Goodbye, *that chicken* is too much for me, combined with the loss of twenty dollars some one stole out of my purse and the scorching of the skirt you gave me, while I was stirring custard on the stove for a wounded man . . . circumstances too hard to bear.

Give my love and a kiss (till I can give it myself) to Gen. Gilmer, tell him I shall only consider it a pleasure deferred. Most lovingly yours

PHOEBE PEMBER

---

[16] After George Wythe Randolph had resigned as Secretary of War on November 15, 1862, he remained in Richmond to help organize volunteers for its defense, and resume his law practice. In late 1864, he and his family went to Europe for his health.

12. ELIZABETH L. VAN LEW

"Threats"

> Without mentioning names, a Richmond newspaper de-
> voted a column to the shocking activities of "two ladies,
> mother and daughter, living on Church Hill." It said that the
> two women had attracted public notice "by their assiduous
> attentions to the Yankee prisoners."
> It was true. Elizabeth and her mother provided many deli-
> cacies to "the miscreants who have invaded our sacred soil."
> On the other hand they refused to make shirts for Confederate
> soldiers. When days designated as "Fast Days" by President
> Davis were strictly observed in Richmond, the Van Lews
> dined in abundant style.

If you spoke in your parlour or chamber to your next of heart
you whispered, you looked under the couches and beds. The
threats, the scowls, the frowns of an infuriated community—who
can write them? I have had brave men shake their fingers in my
face and say terrible things. We had threats of being driven
away, threats of fire, and threats of death. "You dare to show
sympathy for any of these prisoners," said a gentleman, shaking
his finger in my face. "I would shoot them as I would blackbirds
—and there is something on foot up against you *now!*" One day
I could speak for my country, the next I was threatened with
death. Surely madness was upon the people! . . .

I was afraid even to pass the prison; I have had occasion to
stop near it when I *dared* not look up at the windows. I have
turned to speak to a friend and found a detective at my elbow.
Strange faces could sometimes be seen peeping around the col-
umns and pillars of the back portico.

Once I went to Jefferson Davis himself to see if we could not
obtain some protection. He was in Cabinet session, but I saw . . .
his private secretary; he told me I had better apply to the
Mayor. . . .

Receiving personal threats, on being asked and refusing to make shirts for those South Carolina soldiers, mother and I went again to see them and carried in a large basket a set of *Chambers' Miscellanies,* a few other books and some flowers. This we considered very innocent "aid and comfort" and it added much to *our own* comfort. . . .

13. BELLE BOYD

"I Was Besieged with Company"

Belle Boyd, the famous Confederate spy of Martinsburg, Virginia, had visited Richmond in the fall of 1862, after being released from Old Capitol Prison in Washington. Her picture and a story about her appeared in *The Southern Illustrated News,* October 18, 1862. She had been the subject also of an article by the army correspondent of the Philadelphia *Inquirer,* part of which was reprinted in the same magazine:

"The chief of these spies is the celebrated Belle Boyd. Her acknowledged superiority for machination and intrigue has given her the leadership and control of the female spies of the valley of Virginia. . . . Last summer, whilst Patterson's army lay at Martinsburg, she wore a revolver in her belt, and was courted and flattered by every Lieutenant and Captain in the service who ever saw her. There was a kind of Di Vernon dash about her, a smart pertness, a quickness of retort, and utter abandonment of manner and bearing which were attractive from the very romantic unwontedness. . . . Well, this woman I saw practicing her arts upon our young lieutenants and inexperienced captains, and in each case I uniformly felt it my duty to call them aside and warn them of whom she was. To one she had been introduced as Miss Anderson, to another as Miss Faulkner. She is so well known now that she can only practice her blandishments upon new raw levies and their officers. But from them she obtains the number of their regiments and force. She has, however, a trained band of coadjutors, who report to her daily—girls aged from 16 upward—women who have the common sense not to make themselves as conspicuous as she, and who remain unknown, save

to her, and are therefore effective. . . . During the past campaigns in the Valley this woman has been of immense service
to the enemy. She will be now if she can."

Acting on General Jackson's advice, Belle left Virginia to
travel through the South. After her hero's death, she returned
to Martinsburg, was again arrested, conveyed to Washington,
and confined in Carroll Prison. Her worried father followed
her to Washington. Belle contracted typhoid fever, which
led to her release on December 1, 1863. She was sent to
Fortress Monroe and placed on board an exchange steamer,
the *City of New York*. At City Point, she was transferred to a
Confederate flag-of-truce boat.

"Here, under my own country's flag, I felt free and comparatively happy," Belle declared. She continues her story:

On our way up the river to Richmond we had to pass the
obstructions situated between Chapin's and Drury's Bluffs.
These places take their names from the bold appearance that the
shores here present. The obstructions designed to impede a
hostile squadron became accidently hurtful to our Confederate
vessel. She ran foul of them, and it was found utterly impossible
to continue the voyage.

At Drury's Bluff, therefore, we went on board a tug, in which
we proceeded to Richmond. When we arrived, at 8 P.M., I went
immediately to the Spotswood House, and, tired and worn out
with the fatigue of my journey, I retired to rest, refusing to see
any one that evening.

When I came down to breakfast on the following day, my
many acquaintances and friends in the hotel were astonished to
see me, for few had expected that I should be released, and none
that I should so soon arrive at Richmond. The morning papers
announced my return in flattering terms; and, as it thus became
generally known, I was at once besieged with company, and
every afternoon and evening I held a perfect drawing-room. My
reception was everything that I could wish; but, alas! my happiness was of short duration, and my freedom was dearly bought.

I was at a large dinner-party on a Saturday evening exactly one week after the day I had arrived. I was joyous and light-hearted, little dreaming of the blow that was to overwhelm me with sadness. . . .

On Monday morning, the 14th [December 1863], before I had risen, I received a little note from Captain Hatch, in which he expressed great sorrow at having to be the bearer of mournful tidings, and said that, as soon as I was dressed, he would call in person with the wife of the proprietor of the hotel. For one moment I could not imagine what he meant, but, dressing myself as speedily as I possibly could, I sent for them. They came: Captain Hatch held in his hands a newspaper. He approached me, saying—

"Miss Belle, you are aware that you left your father ill?"

In one moment I comprehended everything, and exclaiming, "My God! is he dead?" I sank fainting to the floor.

The swoon was followed by severe illness; and I felt all the loneliness of my position. An exile (for the Yankees held possession of Martinsburg) and an orphan—these words described me; and oh! how hard they seemed!

One of those strange warnings that are sometimes given to mortals, or that are, some would say, the imaginings of an excited brain shaken by sickness, ought to have prepared me for my sad bereavement.

The night upon which my father died I had retired to rest somewhat earlier than usual. How long I slept I do not know, but I suddenly awoke, or seemed to awaken, from my sleep, although I had neither the power nor the wish to move. In the centre of the room I saw General Jackson, whose eyes rested sorrowfully upon me. Beside him stood my father, gazing at me, but saying nothing. I was dumb, or I should have spoken, for I did not feel alarmed. As I looked upon those two standing together, General Jackson turned and spoke to my father. I remember the words distinctly.

"It is time for us to go," he said; and, taking my father's hand, he led him away, adding as he did so, "Poor child!"

I afterward learnt by a letter from my mother that my beloved father, at the news of my being sent south, where I should have to battle alone with the world, had grown rapidly worse, and had expired the very next day after my arrival in Richmond. My mother and the children had been sent for, and reached my father just before he died. . . .

Several of our senators and exchange officers, with many other influential persons, wrote to the Federal Government to try and obtain permission for me to return to my sorrowing mother. I myself wrote to the Northern President and Secretary Stanton, at the suggestion of my friends, and appealed to them as a Mason's daughter. But no, every appeal was refused. . . .

My health was very bad and my constitution greatly undermined. . . .

During my illness in Richmond I was well cared for; and amongst the warmest of my friends must be ranked the wife of the world-renowned Captain Semmes (afterwards Admiral Semmes), of the ill-fated *Alabama*.

Mrs. Semmes[17] treated me with as much attention as though I had been her own daughter. . . . I had always been termed "the child of the army"; and, no matter where I went, I was welcomed both by gentry and the people. . . .

14. ANITA DWYER WITHERS

"We Bought a Servant Yesterday"

We do not know what the Withers family paid for Susan, their eighteen-year-old servant, but in the summer of 1863 the slave William was bought in Richmond for $2,400, and Isaac in Lynchburg for $3,105. In the summer of 1864 a slave girl of Susan's age was sold at Augusta, Georgia, for $4,250.

[17] Anne Elizabeth Spencer Semmes.

Sunday, November 1st, 1863. Feast of All Saints. A beautiful day. The Capt. is going out to the country to Mr. Grant's to spend the day. We bought a servant yesterday. I trust she may suit us. Susan seems to be a good-natured woman, and says she is only eighteen. . . .

Nov. 28th. Susan seems to get along pretty well. Johnny knows her already. . . . I have just been around to call on Mrs. Semmes who is our neighbor. . . .

December 25th. On Christmas day Col. Williams & his family, Capt. Wade & Capt. Myers & wife dined with us. We had a mighty nice dinner—cake, Jelly, Blanc Mange and many nice things. The gentlemen gave several parties. My husband was invited to Mr. Grant's, Maury's and Dr. Cabell's. . . .

V

BUT RICHMOND WAS SAFE

January—May 1864

"Soldiers," said President Davis in a February proclamation, "the coming spring campaign will open under auspices well calculated to sustain your hopes. . . . Assured success awaits us in our holy struggle. . . ."

On March 1, 1864, General Judson Kilpatrick and Colonel Ulric Dahlgren attempted a daring raid on Richmond.

Nine days later, General Ulysses S. Grant assumed command of the Union armies. He began his spring campaign for the capture of Richmond at the Battle of the Wilderness (May 5-7). Then followed the battles of Spottsylvania Court House (May 8-18), the North Anna and Totopotomay Creek (May 23-28), and Cold Harbor (June 1-3). The campaign of one month—from May 4 to June 4—cost Grant 55,000 men and Lee less than 20,000, but he could ill afford to spare them.

Seven miles from Richmond is the battlefield of Yellow Tavern. A monument on the hillside marks the spot where General J. E. B. Stuart fell, and in the city a tablet marks the site of the house at 210 West Grace Street, where he died on May 12, 1864. The inscription ends with his own chivalrous declaration, "I must save the women of Richmond."

General Stuart directed that his golden spurs be given to Mrs. Robert E. Lee as a dying memento of his love and esteem for her husband.

There was a change in President Davis' Cabinet. Thomas Hill Watts of Alabama, whose wife was Eliza B. Allen Watts, resigned as Attorney General in December 1863. In January,

George Davis of North Carolina succeeded him. Recently,
Davis had married Monimia Fairfax, daughter of Dr. Fairfax,
formerly of Alexandria, and then living in Richmond.

1. JUDITH BROCKENBROUGH McGUIRE

"Something Told Her He Would Never Get Back"

Mrs. McGuire was appointed a clerk in the Commissary
Department at a salary of $125 per month. She also continued
her hospital duties.

Sadness had come to her in the death of her nephew,
Captain Newton, who once had marched gaily through the
streets of Richmond on his way to fight at Williamsburg.
After his release from Fort Delaware, he had rejoined his
regiment, the Fourth Cavalry, and was mortally wounded in
October 1863.

January 3, 1864. Entered on the duties of my office on the
30th of December. So far I like it well. "The Major" is very
kind, and considerate of our comfort; the duties of the office are
not very onerous, but rather confining for one who left school
thirty-four years ago, and has had no restraint of the kind during
the interim. The ladies, thirty-five in number, are of all ages,
and representing various parts of Virginia, also Maryland and
Louisiana. Many of them are refugees. It is melancholy to see
how many wear mourning for brothers or other relatives, the
victims of war. One sad young girl sits near me, whose two
brothers have fallen on the field, but she is too poor to buy
mourning. I found many acquaintances, and when I learned the
history of others, it was often that of fallen fortunes and destroyed homes. One young lady, of high-sounding Maryland
name, was banished from Baltimore, because of her zeal in going
to the assistance of our Gettysburg wounded. . . . I am now
obliged to visit the hospital in the afternoon, and I give it two
evenings in the week. It is a cross to me not to be able to give it

more time; but we have very few patients just now, so that it makes very little difference.

Jan. 15. Nothing new from the armies—all quiet. . . . My occupation at home just now is as new as that in the office—it is shoe-making. I am busy upon the second pair of gaiter boots. They are made of canvas, presented me by a friend. It was taken from one of our James River vessels, and has been often spread to the breeze, under the "Stars and Bars." The vessel was sunk among the obstructions at Drury's Bluff. The gaiters are cut out by a shoemaker, stitched and bound by the ladies, then soled by a shoemaker, for the moderate sum of 50 dollars. Last year he put soles on a pair for ten dollars. They were then blacked with the material used for blacking guns in the Navy. They are very handsome gaiters, and bear polishing by blacking and the shoe-brush as well as Morocco. They are lasting, and very cheap when compared with those we buy, which are from $125 to $150 per pair. We are certainly becoming very independent of foreign aid. The girls make beautifully fitting gloves, of dark flannel, cloth, linen, and any other material we can command. We make very nice blacking, and a friend has just sent me a bottle of brilliant black ink, made of elderberries. . . .

February 28th. Our hearts ache for the poor. A few days ago, as E. was walking out, she met a wretchedly dressed woman, of miserable appearance, who said she was seeking the Young Men's Christian Association, where she hoped to get assistance and work to do. E. carried her to the door, but it was closed, and the poor woman's wants were pressing. She then brought her home, supplied her with food, and told her to return to see me the following afternoon. She came, and with an honest counte-nance and manner told me her history. Her name is Brown; her husband had been a workman in Fredericksburg; he joined the army, and was killed at the second battle of Manassas. Many of her acquaintances in Fredericksburg fled last winter during the bombardment; she became alarmed, and with her three little children fled too. She has tried to get work in Richmond, sometimes she succeeded, but could not supply her wants. A kind woman had lent her a room and a part of a garden, but it was outside of the corporation; and although it saved house-rent, it disbarred her from the relief of the association formed for supplying the city poor with meal, wood, etc. When I gave her meat for her children, taken from the bounty of our Essex friends, tears of gratitude ran down her cheeks; she said they "had not seen meat for so long." Poor thing, I promised her that her case should be known, and that she should not suffer so again. A soldier's widow shall not suffer from hunger in Richmond. . . .

This evening Mrs. R. and myself went in pursuit of her, but though we went through all the streets and lanes of "Butcher Flat" and other vicinities, we could get no clue to her. We went into many small and squalid-looking houses, yet we saw no such abject poverty as Mrs. Brown's—all who needed it were supplied with meal by the corporation, and many were supporting themselves with Government work. One woman stood at a table cutting out work; we asked her the stereotyped question—"Is there a very poor widow named Brown in this direction?"

"No, ladies. . . ." We turned away; but she suddenly exclaimed, "Ladies, will one of you read my husband's last letter to me? for you see I can't read writing."

As Mrs. R. took it, she remarked that it was four weeks old, and asked if no one had read it to her?

"Oh, yes, a gentleman has read it to me four or five times; but you see I loves to hear it, for maybe I shan't hear from him no more." The tears now poured down her cheeks. . . .

Mrs. R. read the badly written but affectionate letter in which he expressed his anxiety to see her and his children, and his inability to get a furlough. She then turned to her mantelpiece, and with evident pride took from a nail an old felt hat, through the crown of which were two bullet-holes. It was her husband's hat, through which a bullet had passed in the battle of Chancellorsville, and, as she remarked, must have come "very nigh grazing his head." . . . She then hung it up carefully, saying that it was just opposite her bed, and she never let it out of her sight. She said she wanted her husband to fight for his country, and not "to stand back like some women's husbands, to be drafted; she would have been ashamed of that, but she felt uneasy, because something told her that he would never get back." Poor woman. . . .

2. MARY BOYKIN CHESNUT

"We Go On As Before"

Richmond gave a great ovation to General John Hunt Morgan and his beautiful wife, née Mattie Ready, of Tennessee. On November 26, 1863, after his spectacular raid into Indiana and Ohio, General Morgan had escaped from the Columbus penitentiary.

Mrs. Chesnut was on hand to hear General J. E. B. Stuart praise the hero to the crowd. She missed the reception later in the month at the President's home when both a fire and a robbery occurred. Perhaps Elizabeth Van Lew had something to do with those troubles. One of her former slaves, who reported regularly to her, was still with the Davis household as a servant. Mary Chesnut hinted at other sinister happenings in the Davis residence.

January 9th. Met Mrs. Wigfall. She wants me to take Halsey to Mrs. Randolph's theatricals. I am to get him up as Sir Walter Raleigh. Now, General Breckinridge has come. I like him better than any of them. Morgan also is here. These huge Kentuckians fill the town. . . .

The President's man, Jim, that he believed in as we all believe in our own servants, "our own people," as we call them, and

Betsy, Mrs. Davis's maid, decamped last night. It is miraculous that they had the fortitude to resist the temptation so long. At Mrs. Davis's the hired servants all have been birds of passage. First they were seen with gold galore, and then they would fly to the Yankees, and I am sure they had nothing to tell. It is Yankee money wasted. I do not think it had ever crossed Mrs. Davis's brain that those two could leave her. She knew, however, that Betsy had eighty dollars in gold and two thousand four hundred dollars in Confederate notes.

Everybody who comes in brings a little bad news—not much, in itself, but by cumulative process the effect is depressing, indeed.

January 12th. To-night there will be a great gathering of Kentuckians. Morgan gives them a dinner. The city of Richmond entertains John Morgan. He is at free quarters. The girls dined here. Conny Cary came back for more white feathers [for theatricals] Isabella[1] had appropriated two sets and obstinately refused Constance Cary a single feather from her pile. . . .

January 14th. Gave Mrs. White twenty-three dollars for a turkey. Came home wondering all the way why she did not ask twenty-five; two more dollars could not have made me balk at the bargain, and twenty-three sounds odd.

January 15th. What a day the Kentuckians have had! Mrs. Webb gave them a breakfast; from there they proceeded *en masse* to General Lawton's dinner, and then came straight here, all of which seems equal to one of Stonewall's forced marches. General Lawton took me in to supper. In spite of his dinner he had misgivings. "My heart is heavy," said he, "even here. All seems too light, too careless, for such terrible times. It seems out of place here in battle-scarred Richmond."

---

[1] Isabella Martin, daughter of the Reverend William Martin.

"I have heard something of that kind at home," I replied. "Hope and fear are both gone, and it is distraction or death with us. I do not see how sadness and despondency would help us. If it would do any good, we would be sad enough."

We laughed at General Hood. General Lawton thought him better fitted for gallantry on the battle-field than playing a lute in my lady's chamber. . . .

Not only had my house been rifled for theatrical properties, but as the play went on they came for my black velvet cloak. When it was over, I thought I should never get away, my cloak was so hard to find. But it gave me an opportunity to witness many things behind the scenes—that cloak hunt. Behind the scenes! I know a little what that means now.

General Jeb Stuart was at Mrs. Randolph's in his cavalry jacket and high boots. He was devoted to Hetty Cary. Constance Cary said to me, pointing to his stars, "Hetty likes them that way, you know—gilt-edged and with stars."

January 16th. A visit from the President's handsome and accomplished secretary, Burton Harrison. I lent him *Country Clergyman in Town* and *Elective Affinities.* . . .

Every Sunday Mr. Minnegerode cries aloud in anguish his litany, "from pestilence and famine, battle, murder, and sudden death," and we wailed on our knees, "Good Lord deliver us," and on Monday, and all the week long, we go on as before, hearing of nothing but battle, murder, and sudden death, which are daily events. Now I have a new book; that is the unlooked for thing, a pleasing incident in this life of monotonous misery. We live in a huge barrack. We are shut in, guarded from light without. . . .

January 18th. Invited to Dr. Haxall's last night to meet the Lawtons. Mr. Benjamin dropped in. He is a friend of the house. Mrs. Haxall is a Richmond leader of society, a *ci-devant* beauty and belle, a charming person still, and her hospitality is of the genuine Virginia type. Everything Mr. Benjamin said we listened to, bore in mind, and gave heed to it diligently. He is a Delphic oracle, of the innermost shrine, and is supposed to enjoy the honor of Mr. Davis's unreserved confidence.

Lamar was asked to dinner here yesterday, so he came to-day. We had our wild turkey cooked for him yesterday, and I dressed myself within an inch of my life with the best of my four-year-old finery. Two of us, my husband and I, did not damage the wild turkey seriously. So Lamar enjoyed the *réchauffé,* and commended the art with which Molly had hid the slight loss we had inflicted upon its mighty breast. She had piled fried oysters over the turkey so skilfully, that unless we had told about it, no one would ever have known that the huge bird was making his second appearance on the board.

Lamar was more absent-minded and distrait than ever. My husband behaved like a trump—a well-bred man, with all his wits about him; so things went off smoothly enough. . . .

January 20th. . . . Our Congress is so demoralized, so confused, so depressed. They have asked the President, whom they have so hated, so insulted, so crossed and opposed and thwarted in every way, to speak to them, and advise them what to do.

January 21. Both of us were too ill to attend Mrs. Davis's reception. It proved a very sensational one. First, a fire in the house, then a robbery—said to be an arranged plan of the usual bribed servants there and some escaped Yankee prisoners. . . .

January 22d. . . . Went to Mrs. Davis's. It was sad enough. Fancy having to be always ready to have your servants set your house on fire, being bribed to do it. Such constant robberies, such servants coming and going daily to the Yankees, carrying one's silver, one's other possessions, does not conduce to home happiness. . . .

I imparted a plan of mine to Brewster.[2] I would have a breakfast, a luncheon, a matinee, call it what you please, but I would
try and return some of the hospitalities of this most hospitable
people. Just think of the dinners, suppers, breakfasts we have
been to. People have no variety in war times, but they make up
for that lack in exquisite cooking.

"Variety?" said he. "You are hard to please, with terrapin
stew, gumbo, fish, oysters in every shape, game, and wine—as
good as wine ever is. I do not mention juleps, claret cup, apple
toddy, whisky punches and all that. I tell you it is good enough
for me. Variety would spoil it. Such hams as these Virginia
people cure; such home-made bread—there is no such bread in
the world. Call yours a 'cold collation.' "

"Yes, I have eggs, butter, hams, game, everything from home;
no stint just now; even fruit."

"You ought to do your best. They are so generous and hospitable and so unconscious of any merit, or exceptional credit,
in the matter of hospitality." . . .

January 23d. My luncheon was a female affair exclusively.
Mrs. Davis came early and found Annie and Tudie making
chocolate. Lawrence had gone South with my husband, so we
had only Molly for cook and parlor-maid. . . .

Later in the afternoon, when it was over and I was safe, for
all had gone well and Molly had not disgraced herself before
the mistresses of those wonderful Virginia cooks, Mrs. Davis and
I went out for a walk. . . .

3. ELIZABETH L. VAN LEW

"Beware"

The selection from Miss Van Lew's journal is followed by
her letter to General Benjamin F. Butler at Fortress Monroe.

---

[2] Henry P. Brewster, Hood's aide.

General Butler reported to Secretary of War Stanton on February 5; "I sent enclosed for your perusal the information I have acquired of the enemy's forces and dispositions about Richmond. The letter . . . is a cipher letter to me from a lady in Richmond, with whom I am in correspondence. There are not now in Lee's army or about Richmond 30,000 men. . . . Forty thousand men on the south side of the James would be sufficient for the object of taking and permanently holding Richmond. . . . Now or never is the time to strike. . . ."

January 24, 1864. Alas for the suffering of the very poor. Women are begging for bread with tears in their eyes—and a different class from ordinary beggars. On Thursday I went through the city for meal and I could not get a particle anywhere. I went to the City Mills; they told me they had no corn and could procure none, they were only grinding for toll as persons would bring them corn, that "the people" would come crying to them for meal and they did not know what to do—they had none to give them and people must starve. The miller told me they were grinding at the little mill on the dock. I went immediately there and found it was so, but they would not let one family have more than a peck at any price. There were crowds of persons coming and going, each for or with their peck, and for this peck they paid five dollars, which was cheap. . . .

No boy over fourteen is permitted to leave the Confederacy. I meet everywhere the rough board coffins of the wretched prisoners. . . . I cannot go to church. I went last of all to the Friends meeting, and heard the preacher . . . pray "God bless the Confederate Congress"—and this I could not do.

January 30, 1864

To General Benjamin F. Butler:
Dear Sir: It is intended to remove to Georgia very soon all the Federal prisoners; butchers and bakers to go at once. They are already notified and selected. Quaker [a Union man whom

I know. S. F. B.] knows this to be true. Are building batteries on
the Danville road.

This from Quaker: Beware of new and rash council! Beware!
This I send you by direction of all your friends. No attempt
should be made with less than 30,000 cavalry, from 10,000 to
15,000 infantry to support them, amounting in all to 40,000 to
45,000 troops. Do not underrate their strength and desperation.
Forces could probably be called into action in from 5 to 10 days;
25,000 mostly artillery Hoke's[3] and Kemper's[4] brigades gone to
North Carolina; Pickett's[5] in or about Petersburg. Three regiments of cavalry disbanded by General Lee for want of horses.
Morgan[6] is applying for 1,000 choice men for a raid.

4. AGNES
"Champagne Is $350 a Dozen"

A foreign visitor to Richmond was surprised to find so
much gaiety. In *A Visit to the Cities and Camps of the Confederate States,* published in Edinburgh and London about
the time General Lee began his march toward Appomattox,
Captain Fitzgerald Ross writes, "Congress, as well as the
State Legislature of Virginia, was in session; the shops were
full of stores, and crowded with purchasers; hosts of fur-
loughed officers and soldiers perambulated the streets; hotels,
restaurants, and bar-rooms were crowded with guests, and
the whole city presented a lively appearance. . . . Balls,
tableaux vivants, and all kinds of social gatherings, were the
order of the day."

Agnes, our Christian-name-only friend, took part in these
gaieties. Mrs. Pryor, to whom she writes about them, was in
Petersburg.

Richmond, January 30th, 1864

. . . How can you be even dreaming of new cups and saucers?

---

[3] General Robert Frederick Hoke, of North Carolina.
[4] General James Lawson Kemper.
[5] General George E. Pickett.
[6] General John Hunt Morgan.

Mend your old ones, my dear, with white lead. That is what we
are doing here; and when the cup is "angular" lines of white
give it quite a Japanesque effect. There is not a bit of china for
sale in the capital of the Confederacy. A forlorn little chipped set
—twelve odd pieces—sold last week at auction for $200—and as
to hats and bonnets! We are washing the old ones and plaiting
straw for the new. . . .

President and Mrs. Davis gave a large reception last week, and
all the ladies looked positively gorgeous. Mrs. Davis is in mourning for her father. We should not expect suppers in these times,
but we do have them! Champagne is $350 a dozen, but we some-
times have champagne! The confectioners charge $15 for a cake,
but we have cake. My flounced gray silk is behaving admirably,
but I am afraid my Washington friends remember it as an old
acquaintance. I never go out without meeting them. I have seen
Dr. Garnett and Judge Scarborough and Mr. Dimitri on the
street, and often meet Mr. Hunter, running about, in his enthusiasm, like a boy. But what do you think? I never could bear
that Lord Lyons,[7] with his red face and small eyes like ferrets';
and now we have reason to suppose that England would have
recognized us but for his animosity against us. He says "the
Confederacy is on its last legs." We have heard from dear old
Dudley Mann;[8] but of course he can do nothing for us in England, and he had as well come home and go with me to receptions. Mrs. Davis receives every Tuesday, and Mr. Mann is a
better squire of dames than he is a diplomat. . . .

5. ELIZABETH L. VAN LEW

"109 Prisoners Escaped"

> Libby Prison was on the corner of Twentieth and Cary
> Streets. It was formerly a tobacco warehouse which had been

[7] British Minister at Washington, 1859-1864.

[8] Ambrose Dudley Mann, diplomatic commissioner of the Confederacy
in London, Brussels, and the Vatican.

acquired by General John H. Winder from Libby & Son
when captives after First Manassas had overcrowded all
Richmond jails.

Miss Van Lew certainly lent a hand in the mass escape of
Thursday, February 9, 1864, which she describes.

15th of Feb., 1864. I shall remember the 15th of February
because of a great alarm I had for others. Colonel Streight[9] and
three of the prisoners (who had escaped from the Libby) were
at Howard's Grove. After passing through the tunnel, they were
led by a Mrs. Green to an humble home on the outskirts of the
City. Here Mrs. Rice received them. She waited upon them
herself though in poor health—walking to and from town. Peril
and fatigue she counted not so they might escape their pursuers.
By request of some of their number she came in a carriage for
me and I went with her to see them. (This place is thickly settled
and in this plain neighborhood any display of equipage would
create an excitement.) I followed Mrs. Rice into the house, the
front door of which opened into the parlor or sitting room, and
I found myself in the presence of the four fugitives. I was so
overcome with terror for them that I quite lost my voice for
some time. Two of these gentlemen were quite sick and looked
very feeble.

Colonel Streight seemed in good condition. I mentioned that
there was particular enmity towards him, because he had commanded, it was said, a Negro regiment. He replied, "I did not,
but would have had no objection." He asked me my opinion of
the cause of this war. I tried to say, Democracy, though in my
heart I thought it was slavery. . . . I had a very pleasant visit.
How my heart ached all the while for their peril!

I was particularly delighted with the man who made the
tunnel—Col. McDonald, I think was his name. . . . It was a
pleasure to take the hand which had worked so faithfully, so
hard, to deliver himself and fellow prisoners. He put into my

---

[9] Colonel Abel D. Streight, of Indiana, had been captured by General
Forrest while on a raid into Alabama.

hand the chisel with which alone he made the passage. I wanted
him to leave it with me to take care of for him, but he preferred
carrying it with him. . . .

By this ingenious tunnel 109 prisoners escaped, 65 of whom
were recaptured. Their escape was not known until 8 o'clock in
the morning—thus giving them much time. . . .

We had a little laughing and talking and then I said good
bye, with the most fervent God bless you in my heart towards all
of them. Mrs. Rice came home with me. We were afraid of the
hack driver, and he took advantage of it to ask a round sum in
Confederate dollars. It was not safe for me to go again to see these
gentlemen, but I heard from them. . . .

I knew the night these gentlemen set out—a few Union people
had done for them what they could—but they were poorly provided for the weather, which became intensely cold—so cold that
some poor fellows in the Confederate service froze to death and
the prisoners on Belle Isle suffered beyond description. The
man, who agreed to go with them as guide, and on whom they
depended, realizing his perilous situation, deserted them and
returned in a few hours to his home. Their safe arrival, after
many days of suffering and wandering, gladdened our hearts. . . .

6. VARINA HOWELL DAVIS

"I Could Not Reconcile the Two Ulrics"

> Colonel Ulric Dahlgren, twenty-two-year old son of Ad-
> miral John A. Dahlgren, headed a company of several hun-
> dred cavalrymen in a raid of deadly intent. Instead, he lost
> his own life, on March 4, 1864.
> According to the plan, two forces of picked cavalry were to
> make a dash on Richmond, release the prisoners, burn the
> city, and escape by way of the Peninsula to Old Point Com-
> fort. On February 29, Dahlgren set out to cross the James
> River at some point in Goochland County. General Judson
> Kilpatrick was to make an attack on the city from the west,
> while Dahlgren rode in from the north. The plan failed.

Along the way, Dahlgren stopped at Sabot Hill, home of
Secretary of War Seddon, twenty miles above Richmond.
The Secretary was in Richmond, but Mrs. Seddon entertained
the young raider with blackberry wine of the vintage of
1844, and anecdotes of Commodore Dahlgren as one of her
mother's old beaux and schoolmates. In the meantime, a
courier galloped off to warn officials in Richmond of the
enemy's proximity. "Mrs. Seddon saved Richmond," said William Preston Cabell.

Mrs. Davis, who had known the Dahlgrens in happier
days, tells the story of the raid.

Just before daylight of March 1st, the Marylanders struck one
of Kilpatrick's flanking parties and drove them in on the main
body. They followed the enemy through Ashland down to the
outer defences of Richmond; there Kilpatrick had dismounted
his twenty-five hundred men and was making a regular attack
on the works. General Wade Hampton heard that the Federal
cavalry was approaching the city, and immediately moved out to
attack him.

The Marylanders drew upon his rear picket just as, by a happy
chance, an officer and five men bearing a despatch from Dahlgren galloped into their arms. The despatch informed Kilpatrick that Dahlgren would attack on the Broad Road at sunset,
that Kilpatrick must attack at the same time, and together they
would ride into Richmond. Colonel Johnson[10] at once drove in
Kilpatrick's picket, who, finding himself attacked in rear at once
retreated toward the White House.[11] The Marylanders followed
him, never losing sight of his rear-guard, and driving it in on him
whenever the ground allowed, until he got to Tunstall's, under
the protection of infantry sent from Williamsburg or Yorktown
for his rescue.

---

[10] Colonel Bradley T. Johnson. For having saved Richmond from capture,
General Hampton presented him with a saber.

[11] White House Landing on the Pamunkey River, twenty miles east of
Richmond, had been used as a Federal base by McClellan.

Dahlgren, hearing the firing, concluded that for reasons un-known to him, Kilpatrick had attacked four hours before the appointed time, and kept under cover until dark, when he made an attack upon the north side of the city. Here, March 1st, he encountered the company of Richmond boys (under eighteen years of age) at the outer intrenchments, and their fire becoming "too hot, he sounded the retreat, leaving forty men on the field."

Continuing his retreat down the Peninsula, he was met by a few men of the Fifth and Ninth Virginia Cavalry and some home guards, all under command of Lieutenant James Pollard, Com-pany H, Ninth Virginia Cavalry, who, placing his men in am-bush, waited until the Federals were close upon them, when a volley was fired, and Colonel Dahlgren, who had ridden for-ward and tried to discharge his pistol, fell dead, and his com-mand were taken prisoners.

The following special orders were discovered on the body of Colonel Dahlgren: ". . . We will try and secure the bridge to the city (one mile below Belle Isle) and release the prisoners at the same time. If we do not succeed, they must then dash down, and we will try and carry the bridge from each side. The bridges once secured and the prisoners loose and over the river, the bridges will be secured and the city destroyed. The men must keep together and well in hand, and once in the city, it must be destroyed, and *Jeff Davis* and Cabinet killed. Prisoners will go along with combustible material. The officers must use dis-cretion about the time of assisting us. Horses and cattle which we do not need immediately must be shot rather than left. Every-thing on the canal and elsewhere of service to the rebels must be destroyed. . . ."

When Mr. Blair[12] came to Richmond I mentioned Colonel Dahlgren's special orders, and he said, "Did you believe it?" I

[12] Francis P. Blair, Sr., paid an unofficial visit to Richmond in January 1865, and took the initiative in peace negotiations between the North and South. He was a guest at the Confederate White House.

said that there had been no time for such a forgery, and that there was an itinerary in the same hand also. Upon Mr. Blair making some laughing remark of disbelief, I offered to send for the book, and said it had been photographed and sent to General Meade, who was then in our front—"with an inquiry as to whether such practices were authorized by his Government; and also to say that if any question was raised as to the copies, the original paper would be submitted." No such question was then made, and the denial that Dahlgren's conduct had been authorized was accepted.

Mr. Blair laughed again and said: "Now, the fact is I do not want to believe it, and if you could convince me I would rather not look at it."

I had felt much the same unwillingness, having been intimate with his parents. Once Commodore Dahlgren had brought the little fair-haired boy to show me how pretty he looked in his black velvet suit and Vandyke collar, and I could not reconcile the two Ulrics. . . .

7. VIRGINIA NICHOLAS SANDERS
"The Battle Raid Interferes"

Among the friends who were in Richmond during General and Mrs. Morgan's visit early in the year were Virginia Sanders and her mother, native Kentuckians. From Richmond, the Morgans went on to Atlanta, where Mrs. Morgan found she needed a new hat. She called for Miss Sanders' help. Unfortunately, the Kilpatrick and Dahlgren raid interrupted her endeavors. We hope the General's wife got her hat!

Richmond, Virginia
Tuesday 1st March 1864

Dear Mrs. Morgan
Your sweet note of Feb 23d reached me last night. I will spare

no pains to fulfill your request perfectly. I am glad you called upon me and will try to execute the commission so satisfactorily you will be sure to let me serve you again.

I have had the box addressed to you at Atlanta, Ga.

I am every day more satisfied at having commended to General Morgan the noble Ashby's[13] gallant deed—as Senator Lewis remarks "they were indeed congenial spirits." Every day his [Morgan's] name grows brighter as his dashing deeds during three years of unpaid service which he so modestly conceals are brought to light by the praise of a grateful people. I suppose you heard of the war horse lately presented to him by the counties of Shenandoah and Fredericksburg.

Mama joins me in cordial & affectionate greetings and requests me to acknowledge the receipt of the General's beautiful letter. Thank you for your general message from him. I know you are a woman to appreciate it so in return I send him my love, my prayers shall indeed be around him. God bless my gallant countryman & bless our dear old Commonwealth.

And you my lovely friend are a jewel worthy the brilliant setting you have won giving & receiving lustre.

Tell the gentle lady Alice[14] with my love I hope she and I may one day be equally fortunate.

With appreciative regards to the accomplished Col. Alston & Dr. Goode.

Your earnest friend

VIRGINIA NICHOLAS SANDERS

Thursday, 3rd March. I have been to see the man who dwells at the sign of the gold hat. He said the price had gone up from $50 to 75. I hesitated but consulted Col. Pickett who advised me to buy now as you must be aware of the immense change in

---

[13] Turner Ashby, Virginia's beloved cavalryman, was killed in June 1862. Ashby once wrote that he had fought thirty fights in twenty-eight days.

[14] Alice Ready was Mrs. Morgan's young sister.

the currency & might be disappointed by delay. Mr. Dooley said you must be mistaken in the size as 7½ would make an enormous man's hat whereupon I ordered the largest ladies size. I expect it will be enroute tomorrow. I am going down directly to see about it again. V. N. S.

I am going to send you a leaf from Gen. Stonewall Jackson's grave.

The Battle raid interferes with the expressing of the hat. But will try to get a friend to take it.

8. CLARA MINOR LYNN

"The City Might Be Shelled"

> Clara Lynn tells of the noncombatants' trials in traveling south from Richmond by government order. After many adventures along the way, she and her mother and young sisters finally reached their home near Norfolk. She ordered a pair of shoes from Richmond which cost her $150.00. When the county troop came home to recruit at Christmas and "we made merry with them as we were in duty bound," Clara wrote, "I danced these same shoes out in a week."

In the spring of '64, orders were given for all noncombatants to leave Richmond, who could possibly do so. At any time the city might be shelled, and provisions were *more* than scarce.

For educational purposes we had gone there . . . and of course now we had to go with the rest. All of the schools were closed at once. Only in one direction was there safety and a country not absolutely devastated by the passage of both armies. As it led to our home thither we fled, or rather tried to flee, along with many thousands; but for the first two mornings, we got no further than the depot. The train service was absolutely inadequate to carry off such a crowd. On the third morning we secured a corner seat—mother, our fat black mammy and the two children, in the seat. As for me, I sat (when I was not on the floor) on the empty stove which had a round top.

Two mortal hours it took that train to start. With the most unearthly groans and rattling of all the internal machinery, we'd get a little start, then something would break or threaten to break, so we'd back up again and be patched. In the meantime doors were locked, for every seat was full.

Every now and then a soldier with one arm or on crutches, for only able bodied men staid in the city, and all the hospitals were emptied as far as possible—well, one of these would put his head in the window and whisper to the mother sitting nearest to him "madam please lend me your baby." The baby was without a question handed out of the window, and in a few moments soldier and baby appeared at the door and demanded admittance of the guard.

The rule had prevailed on all rail-roads leading out of Richmond, for more than a year, that the ladies coaches were reserved strictly for women and children, and only the men belonging to them—or, more properly speaking, to whom they belonged—were admitted. But the authorities did not reckon with the willingness of the Confederate women to secure a soldier a little comfort, even to the extent of lending her baby. The guard must have been in the secret, for I have seen the same baby act as door-opener to half a dozen soldiers in almost as many minutes; making a steady round, out at the window, and in at the door, as fast as it could be managed.

As we waited, Negroes brought lunches, or as we called them "snacks," for sale to the windows; "Heah, Mistress, heah yo' haim an' aigs, nice haim an' two fresh aigs, yes' three dollar for it all." "Heah a nice tender chicken laig an' a piece uv mush, and I ain' gwine ax you but fo' dollars for it." . . .

At least we got off with many a thump and bump. . . .

9. ANITA DWYER WITHERS
"We Went to Church"

The young wife of Captain John Withers made only a few entries in her diary during this spring of raids, tragedies and threatened attacks, but those she recorded were sad indeed. She recounts the accidental death of little Joe Davis, about which more will be said later, and she feels acutely for the girlish widow of General Stuart. At Yellow Tavern, where he had got between Sheridan and near-by Richmond, the daring "Jeb," who had never been touched by bullet or saber in all his many encounters with the enemy, was shot by a dismounted Union trooper. "I can scarcely think of him without weeping," said General Lee.

April 30th. A terrible accident occurred yesterday. The President's little boy Joe was killed—fell from up stairs down in the area, a servant found the child first but already life had left him. His Mother and Father had walked out.

May 1st. Sunday. We went to Church although it was raining. Father Huber preached about the blessed Virgin.

The President's child will be buried this evening.

May 12th. Thursday. I left Richmond for Mecklenburg. I did not intend going to the country until June, but the great excitement in Richmond, and my being sick, determined my Husband to send me sooner. . . .

General Lee's army had been fighting Grant's for about a week before I left, and is still fighting I believe.

The Yankees attempted to advance on Richmond by different directions. Beauregard whipped them or checked them near Drury's Bluff.[15]

---

[15] On May 16, at the battle of Drury's Bluff, Beauregard battled and checked General B. F. Butler, who had come from Fortress Monroe. President Davis was there, and one of the enemy's shells struck at his feet.

Poor Gen. J. E. B. Stuart was wounded on the 11th and died on the 12th of May. I feel *so* much for his *poor wife*. . . .

10. VIRGINIA TUNSTALL CLAY

"My Precious Husband Left Me"

Mr. Clay accepted a diplomatic mission to Canada in the early spring of 1864, "with a view," said Mrs. Clay, "to arousing in the public mind of this near-by British territory a sympathy for our cause and country that should induce a suspension of hostilities." With her husband were Jacob Thompson of Mississippi and James P. Holcombe of Virginia.

After her husband's departure, Mrs. Clay became a refugee. She left the Confederate capital and went to Petersburg. Fleeing from that city, she sought friends and relatives in Georgia and South Carolina. The Clay home in Huntsville, Alabama, was in enemy hands.

In July, Northern papers published an account of a peace conference which took place in Canada between Clay and Holcombe, for the Confederacy, and Horace Greeley, of New York, "acting with authority of President Lincoln."

April 30th, '64. A sad, sad day for me. My precious husband left me at ½ past 10 o'clock, for a long & perilous journey. God in mercy grant him a safe & speedy return! Wrote a letter to him on the Evening of the day, & sent it to Wilmington. . . . I walked, —read my Bible, prayed to God for my dear husband, & retired.

1st May. Sunday. Rained all day till P.M. I read the "Sermon on the Mount." Walked in the afternoon . . . & went to church at night. . . . Have thought often & sadly of my own dear husband & pray God to keep him under the wings of His love.

3d May. . . . Walked with Cousin Mary Tanner. Came home wretchedly depressed. Lay thinking of & weeping for my precious absent husband. My heart went to him on the perilous deep, & I begged God to keep him in safety.

May 4th. I wrote a letter of condolence to Mr. & Mrs. Davis who mourn my dear husband's little god-son, Joseph Evan Davis. Wrote to Dr. Withers, carried it to the office but found no letter from my darling, a bitter disappointment, but will try to await tomorrow. Still regret not accompanying my only love.

May 5th. Went twice to church, it being Ascension Day. *Heard prayers for my Darling* at Sea. Rec'd his farewell letter from W.[ilmington]. Wrote to him in the P.M. & sent to care of Salomon to forward. Feel better in body & mind. Hope my husband is at *Bermuda,* enroute. . . .

May 7th. At 2 o'clock heard that the enemy was in 6 miles of Petersburg[16]—city would be shelled ere night! Packed & skee-dadled in double quick—bag & baggage. Spent the night at the Junction. . . .

11. ANGELA MORENO MALLORY

"I Feel Very Uneasy"

> Mrs. Mallory, who was described as a "most amiable and the sweetest looking of matrons," enjoyed the love and friendship of all who knew her in Richmond. "I am sure she could not speak or do evil to any one," observed one of her acquaintances.
>
> Among the guests who enjoyed the hospitality of the Mallory home was the historian Thomas Cooper DeLeon. Mr. Mallory, he discovered, could brew a punch as good as his

---

[16] Following Grant's orders, Butler had come up from Fortress Monroe on May 4, and entrenched himself at Bermuda Hundred, the peninsula opposite City Point on the James River. He threatened Petersburg but did not shell the city; Beauregard's arrival prevented that.

stories and *mots,* while Mrs. Mallory "knew tricks of Southern salads and of *'daube a la Créole'* that made many . . .
eyes wink and mouths water."

The Mallory's oldest daughter, Margaret, had married a
Mr. Bishop, of Bridgeport, Connecticut. Stephen, Jr., was in
the Confederate Navy, and the young children, Ruby and
Attie, were with their parents in Richmond. Mrs. Mallory
divided her time between Richmond and the handsome home
in Pensacola.

The "Darling Friend" is Mrs. Clement Clay, who, as we
know, was leaving the city.

Richmond, 6th May, '64

My Darling Friend,

Your welcome note of the 2nd inst. has been in my possession
two days, and though I have endeavoured to answer it sooner,
my interruptions and botherations are so numerous (as you
know) that I have not been able to accomplish my desire sooner.
I hope to be permitted to finish this uninterrupted.

I was surprised to see your note dated Petersburg, as I was told
that you were in Wilmington. I heartily sympathize with you in
your loneliness. I know what the feeling is, to be left alone, for
no matter who I have with me, I feel all alone if my husband is
absent. Oh! the tears that I have shed at being left! I am certain
had they been collected they would float the whole Confederate
Navy.

The only consolation I can offer you my dear friend is to pray
fervently to our heavenly Father to give you the faith to believe
that this separation is for the good of our bleeding country. I
am sure if you pray fervently and trustingly, that God will hear
you. I have the most implicit faith in prayer and when we meet
again (which I hope will be very soon) I will tell you my experience, and I know you will think that I have good reason for my
faith. If your husband succeeds in accomplishing his mission,
and by so doing will be the means of bringing about an honor-

able peace, will you not feel that you are the most fortunate woman in the Confederacy? Yes I know you will, and you will think that this sacrifice which you have made will be richly compensated. God grant it. I hope that you will come to see us soon again, and I will try to cheer you or at least keep your thoughts from the sad subject, by telling you my troubles and tribulations.

I was greatly disturbed last night by Mr. Mallory's being notified that several Yankee Gun boats and numberless transports were coming up the river, and were within fifteen miles of Drury's Bluff. Mr. Mallory immediately went off to look after his boats and men and did not return until very late. I was so sleepy that I could not ask him a question when he returned and did not learn anything about it until this morning.

I regretted so much that you had to leave when you did. The next day I was invited by Mrs. Ould[17] to join a party to City Point. I went, and we had a rather pleasant day but the sight of the poor sick men who were exchanged made me feel so badly, *and the thought that people who a short time since were as one, should now be willing to destroy each other,* made me very sad and I do not know but I regret having gone.

Mrs. Ould and Mrs. Allen with all their children have gone down to Mr. Allen's plantation. They went last evening in a flag-of-truce boat and expected to remain several days on the plantation, and Mr. Allen came to Richmond last night with all his Negroes to keep them from the Yankees. I presume they will return this evening on the boat.

I feel very uneasy about the determination that the Yankees show of getting in Richmond very soon. Not that I believe they will, but I suppose I will have to go away. I dread it so much that I think of it all the time.

---

[17] Mrs. Robert Ould, whose husband was commissioner of prison exchange. More than a thousand prisoners were exchanged on that day at City Point.

Poor Mrs. Davis. Her bereavement has been very great. She used to call him her black-eyed blessing and I thought she loved him more than the others, but that can hardly be. He was a beautiful boy, and his parents' loss has been his gain for he is now where the rumors of war never enter. Oh, if I could only be there too, with all those who are dear to me!

I had a visit of two days from my brother-in-law, Col. J. P. Jones. He is Gen. Bragg's Inspector General. He left for Charleston this morning. Mrs. Bragg[18] and the General called to see you and me, yesterday. They both regretted very much that they did not see you. They are not the only ones who regret your departure. I have seen many who expressed their regrets of your absence.

I have not been visiting except to breakfast with Mrs. Ould, and Tea with Mrs. Purcell, since you left. Mrs. Ives expressed her regrets that we were not at her Tea party. From all I hear about it, we did not miss much, as her company did not all come until after ten o'clock, and her Tea was kept waiting for them. . . . I would not be surprised if some of the company wished they had peanuts and suet when they went home.

I hope that we shall soon have the pleasure of seeing you again and then we will console each other and if we can get nothing else to eat we will always find peanuts and suet. I have plenty of ham. I received three a few days since so we can't starve for some time. Come soon is the hope of your devoted friend.

ANGELA M. MALLORY

Mr. Mallory has gone to Drury's Bluff this morning. The children send much love. Do not trouble yourself about Ruby's boots. I am having a blue pair made for her. When you write your husband give my love to him.

---

18 Eliza Brooks Ellis, of Terrebonne Parish, Louisiana, had married Braxton Bragg in 1849. She became a refugee when Federal troops invaded "Bivouac," their plantation in Lafourche Parish, Louisiana.

12. ELIZABETH L. VAN LEW

"Oh, the Yearning for a Deliverance"

Elizabeth could boast that she was in close communication
with General Grant as he waged his Richmond campaign.
Not only did she send him information, but flowers from her
garden appeared on his dining table.

As May turned into summer and she yearned for deliverance, General Grant was having his problems. After his
month's campaign, with its dreadful death toll, Northern
papers began referring to his "funeral march."

May 1864. The excitement is great throughout the city and
many are the rumors. Gen. Lee has telegraphed a victory, that
Johnson[19] and Vance were killed yesterday is heard too. The
fight commenced without our knowledge. This is the first day
we have had any intimation of fighting. I do not feel as if the
Federals would get here this spring, but I know nothing. I saw
—— yesterday; from his position he should know and he expected them. He almost told me so. It seems to me we have suffered past all excitement. *Nothing* elates me. I have a calm hope,
but there is much heart sadness with it. A few days since and he
who was only sixteen has been taken. . . .

The firing this morning in the direction of the Bluff was very
heavy and jarred the windows. We hear Gen. Stuart is seriously
wounded and said to be in a dying state. . . .

Just at dark the servants bring in a report that the Bluffs have
been taken! the truth of this we shall know soon however. Some
soldiers report it, but we are disposed to doubt it. One cannot
imagine the gloom of this place now. Since Monday the atmosphere has been heavy with the smoke of battle. The stores are all
closed, men are not to be seen on the streets. The alarm bell has

---

[19] General Edward Johnson and his division were captured at Spottsylvania Court House by the Federal General W. S. Hancock, on May 12, 1864.

sounded until today, and now there are no more to be called by it. The burning woods we saw yesterday and the day before, the papers tell us, consumed many wounded Yankees lying there. Oh death and carnage so near!

May 14. Awakened by the cannon—firing has been uninterrupted all day and so loud as to jar the windows. Much of the day passed upon the house top. Who can sit still, who can blame us? We look from the windows—from the grounds—from the house top. . . . Oh, the yearning for a deliverance. . . .

I saw Capt. ——, who has passed through so many hard fought battles, turn deathly pale, when ordered to join Gen. Lee. "I would as soon go into the crater of a volcano," said he.

Friday, May 27. We are on the eve of fearful bloodshed. There is a portentous calm—a great moving of troops. Mr. ——, of —— County, told me that as many as fifteen thousand passed through Richmond last night, and that in the last few days Lee has received 30,000 troops. . . .

13. VARINA HOWELL DAVIS

"I Am Not Rebellious"

It had been almost a month since the tragic death of little Joseph Emory Davis shocked all Richmond. Within another month, Mrs. Davis would give birth to Varina Anne Davis, who was called "Winnie, the daughter of the Confederacy." Baby shoes in Richmond cost twenty dollars that summer.

To her mother, Margaret Louisa Kempe Howell, Mrs. Davis wrote this letter:

May 22nd '64

. . . . I feel hourly how much I have to be thankful for, and I am not rebellious, only grieved.

Jeff as you surmise has been forced from home constantly, and in the various battles around Richmond has been pretty constantly upon the field. . . . I think I shall send Maggie to Mrs. Preston's and then to Mrs. Chesnut's for a visit, and it may be send the children also.[20] Certainly if events take the turn I expect I shall do so, even if I cannot go myself which I will do if I can make up my mind to leave home. . . . Jeff is much worried by anxiety. He seems to have gotten nearly as bad as I am and I hear the roar of artillery and crack of muskets it seems to me all the time.

There is an immense deal of suffering here now, so much so that they are impressing servants in the street to nurse the wounded. Erysipelas has appeared in some of the hospitals and there are many deaths from slight wounds. . . .

Poor Jeb Stuart was shot through the kidney, and his liver grazed also. He lay in the bloom of youth and apparently in high health, strong in voice and patience and resignation to his fate at eleven o'clock in the morning; at five that evening was dead without seeing his wife who was traveling to get him. Poor young man, the city he did so much to save mourned him sincerely. . . .

---

[20] Margaret Howell visited the Prestons and Chesnuts in Columbia in late summer, but Mrs. Davis and her children remained in Richmond.

VI

CLOUD OF SORROW

June—December 15, 1864

> Up and down, through the wards, where the fever
> Stalks noisome, and gaunt, and impure,
> You must go, with your steadfast endeavor
> To comfort, to counsel, to cure!
> I grant that the task's superhuman,
> But strength will be given to you
> To do for these dear ones what woman
> Alone in her pity can do.
> —From *The Ladies of Richmond*

The Federal attacks on Petersburg, which began in the middle of June, were met by Beauregard, who was reinforced by General Lee on June 18. The long, long siege that began would last until April 1, 1865.

On July 18, 1864, George Alfred Trenholm, of Charleston, succeeded C. G. Memminger as Secretary of the Treasury. Mrs. Trenholm, who was born Anna Helen Holmes, of Johns Island, South Carolina, and her daughters Helen and Eliza accompanied him to Richmond.

1. SALLIE ANN BROCK PUTNAM

"The Safest Place in the Confederacy"

Mrs. Putnam spent many hours as a volunteer nurse in the hospitals of Richmond performing "simple acts of attention

that duty dignified into pleasure, and that pleasure exalted
into duty."

Surgeon General Samuel Preston Moore directed the Medical Department of the Confederate Army. Mrs. Putnam
found him "an exacting and conscientious officer."

Richmond, without undue assumption, could style itself the
"Hub of the Confederacy." Never was her spirit more buoyant
than over the results of the various campaigns of the summer of
1864. Peace and independence seemed dependent only on the
endurance of the Southern people. Of that they had already
given the most indubitable evidence.

So long had the camp-fires glowed around Richmond—so long
had we breathed the sulphurous vapors of battle—so accustomed
had our ears become to the dread music of artillery—so signal
had been our deliverance from the most elaborate combinations
for the capture of our city, that more surely than ever before we
felt at this time that our Confederate house was built "upon a
rock."

We were practically solving a curious question, and one which
most nearly involved the vital interests of the population of the
city of Richmond. So enormous had become the expenses of living that the question had grown to be one of moment: "On what
can we subsist that will furnish the greatest amount of nutriment
for the least amount of money?" In our social gatherings the war
topic was most frequently varied in the discussion of rich dishes,
and the luxurious tables of days of yore. Sometimes would arise
the question: "I wonder if we shall ever see the like again?"
Often were we forcibly reminded of our former discontent and
dissatisfaction with the luxuries under which our tables groaned,
when we contrasted them with the severe and simple style to
which we were now compelled to submit. Yet we sipped our
Confederate tea, swallowed quickly our Confederate coffee, (frequently without sugar,) dined on fat bacon and Indian peas, and
took our dessert of sorghum-syrup and corn bread, with as much

cheerfulness and apparent relish as we formerly discussed the rich viands on the well-filled boards of the old Virginia housewives.

Richmond was growing rusty, dilapidated, and began to assume a war-torn appearance. Very few of the buildings has been brightened by a fresh application of paint since the commencement of hostilities, and where a plank fell off or a screw got loose, or a gate fell from its hinges, or a bolt gave way, or a lock was broken, it was most likely to remain for a time unrepaired; for the majority of our mechanics were in the field and those left in the city were generally in the employment of the government, and we were forced to wait for a needful job, until patience would become almost exhausted.

The fashion for dress would have seemed absurdly simple to the fashionable belle of New York, yet despite the rigor of the blockade, the latest mode would now and then struggle through in *Godey's Book,* or *Frank Leslie's Magazine,* or *Le Bon Ton.* When we consider the times, we may say our stores were pretty well stocked with goods, such as they were, but at prices marvellous to contemplate, even in Confederate money.

The summer's work at the hospitals in the year 1864 commenced in all its fullness early in May, after the battles of the Wilderness. It was attended with multiplied disadvantages, owing to the increased scarcity of provisions. The sick, mutilated and miserable, as ever before, uttered warm expressions of gratitude. . . .

Early in June, the officers' hospital in the Baptist Female College buildings was infected with pyaemia—the most malignant disease which can attack the wounded—a malady for which no specific has ever yet been found, and from which many more died than from the wound itself. In this disease the virus that should be discharged by suppuration is disseminated through the circulatory system, causing chills, and soon death supervenes. For a while this hospital was a charnel house, and it was found necessary to remove the patients to the city alms-house, after which the disease disappeared, and our hearts were more rarely sickened by the sight of military funerals through our streets. Still death did not cease its revels in our hospitals. This was evidenced by the continually enlarging dimensions of our cemeteries, and the multiplication of mounds that marked the soldiers' graves. . . .

Our delightful watering-places, which had formerly been favorite resorts of the Southern people, for health or pleasure, were most of them closed up, or occupied as hospitals, or otherwise, for war purposes. However much the system, relaxed or depressed by long confinement to the hot impure atmosphere of the city, needed the bracing and healthy influence of the mountain air, and the healing waters, our situation was such that if we dared to travel fifty or a hundred miles, we might be cut off, and subjected to nameless inconveniences and troubles in getting back to our homes. While the war lasted, the most of us were fixtures in Richmond. We ventured outside the city limits only when the skillful maneuvering of our army made it possible to go with a certainty of being able to return when we desired. . . .

The tide of exiles and refugees which set toward Richmond from the commencement of the war, continued until its close. Notwithstanding the repeated attempts to capture it, those driven from their homes crowded into the capital. Their stories of terror and distress were generally concluded with the exclamation, "Oh, we are too happy in getting to Richmond! It is after all the safest place in the Confederacy!"

Where to quarter the refugees, had long been a question of serious importance. From the second year of the war, the floating population quite equalled, if it did not exceed in numbers the resident inhabitants. Every influx of these unhappy wanderers occasioned grave consideration as to where they might find resting places, and the means of livelihood. There were few hotels, and boarding-houses might then have been counted on the fingers. The Spotswood Hotel, the American and the Powhatan, were all of the larger hotels then open for public accommodation; and so enormous were expenses at those places, that very few of the miserable refugees, who had been compelled to fly from their homes of ease and comfort, could afford the luxury of living in them. Lodgings were hired which seemed of India-rubber capacity, from the numbers frequently packed in them, and to tell of the contingent expenses of house-keeping at this time would sound like stories of wildest fable.

We were frequently awakened from a temporary dream of quiet and security, by the sudden ringing of alarm bells, occasioned often by only a reconnoissance of the enemy, but of a character sufficiently threatening to call out our forces for local defence, which consisted mainly of the battalion of government clerks under Major Henly, and the battalion of armorers and artisans from the government work-shops.

After the explosion of the mine at Petersburg, there was quiet on the Richmond lines during the remainder of the summer, broken only by a demonstration at Bottom's Bridge, in August, which, in practical results, was scarcely of sufficient importance at that period of the war to deserve notice. But our trials were becoming more and more severe, and we looked forward with shuddering apprehensions to the approaching winter.

2. ELIZA MIDDLETON HUGER SMITH

"This Abode of Misery"

One of the many mothers who were called to Richmond to the bedside of a sick and wounded son was Mrs. William Mason Smith, of Charleston, South Carolina.

Her eldest son, twenty-one-year-old Mason Smith, Jr., after serving in the defense of Charleston, had been sent with the 27th Regiment of South Carolina Volunteers to Virginia in May. On June 3, he was wounded at Cold Harbor. His mother hurried to Richmond, where he had been carried to Stuart Hospital. He died there on August 16. "I could not bring him home," sighed his mother. "He lies in Hollywood."

From the bedside of her son in "this abode of misery," she wrote the following letters to her brother-in-law, J. J. Pringle, of Charleston:

[Stuart Hospital], June 11th [1864]

Dear Pringle, I can only write by snatches between attending to Mason, & acknowledging the kind attentions of the ladies who keep him supplied with all sorts of comforts even luxuries. . . .

Now for his state. . . . It is to be a long business & there is to be great uncertainty to the end, altho' Dr. Meredith says it is his opinion that he will recover. His wound is so peculiar that the Drs. come to look at it. In such a delicate place, among those vital organs & yet not one severed. Dr. Meredith (Chief Surgeon of this Hospital) says no human hand could have made such a wound. His expression is that "the ball meandered so as just to avoid the intestines" also the bladder. His right leg is useless to him, & some of the Drs. think he may not recover it. Where the ball is they do not know yet.

It is impossible for me to do more writing that I have done to you. . . . No mails are going out of Richmond. The P.O. Clerks are in the trenches. I am at Mrs. Huger's[1] at night, all day in this abode of misery. . . . Oh! the unavoidable dirt & misery of this place. Our men bear so bravely & patiently too, that it excites admiration & wonder. . . . There is no one here that I know, & this Hospital is in suburbs so that I can not do more than come here. . . . Men are dying for want of stimulants—the best here is bad whiskey, but for the ladies the men would die. Mr. & Mrs. Miles[2] are unbounded in their offers too, & Mason prefers going

---

[1] Celestine Pinckney Huger, "Cousin Celly," wife of General Benjamin Huger.

[2] William Porcher Miles, of Charleston, member of the Confederate Congress, and his wife, Elizabeth Bierne Miles.

to them when he can be moved, but it will be some time yet; but he has been moved into a private room much to my relief, for in the ward there were 3 men desperately ill with Typhoid fever in the same corner with him. . . .

My heart sinks sometimes in spite of many causes for thankfulness.

Hospital, Wednesday, 19th June

Dear Pringle, Mason is going on pretty well but that means that he is not desperately ill or dying, but very suffering & by no means out of danger. . . . Mason cannot take stimulants yet; 2 kind ladies send him strong soup, tea, bread & ice cream also milk. All honour to these Richmond ladies. It is thought very hard that the President will not relieve the P.O. Clerks. . . .

Stuart Hospital, Thursday, June 23rd

Dear Pringle, . . . Mason is getting on slowly but his Drs. hope surely. Dr. Rivers is very kind & Dr. Louis, Chief Surg., is polite & considerate. Cousin Celly is very, very good & many others do what they can.

This must be a very expensive business but I am sure you will agree with me that he must have what is necessary. The very breath one draws here costs money—1 bushel of meal $100, a bbl. of flour $500, so just think of the expense of living. Brandy & wine are what he needs now. I have bought some whiskey at a high price to do until you can send me some. . . . I have drawn $500 on Fraser & Co.'s letter. I cannot stay here without making donations from time to time to the Hospital, or I should feel that I am devouring the Soldier's spare diet. The Ladies who brought so many things are shut out by this Dr., because he thinks they worry his patients, many of whom are fearfully reduced, and wounded, & did not like to be inspected by the ladies, so Dr. L. said.

Mason has a very good Servt. belonging to the Regt. left with him until he can dispense with his services. He draws Mason's rations, besides what Mason eats. . . . I can't write much for I write on my knees & by snatches. . . .

June 30th

Dear Pringle. . . . Mason suffers dreadfully. . . . It is fortunate that I am here but I cannot write about myself, or it will be up with me. Oh! this Hospital experience is subduing indeed. Sometimes my heart seems hard as a nether mill stone, then again my faith fails for a little moment & it all seems black, but I know that God reigns & no matter at what human cost I want his "will done on earth, as it is in Heaven," but He must give me strength.

There is less chance for a gentleman in these Hospitals than you would think reasonable. The mass are so animal & vulgar, & the rules & regulations are made for the mass. . . . Those whose friends are *passed instantaneously* have much to be thankful for; some linger & suffer & die after all, & often times the sufferings are so aggravated.

This interruption to communication has been very painful & trying to all parties. . . .

Hospital, [June]

Dear Pringle, Mason is asleep under the influence of Morphine. He had a 6 by 8 blister put on him last evening. They say only one lung is affected but he has much shortness of breath at times. They call it Pneumonia, the result of 12 hours exposure on the wet ground after his wound or of lying on a stretcher wet with cold water for 4 days. . . . Mason's mind is tranquil; he is very grateful to God for his mercies & finds comfort in two or three hymns being repeated to him every now and then. He begins to look very ill, but whenever I feel depressed about him I go into one of the wards & there see such aggravated suffering that I come back cheerful. . . . What a mercy it is that I came. This is a first duty. You will know before I do the result of the threat at Petersburg. What a curse War is. . . .

Stuart Hospital, Richmond, July 2

Dear Pringle, Now that Mason is better, & able to put things together, I find that his hold on March[3] is very uncertain, & yet he is likely to suffer if he has to give him up as he is entirely dependent on a capable servt. I thought he could keep him by paying his Wages & taking him home, but he cannot do this if Capt. Clarkson's Co. is not disbanded & if Capt. C. is coming to Virginia. I suppose he has straightened his affairs. Do, if you can, see Capt. C. & ascertain if we can keep the Servt. & at what cost; if we cannot keep him, send us by some early opportunity Jeffrey or some Servt. that can be useful in a civilized way. Now I feel January's failure, & that I have no *maid Servt.* . . . Soap for 2 days washing costs $5, & so on. I am preparing to face ruin, or rather great expense, and no means at home. I shall get him home just as soon as I can. . . .

Stuart Hospital, Monday, July 4th

My dear Pringle, . . . The Drs. still speak hopefully, but I feel discouraged—31 days & this his present state! God knows I try to be patient & believing. The poor boy is worn out. I don't let myself think about *home* for it is of no use. . . . About 80 wounded were brought in yesterday; it is very fearful. I see dead bodies carried by the windows two or three times a day & have seen worse sights than that. . . . Mothers or friends would be of no use in many cases I see around me. It would just be torture for the friends to witness it all. . . . Some part of Hospital practice I do abhor—they bury the dead like animals, without any religious service & without clothes *almost* if not entirely. They say the

---

[3] March was the servant who belonged to Mason's regiment.

Confederacy cannot afford to lose the clothes. I am amazed at the Clergy in Richmond not dividing the duty between them. . . .

Sunday, July 10th, Hospital

Dear Pringle, When I sent that Telegram "Not so well" . . . I thought Mason's hours numbered & his Drs. were very anxious too. His pulse sunk so, that I made up my mind to be prepared to see God do his own work, & only prayed that it might be a gentle departure; but not so has it been appointed. . . . He told me some days ago that he did not wish to die, but was not afraid if so God willed it. I asked if he would do again, knowing the results, as he had done about coming to Virginia. He said "Yes, for I came from a sense of duty in the sight of God, & with the hope of the approval of my Uncles & those I love, also of those whose opinion I respect in the community." . . .

The ladies are shut off from this Hospital now, & we miss their delicacies. . . .

[July 30, 1864]

Dear Pringle, . . . Mason's mind is still so weak & weary. . . . Nevertheless he improves daily, & all around pet him as if to reward him for recovering. . . . I get no letters but those by courier now. They expect a severe Battle on the Front side daily. Oh Lord! think of the wounded. . . .

3. EMMA MORDECAI

"Camp Winder Hospital"

> Emma Mordecai, whom we have met, moved from Richmond, in the spring of 1864, to Rosewood, one of the family homes close outside the city. At the same time she began a diary, which she kept until May 30, 1865. It records the many visits she paid to Camp Winder Hospital and her experiences as a volunteer helper.

Rosewood

June 16th [1864]. Morning very cool, but found the sun very hot, walking to take the cars & afterwards about town. Went to Miss Deborah Couch's to make arrangements about visiting Camp Winder. Rode out there with Miss Deborah & Mrs. Ballard. Other ladies went in a Hospital wagon & took many nice things. I went with them through the different wards to assist in serving these out to the men. Everything appeared clean & comfortable, & there were fewer patients than I expected to find. Returned from there about one. Went on Broad Street & for 15 dollars got 1½ lb. sugar, for 5 dollars 2 lbs. rice, for 2 dollars 1 qt. of wheat to make coffee of. This may, in some future day, be read with amazement.

June 17th. Went in again to visit Camp Winder Hospital. Took a bottle of Buttermilk to Mrs. Capt. Sinclair before going to the rendevous at Miss Deborah's. Found her greatly improved, & as sweet & pleasant as ever. Got to Miss D's in full time for the Hospital wagon. Many nice things had been sent there for the lady visitors to take to the patients. Large quantities of bread & butter, at least 2 gals. of rice-custard, 2 gals. buttermilk, 4 bottles raspberry vinegar, 2 gals. stewed peaches, & some other things. Mrs. Rogers, a pleasant, kind & cheerful woman, who has something cheering to say to all the men, was the only lady out besides myself. It took me nearly three hours to go round to all the patients in the fifteen wards of the 3rd Division, and to serve each with the refreshments we had for them, and we wasted no time.

I just managed to reach the cars in time to get home. Heard that Beauregard had attacked the enemy last night & this morning near Petersburg and driven them several miles. An old lady in the cars, who lives at Ashland and writes in one of the departments in Richmond was employing herself enroute, in ravelling stocking-tops to double and twist for sewing cotton. She told me she was a refugee from Fredericksburg, that she had been stripped of everything three times by the Yankees. "So," she added, "you may suppose that I have to enonomize in every way." She employs her leisure time in plaiting straw & making hats, which she sells according to quality, from 5 to 15 dollars. She eats no meat, but gets butter at 12 dols. a lb. & uses that as the cheapest substitute. Some one gave her an old cow, which gives about three pints at a milking, and on this & bread she lives. . . .

When I got home I found a number of men at the well, and incessant applications to Rosina for milk & vegetables, wash-tubs, soap, pens & ink, & everything else that can be thought of. The dry weather continues. The dust from so many horses passing to & from water & to look for pasture fills the atmosphere. The very woods are full of dust, & it settles over the garden & fields as if they were public roads.

June 18th. Still very dry, but cool & pleasant in the shade. Passed a day of rest & quiet. The usual thronging to the house all day, but this disturbed Rose no more than it did me. She is so kind & indulgent to our soldiers that she thinks nothing a trouble that she can do for them, & never refuses them anything if she can possibly spare it. One of them left a poor broken-down horse here to be taken care of. He had some bad sores, which Rose & I had well washed and dressed, & she had him well grazed in the garden walks. He had "U.S." branded on him, but I have no hatred of the Yankee *horses*. . . . Heard heavy cannonading all day, & men who were on guard duty say they heard it all last night. . . .

4. EMILY MASON

Hospital Scenes

> Miss Emily Mason, whom we met in Washington, dedicated her life to the patients of Winder Hospital. To her soldiers she was affectionately known as "Cap'n."

There is a happy ending to her story of the "runaway boy" patient. After the war, he returned to America from England and brought her a "fine present." He visited his mother's family in Charleston, and there fell in love with one of his own family connections. "They were married and lived happily ever after," Miss Mason reported.

Mrs. Lee spent most of her time in making gloves and socks for the soldiers. She gave me at one time several pair of General Lee's old socks, so darned that we saw they had been well worn by our hero. We kept these to apply to the feet of those laggard "old soldiers" who were suspected of preferring the "luxury" of hospital life to the activity of the field. And such was the effect of the application of these warlike socks that even a threat of it had the effect of sending a man to his regiment who had been lingering months in inactivity. It came to be a standing joke in the hospital infinitely enjoyed by the men. If a poor wretch was out of his bed over a week he would be threatened with "General Lee's socks," and through this means some most obstinate chronic cases were cured. Four of the most determined rheumatic patients who had resisted scarifying of the limbs, and what was worse, the smallest and thinnest of diets, were sent to their regiments and did good service afterwards. With these men the socks had to be left on several hours, amidst shouts of laughter from the "assistants," showing that though men may resist pain and starvation they succumb directly to ridicule. . . .

It was after the battle of Fredericksburg—the Wilderness perhaps—that we were ordered to have ready eight hundred beds, for so many our great field hospital accommodated. The convalescents and the "old soldiers," with rheumatism and chronic disorders, who would not get well, were sent to town hospitals, and we made ready for the night when should come in the eight hundred. They came so fast it was impossible to dress and examine them. So upon the floor of the receiving wards (long, low buildings hastily put up) the nurses placed in rows on each side their ghastly burdens, covered with blood and dirt, stiff with mud and gravel from the little streams in which they often fell. The female nurses, armed with pails of toddy or milk, passed up and down giving to each man a reviving drink to prepare him for the examination of the surgeons, while others, with water and sponges, wet the stiff bandages.

As I passed round looking to see who was most in need of help and should first be washed and borne to his bed, I was especially attracted by one group. A young officer lay with his head upon the lap of another equally distinguished-looking man, while a Negro man-servant stood by in great distress.

I offered a drink to the wounded man, saying: "You are badly hurt, I fear."

"Oh, no," he replied. "Do not mind me, but help the poor fellow next to me, who is groaning and crying. He is wounded in the wrist. There is nothing so painful as this. Besides, you see, I have my friend, a young physician, with me, and a servant to ask for what I need."

So passing on to the man with the wounded wrist, I stopped to wet it again and again, to loosen the tight bandage and say a comforting word, and so on and on, till I lost sight of this interesting group, and forgot it till in the early morning I saw the same persons. The handsome young officer was being borne on a litter to the amputating room, between the two friends.

I followed to see him laid upon the terrible table which had proved fatal to so many. Not only was his leg to be taken off at the thigh, an operation from which few recovered, but he had two wounds besides.

From this moment I never really lost sight of this doomed man. He was of a Louisiana regiment. One could see that he was of refined and cultivated people, that he was the darling of the parents of whom he constantly spoke. Yet he never complained of his rude straw couch or seemed to miss the comforts which we would fain have given him, nor did he lament his untimely fate or utter a murmur over pangs which would have moved the stoutest heart. He could not lie upon his back, for a gaping wound extended from his shoulder far down upon it, nor go upon one side, for there the arm was crushed. We were forced to swing him from the ceiling. And soon the terrible leg became covered with the fatal gangrene, and all the burning of this proud flesh could not keep death from the door. In the burning fevers, in the wild delirium, every word betrayed a pure and noble heart full of love.

Only could he be quieted by the sound of music. We took turns, my sister and I, to sit beside him and sing plaintive hymns, when he would be still. We sung and prayed for three long weeks, till we saw the end draw near, and lowered him in his bed that his "dull ear" might hear our words and his cold hands feel our warm touch. . . .

In another ward lay upon the floor two young men just taken from an ambulance—dead, as we supposed. Their heads were enveloped in bloody bandages, and the little clothing they had was glued to their bodies with mud and gravel. Hastily examining them, the surgeon ordered them to the "Dead House." I prayed they might be left till morning and bent over them with my ear upon the heart to try and detect a faint pulsation, but in vain. But neither of them had the rigidity of death in their limbs, as I heard the surgeon remark. Turning them over he pointed to the wounds below the ear, the jaws shattered, and one or both eyes put out, and reminded me that even could they be brought to life it would be to an existence worse than death—blind, deaf, perhaps unable to eat—and he muttered something about "wasting time on the dead which was needed for the living."

"Life is sweet," I replied, "even to the blind and the deaf and dumb. . . . "

And so I kept my "dead men," and the more I examined the youngest one the more was my interest excited. His hands, small and well formed, betokened the gentleman. His bare feet were of the same type, though cut by stones and covered with sand and gravel. After searching for a mouth in these bundles of rags, we forced a small spoon between the lips with a drop of milk punch and had the satisfaction to perceive that it did not ooze out, but disappeared somewhere, and all night long in making our rounds and passing the "dead men," we pursued the same process.

At length, with the morning, the great pressure was over and we found a surgeon to examine and dress again these wounds, and we were permitted to cut away by bits the stiff rags from their bodies, wash and dress them, pick out the gravel from their torn feet and wrap them in greased linen. With what joy we heard the first faint sigh and felt the first weak pulsation! Hour after hour, day after day, these men lay side by side, and were fed drop by drop from a tube lest we should strangle them. The one least wounded never recovered his mind, which had been shattered with his body. He was of the earth earthy and soon returned to his mother earth, while the younger one, though he could neither speak nor see, and hear but little, showed in a thousand ways that, though his mind wandered at times, he was aware of what went on about him, and was gentle and grateful to all who served him. As he had come in without cap or knapsack, and there was no clue to his identity, over his bed was marked "Name and Regiment Unknown."

In the meantime, by flag of truce from the North had come newspapers and letters making inquiries for a young man who, in a fervor of enthusiasm, had run away from school in England to fight the battles of the South. His mother having been a South Carolinian, he told his father he had gone to fight for his mother country, and for his mother's grave. Traced to Charleston, he was known to have gone to the Army of Northern Virginia, and to have entered the battle of the Wilderness as color-bearer for his regiment, in bare feet. As nothing had been heard of him since the battle, he was reported dead, but his friends begged that the hospitals about Richmond might be examined to see if any trace of him could be found.

We saw instantly that this runaway boy was our unknown patient. Informed of our suspicions, the assistant surgeon-general came himself to see and examine him, being himself a Carolinian and a friend of his mother's family. But the boy either would not or could not understand the questions addressed to him.

And so weeks passed in the dimly lighted room to which he was consigned, and many months went before we could lift the bandage from the one eye; before he could hear with the one ear and eat with the wounded mouth. Fed with soups and milk, he grew strong and cheerful, and was suspected of seeing a little before he confessed it, as I often saw his head elevated to an angle which enabled him to see the pretty girls who came from the city to read to him and bring him dainties. These, moved by compassion for his youth and romantic history, came to help us nurse him, and risked daily choking him in their well-meant endeavors to feed him.

At last all the bandages were removed save a ribbon across the lost eye, and our "dead man" came forth a handsome youth of 18 or 19, graceful and elegant. And now the surgeon-general claimed him for his father, and with much regret we gave him up to the flag-of-truce boat. . . .

5. KATE MASON ROWLAND

"The Band on the Square Played"

> Kate spent the summer of 1864 at Winder Hospital with her mother and her Aunt Emily Mason. Since it was only a short walk from the city, Kate could occasionally visit the Capitol Square and enjoy the concerts. One of the popular numbers performed by the band was "Silver Bells," a lively mazurka by Charles O. Pope which was dedicated to Mrs. Davis.

July 19, 1864. Our army has made a bold dash into Maryland. Early and force frightened all Yankeydom out of its wits—threat-

ened Washington, burnt railroads, and some houses by way of
retaliation; have taken a great number of horses, and cattle with
other stores and are now back across the Potomac before Lincoln,
Seward & Co. have quite opened their eyes to the state of
affairs. . . .

July 26th. I am at work now in earnest—have 3 wards but
fortunately there are very few sick.

July 30th. I am becoming so interested in our patients—have
been cooking for them all the morning.

August 4th. T. & L. came out last night & several gentlemen
spent the evening. We sat out under the stars & all caught colds
but otherwise enjoyed the evening. I was up betimes this morning in spite of late hours last night & made egg-nog for Captain
C. which he was not able to drink. He can take no food this morning & the Doctors think he will lose a *part of his tongue.* I am so
much interested in him & in my work generally.

August 14th. . . . My Captain is getting well fast, he is learning
to talk again & is no longer fed with a spoon. . . .

August 21st. We went to the Square Tuesday. While we were
there some troops passed through—Infantry & Artillery on their
way to the front. What a contrast they presented to the gayly
dressed crowd of officers & no less distingué privates who
mingled with the beautifully dressed ladies—making up such a
gay & brilliant scene. Grim & dark & dirty—yet cheerful & full of
life. The band on the Square played as they passed along & a
cheer rang through their lines as they went by on their march to
battle & death. The Yankees have been within 8 miles often—
heavy skirmishing has been going on for several days. We hear
the booming of the guns. We have lost 2 Brigadier Genls & many
nameless brave ones—no wounded brought here as yet. . . .

6. CORNELIA PEAKE McDONALD

"They Carried Him to Hollywood"

At the outbreak of war, Cornelia Peake McDonald was the wife of Angus W. McDonald, of Winchester, Virginia, and the mother of seven children. Her husband, a West Point graduate of the class of 1817, volunteered his services as an aide to General Stonewall Jackson. In June 1861 he received a commission as Colonel and organized the 7th Virginia Cavalry. Ill-health forced his resignation from the cavalry, and he was assigned to post duty. He was captured near Winchester in June 1864 by General David Hunter's command and transferred to Cumberland, Maryland. He was chained in his jail cell by General Hunter's order.

No town changed hands so often, or so suddenly, as Winchester. When the Federals occupied it, they made free use of the McDonald house.

In the fall of 1863, Cornelia and her young children began the life of refugees in various parts of Virginia. She was in Lexington when she received news of Colonel McDonald's imprisonment. Six months later, after futile appeals for his exchange, his old friend General Ethan Allen Hitchcock, then serving in Washington on the commission for the exchange of prisoners, arranged his parole, and he was sent to Richmond.

At this point, Mrs. McDonald tells her own story:

October, 1864. . . . After the reception of the letter telling of my husband's illness, I felt persuaded that he must be too weak and exhausted to endure even the fatigue of a journey home; and I was full of anxiety, restless and uneasy, so that at all times my nerves were easily affected; if I slept it was to dream sad and uneasy dreams, and all my thoughts by day or night were of the released prisoner now travelling homewards.

One night . . . I had a dream that startled and distressed me greatly. . . . I dreamed that he was to be married, that preparations were going on for the wedding; that I came into a room and saw him sitting alone at a long table covered with a white cloth. On the table just before him was laid a large green wreath; nothing else was on it.

On the 9th of November I received a short letter from him at Richmond. He had arrived there on the 7th; was too fatigued to write much; he would be at home as soon as he could be. . . .

On the 28th I had a letter from Flora, written at his dictation, telling me that he was not as well as he had been; that I must come immediately as he might not be able to travel for some time. I was compelled to wait two days to arrange for the children during my absence. . . .

December, 1864. At dawn on the 1st of December I left the house with the little ones fast asleep, and everything quiet around. It was a bitter cold day, and I could scarcely keep from freezing on the way to the canal boat. It was comfortless on the boat, so cold that everybody had to sit close to the red hot stove. The boat was full, and I never remember to have seen so many people together who displayed so little merriment.

Everyone was sad and anxious. . . .

At Lynchburg we stopped, and I went on to Richmond next morning by rail. I met some friends on the cars, Mrs. Magill and others, and when we were in motion and fairly on the way, I felt light-hearted, even elated; not for months had I had so much lightness of spirit.

I sat all day happy, talking and laughing with friends, and joyfully anticipating my arrival at Richmond.

When we reached the depot, Mr. Ran.[dolph] Tucker came to meet Mrs. Magill. He spoke to me very affectionately, and I remarked to myself how sad he looked, but did not think of it long, for I was occupied in wondering why some one was not there to meet me. Mr. Tucker got me a carriage, and I drove to Mr. Claiborne Green's[4] where he was staying. Mr. Green met me

---

4 Thomas Claiborne Green married Mary McDonald, daughter of Colonel McDonald's first wife, Leacy Ann Naylor.

at the door, and stood rubbing his hands and absently looking at me without saying a word. At last he went out to have the trunk brought in, and I stood in the hall rather at a loss to imagine why no one came to the door to meet me. Soon Mrs. Holliday[5] came out of a room, and in her usual unthinking way pointed to an open door and asked me if I would go in there now. I went, and the object I first saw was my husband's corpse, stretched on a white bed with a large green wreath around his head and shoulders, enclosing them as in a frame.

They had not intended that I should have had such a shock, had not expected me till nine o'clock by the south side train, and when I went in had just finished the wreath and laid it around him, that I might see him first with the horror of death a little softened. Ah! how familiar it looked, that wreath; I had seen it, weeks before; when my body slept, but my spirit was awake. . . .

That same night I heard of the death of my dear sister Lizzy,[6] of the shock and distress of seeing their home invaded and pillaged and everything burnt and destroyed.

Many friends came to sympathize with and try to comfort me. . . . The only thing that gave me comfort was the account they gave of the change in him. He who had always said that he loved his friends and hated his enemy, that he believed revenge was a duty, left word that his sons were not to avenge his death, that they were to let the wicked alone to the vengeance of the Almighty. He said he did not wish the children, the young ones, to remain in the country if it was conquered, that he did not suppose the older ones would survive our defeat, but that the younger ones must not remain in the country to suffer the humiliation. Mary, Anne and Flora[7] were with him. Poor Anne had just that morning gone to her little baby's bed and found it dead. . . .

---

[5] Mrs. Richard Holliday, *née* Millicent McDonald, was the sister of Colonel Angus W. McDonald.

[6] Mrs. Thomas F. Buck, of "Clover Hill" plantation, near Front Royal.

[7] Anne and Flora, like Mary, were children by Colonel McDonald's first wife; Anne was Mrs. James W. Green.

. . . On Sunday he was buried. An immense crowd of people, I was told, was there. The President and all the state and high military officers were mourners. General Cooper and others of his old West Point friends were his pallbearers, and wrapped in the folds of the stars and bars, with bands playing the dead march, they carried him to Hollywood, and there laid him to rest with all the honours of war. Nothing was omitted to do him honour, or to show how deeply his sufferings were regretted. I would have been comforted by the thought that such a burial was the one he would have desired, that his true soldierly spirit, if it could have seen, would have been glad, but for the knowledge that he had been sent to his grave by inhuman treatment; it seemed to me then not so much the will of God as the wickedness of man that had taken him from the world. . . .

Some days passed and many discussions arose with regard to the future of myself and the children. Mr. Green thought I had better come to Richmond where I could find employment in one of the Departments. All thought that the children ought to be distributed among the older members of the family. . . .

I listened, but was resolved no matter what happened not to part with my children. . . .

I thanked all the family for their kindness in offering to help us, but told them . . . that they were all I had, and that I could not consent to part with them. They gave up kindly . . . and so I left them and went back to Lexington. The day before I left I went with Flora to Hollywood to see the place where he was laid. It was bitter cold, and a keen wind blew in our faces all the way. After a long walk we reached the hillside where he was, with Anne's poor little babe by his side.

The wind whistled through the leafless trees, and everything looked so bleak and desolate that I felt as if my heart was broken. The falls of the James River were just below and the melancholy sound and cold look of the icy water added to the dreariness. It was bright sunshine, but a grey and cloudy sky would have harmonized better with the scene and my desolation. We could not stay long with him, but were obliged to hurry away to keep from freezing in the bitter biting wind. So we turned and left him to his lonely sleep, with the bare branches waving over him, and the sound of the rushing water the only one to break the stillness. The hillsides were covered thickly with fresh graves. . . .

7. SALLY NELSON ROBINS

"No. 707 Franklin Street"

Sally Berkeley Nelson, of Gloucester County, was the second wife of William Todd Robins, 9th Regiment of Virginia Cavalry. Before the war ended, eight horses were shot from under him, and he was wounded three times.

Before coming to 707 Franklin Street, to make her home, Mrs. Lee had stayed for a time with the James Caskies. Later, she lived in a small rented house on Leigh Street.

No. 707 is a large brick house. It was in the most fashionable part of Richmond, just two squares from Capitol Park and St. Paul's Church. It was built by Norman Stewart, of Rothsay, Scotland, who came to this country early in the century. The house for its day was handsome and commodious, with walnut woodwork and big windows, wide halls, spacious rooms and broad verandas. When Mr. Norman Stewart died, he left the house to his nephew, Mr. John Stewart of "Brookhill," through whose courtesy General Lee occupied it during the war.

It was nicknamed "The Mess," and, before Mrs. Lee and her daughters arrived, was occupied by the General (when he was in town), General Custis Lee, Major Coxe, Captain Ferdinand C. Hutter, Robert Shirley Carter, Chapman Leigh and others—a merry party of young officers, who made the house ring with jest and song, and who scoffed at danger and defeat. . . .

No. 707 became a common meeting place. People came to talk

of victory or sorrow; they could stay here if they had nowhere else to go; they gathered here to work, the disheartened came for comfort from the tender, loving wife of the commander-in-chief. Mourning mothers came to her in their agony; wives of heroes brought their joy over recent success; friends came without ceremony, and partook of what they could get. Indeed, so free was "The Mess" from any touch of style or ceremony that a young friend called there one day, and was surprised and amused to find a stuttering butler gotten up in a sort of livery, wearing gray clothes and red stripes on his trousers.

Some after Mrs. Lee came to Richmond, a merciless rheumatism bound her to her chair. In the back room, opening on a veranda shadowed by ailanthus trees, her days were spent. . . . She gathered together the young girls and infused into them a working interest. They began to knit and sew, to scrape lint and to make bandages. The Ordnance Department furnished Mrs. Lee with knitting needles by the gross, and she had "Yarn Scouts" working for her all over the country. . . .

The neighborhood of "The Mess" was taken by prominent people; on one side were the Cabells, on the other was General George W. Randolph; next to him were the Tripletts (Mary Triplett, one of the most beautiful women in America, was General Lee's prime favorite); three doors from them lived Dr. Minnigerode, the rector of St. Paul's, and pastor of both Lee and Davis.

The Randolphs were very gay—they had big receptions, and young officers and pretty girls were always around. The Lees were, in contrast, extremely quiet. When they heard of expenditure for social pleasure they could not restrain a groan, they were desperately in earnest about helping the soldiers. . . .

The life at Richmond then was a shifting panorama; sick people were coming in and well ones going out. It was a restless turmoil—one day of hope, a night of anguish, a morning of joy or sorrow. In these varying scenes Mrs. Lee's chamber was a

"Mecca." Seated in her wheeled chair, she listened, and strengthened, and smiled even when her own heart ached.

There was not a man or woman at "The Mess" who ever heard Mrs. Lee complain. The brightness of her nature, amidst uncertainty and pain, was wonderful. Her eyes would shine whenever her husband came in from camp. Often he rode in just to see her for an hour. . . . The soldiers thought of her with tenderest love, and prayed God to bless her for saving their poor frosted feet. The General would take her socks back with him to camp and distribute them to his "boys."

On Sundays when General Lee was at home he read the Episcopal service in Mrs. Lee's room, and the whole family assembled to hear him. . . .

Once alone did her courage seem utterly to forsake her. After the tragedy of "Yellow Tavern" she was indeed disconsolate. "Jackson is dead," she said, "and now Stuart is gone. What will become of us? What will my poor husband do? It seems that God has turned his face from us." But she gathered up her strength, and through the darkest days tried to soothe others by her perfect resignation.

St. Paul's Church, showing Washington monument in the foreground. Reprinted from Varina Howell Davis, *Jefferson Davis: A Memoir.*
The Belford Company, 1890.

The Davis children, Christmas 1864. Reprinted from Varina Howell Davis, *Jefferson Davis: A Memoir*. The Belford Company, 1890.

Little Joe Davis' grave in Hollywood Cemetery, Richmond. W. L. Sheppard.
Reprinted from J. W. Jones, The Davis Memorial Volume. Richmond, Virginia,
B. F. Johnson & Company, 1889.

Miss Elizabeth Van Lew, spy for the Union army who "risked everything that is dear to man." Cook Collection, Valentine Museum, Richmond, Virginia.

Captain Sally Tompkins served as head of the Robertson Hospital. Cook Collection, Valentine Museum, Richmond, Virginia.

Miss Louise Wigfall. The star in this portrait was from the coat collar of General J. E. Johnston. Reprinted from Mrs. D. Giraud Wright, *A Southern Girl in '61.* Doubleday, Page & Company, 1905.

Miss Mary Triplitt (Mrs. Philip Haxall), of Richmond. Reprinted from Mrs. D. Giraud Wright, *A Southern Girl in '61*. Doubleday, Page & Company, 1905.

Miss Hetty Cary. Reprinted from Mrs. D. Giraud Wright, *A Southern Girl in '61*. Doubleday, Page & Company, 1905.

VII

NEVER CRY FOR QUARTER

December 16, 1864—April 2, 1865

All through the winter of 1864-65, the siege of Petersburg continued. Grant sent Sheridan's cavalry to the Shenandoah Valley on a "pilgrimage of terror." Sheridan proclaimed, "I will leave them nothing but their eyes to weep with." This was "total war."

On February 5, 1865, Secretary of War James A. Seddon resigned. His position was filled by General John Cabell Breckinridge, former Vice-President of the United States, Senator from Kentucky, and, more recently, Major General in the Confederate Army. His wife, Mary Cyrene Burch Breckinridge, was with him in Richmond. She was described as a "petite beauty." Early in the war, she was honored by having a cannon named after her, but a fate which she always dreaded for herself befell the "Lady Breckinridge." It was captured at Missionary Ridge.

In the last days of March, General Lee made his final offensive demonstration by attacking the enemy's works at Hare's Hill. His plan ended in failure. At Five Forks, on April 1, Confederate forces were defeated by Sheridan. At sunrise the next day, Lee's lines were broken at Petersburg. That night, Lee and the small remnant of the Army of Northern Virginia evacuated Petersburg and began crossing the Appomattox.

"It is a most remarkable circumstance that the people of Richmond had remained in profound ignorance of the fight-

ing which had been taking place for three days on General
Lee's lines," writes the journalist Edward A. Pollard. "There
was not a rumour of it in the air. Not a newspaper office in
the city had any inkling of what was going on. Indeed for the
past few days there had been visible reassurance in the Confederate capital; there were rumours that Johnston was moving to Lee's lines and a general idea that the combined force
would take the offensive against the enemy. . . . How little
prepared the people of Richmond were on the bright Sabbath morning of the 2d of April for the news that fell upon
them like a thunder-clap from clear skies. . . . "

1. ALICE WEST ALLEN

"The Tree Was a Lovely Holly"

Alice, who was eleven years old in 1864, lived in the Pied-
mont section of Virginia. To avoid the dangers and hazards
of Sheridan's raiders, she and her two little brothers were
packed off to spend Christmas in Richmond. That Christmas
of 1864 was one of the saddest in history, but it proved an
unforgettable event for Alice.

The last Christmas of the war my parents thought our home
would soon be in the enemy's lines, so they decided to send us
to Richmond until all danger was over. We were wild with de-
light at the thought of going to the big city. As we had to leave
in four days, everybody helped the Negro seamstress to get us
ready. The boys were happy with jackets made from old Confederate uniforms, with the brass buttons on them, feeling as
though they were real soldiers.

We left home about daylight to catch the early train, and as
we reached the railroad crossing, which Hampton and Butler
had fought so hard to retain, we saw just ahead of us twelve
Federals well armed. We were terribly frightened, but they gave
us just a glance and went on, as they saw only a jersey wagon
full of frightened children driven by an old Negro man. I must

say that the boys were not so brave then and wished that they could hide their gray jackets, as each moment we expected to be arrested. We told at the station what we had seen, but our fears were laughed at. Later these men were captured after they had torn up several yards of the railroad track. It was some time before it could be repaired, which made us fifteen hours later than we had expected in taking the train to Richmond. When the train came in, it was laden with prisoners bound for Libby prison and many wounded soldiers going to the large hospitals—Chimborazo and others.

We were delighted when we got to Richmond. The next morning our aunt took us out shopping; and as each of us had one hundred dollars to spend, we felt that we could give presents to all at home. We soon found that toys and candy were as costly as food. A dear friend of my mother's found that we were to spend our Christmas in the city, so she invited us to a Christmas tree given to President Davis' children. The tree was a lovely holly laden with homemade candles and dolls made out of hickory nuts and Canton flannel; then there were cotton and Canton flannel rabbits, dogs and cats, and numerous other presents, all homemade, as was everything on the supper table—homemade coffee, tea, sugar, and everything. I have never seen anything that looked so pretty to me. Probably some of it was due to Maggie and Jeff Davis, our President's children. Maggie Davis had the honor of presenting the gifts, and I fell in love with her when I saw her worshipped by all. She and her brother were full of fun and mischief, and we played hide and seek all over the house; they the leaders in every game. Mrs. Davis called me to her side and said: "Your dress, I see, is very much like Maggie's. You are both happy in wearing dresses made from your mothers' wedding gowns." I think she just wanted to make me feel good.

President Davis came in for them. Their home was only four doors away. He was tall and thin and sad, presenting quite a contrast to his wife. . . .

2. VARINA HOWELL DAVIS

"Christmas in the Confederate White House"

Richmond children had been deprived of many things, but they could not say that Santa Claus had entirely forgotten them. Mrs. Davis was determined to give her own four little children—and other children too—a day of joyful remembrance. Winnie, the Davis baby, and three–year–old William, had been born in the Confederate White House. Maggie was nine and Jeff, Jr., was seven.

Christmas season was ushered in under the thickest clouds; every one felt the cataclysm which impended, but the rosy, expectant faces of our little children were a constant reminder that self-sacrifice must be the personal offering of each mother of the family. How to satisfy the children that nothing better could be done than the little makeshifts attainable in the Confederacy was the problem of the older members of each household. There were no currants, raisins or other ingredients to fill the old Virginia recipe for mince pie, and the children considered that at least a slice of the much-coveted dainty was their right. . . . Apple trees grew and bore in spite of war's alarms, so the foundation of the mixture was assured. The many exquisite housekeepers in Richmond had preserved all the fruits attainable and these were substituted for the time-honored raisins and currants. The brandy required for seasoning at one hundred dollars a bottle was forthcoming, the cider was obtained, the suet at a dollar a pound was ordered—and the pies seemed a blessed certainty—but the eggnog—how were the eggs and liquors to be procured, without which Christmas would be a failure to the Negroes?

"Ef it's only a little wineglass," said the Negro rubber in the stables who brought in the back log (our substitute for the Yule log). "I dunno how we gwine get along without the eggnog." So, after redoubled efforts, the eggs and other ingredients were secured in advance.

The little jackets, pieced together out of the cloth remaining when uniforms were turned out by the tailors, were issued to the children of the soldiers, amid the remonstrances of the mothers that the pattern of them "wasn't worth a cent."

Rice, flour, molasses and tiny pieces of meat, most of these sent to the President's wife anonymously to be dispersed to the poor, had all been weighed and issued, and the playtime of the family began, but like a clap of thunder out of a clear sky came the information that the orphans at the Episcopalian Home had been promised a Christmas tree and the toys, candy and cakes must be provided, as well as one pretty prize for the most orderly girl among the orphans. The kind-hearted confectioner was interviewed by our committee of managers, and he promised a certain amount of his simpler kinds of candy, which he sold easily at a dollar and a half a pound, but he drew the line at cornucopias to hold it, and sugared fruits to hang on the tree, and all the other vestiges of Christmas creations which had been on his hands for years. The ladies dispersed in anxious squads of toy-hunters, and each one turned over the store of her children's treasures for a contribution to the orphans' tree. My little ones rushed over the great house looking for their treasures—eyeless dolls, three-legged horses, tops with the upper peg broken off, rubber tops, monkeys with all the squeak gone silent and all the ruck of children's toys that gather in a nursery closet.

Some small feathered chickens and parrots which nodded their heads in obedience to a weight beneath them were furnished with new tail feathers, lambs minus much of their wool were supplied with a cotton wool substitute, rag dolls were plumped out and recovered with clean cloth, and the young ladies painted their fat faces in bright colors and furnished them with beads for eyes.

But the tug of war was how to get something to decorate the

orphans' tree. Our man servant, Robert Brown, was much interested and offered to make the prize toy. He contemplated a "sure enough house, with four rooms." His part in the domestic service was delegated to another and he gave himself over in silence and solitude to the labors of an architect.

My sister painted mantel shelves, door panels, pictures and frames, for the walls and finished with black grates in which there blazed a roaring fire, which was pronounced marvelously realistic. We all made furniture of twigs and paste-board, and my mother made pillows, mattresses, sheets and pillow cases for the two little bedrooms.

Christmas Eve a number of young people were invited to come and string apples and popcorn for the tree: a neighbor very deft in domestic arts had tiny candle moulds made and furnished all the candles for the tree. However, the puzzle and triumph of all was the construction of a large number of cornucopias. At last some one suggested a conical block of wood, about which the drawing paper could be wound and pasted. In a little book shop a number of small, highly colored pictures cut out and ready to apply were unearthed, and our old confectioner friend, Mr. Pizzini, consented to give "all the love verses the young people wanted to roll with the candy."

About twenty young men and girls gathered around small tables in one of the drawing-rooms of the mansion and the cornucopias were begun. The men wrapped the squares of candy, first reading the "sentiments" printed upon them, such as "Roses are red, violets blue, sugar's sweet and so are you," "If you love me as I love you, no knife can cut our love in two." The fresh young faces, wreathed in smiles, nodded attention to the reading, while with their little deft hands they glued the cornucopias and pasted on the pictures. Where were the silk tops to come from? Trunks of old things were turned out and snippings of silk and even woolen of bright colors were found to close the tops, and some of the young people twisted sewing silk into cords with which to draw the bags up. The beauty of these homemade things astonished us all, for they looked quite "custom-made," but when the "sure-enough house" was revealed the young people clapped their approbation while Robert . . . bowed his thanks for our approval.

Then the coveted eggnog was passed around in tiny glass cups and pronounced good. Crisp homemade ginger snaps and snowy lady cake completed the refreshments of Christmas Eve. The children, allowed to sit up and be noisy in their own way as an indulgence, took a sip of the eggnog out of my cup and the eldest boy confided to his father: "Now I just know this is Christmas." . . .

At last quiet settled on the household and the older members of the family began to stuff stockings with molasses candy, red apples, an orange, small whips plaited by the family with high-colored crackers, worsted reins knitted at home, paper dolls, teetotums made of large horn buttons and a match which could spin indefinitely, balls of worsted rags wound hard and covered with old kid gloves, a pair of pretty woolen gloves for each, either cut out of cloth and embroidered on the back or knitted by some deft hand out of homespun wool. For the President there was a pair of chamois-skin riding gauntlets exquisitely embroidered on the back with his monogram in red and white silk, made, as the giver wrote, under the guns of Fortress Monroe late at night for fear of discovery. There was a hemstitched linen handkerchief, with a little sketch in indelible ink in one corner; the children had written him little letters, their grandmother having held their hands, the burthen of which composition was how they loved their dear father. . . .

A bowl of eggnog was sent to the servants, and a part of everything they coveted of the dainties.

On Christmas morning the children awoke early and came in to see their toys. They were followed by the Negro women, who one after another "caught" us by wishing us a merry Christmas before we could say it to them, which gave them a right to a gift. Of course, there was a present for every one, small though it might be, and one who had been born and brought up at our plantation was vocal in her admiration of a gay handkerchief. As she left the room she ejaculated: "Lord knows Mistress knows our insides—she just got the very thing I wanted."

For me there were six cakes of delicious soap, made from the grease of a ham boiled for a family at Farmville, a skein of exquisitely fine gray linen thread spun at home, a pincushion of some plain brown cotton material made by some poor woman and stuffed with wool from her pet sheep, and a little baby hat plaited by the orphans and presented by the industrious little pair who sewed the straw together. Another present was a fine, delicate little baby frock without an inch of lace or embroidery upon it, but the delicate fabric was set with fairy stitches by the dear invalid neighbor who made it, and it was very precious in my eyes. There were also a few of Swinburne's best songs bound in wall-paper and a chamois needlebook left for me by young Mr. P., now succeeded to his title in England. It was a Brobdingnagian thimble—"for my own finger, you know," said the handsome, cheerful young fellow.

After breakfast, at which all the family, great and small, were present, came the walk to St. Paul's Church. We did not use our carriage on Christmas or, if possible to avoid it, on Sunday. The saintly Dr. Minnegerode preached a sermon on Christian love, the introit was sung by a beautiful young woman and the angels might have joyfully listened.

Our chef did wonders with the turkey and roast beef, and drove the children quite out of their propriety by a spun-sugar hen, life-size, on a nest of blanc-mange eggs. The mince pie and plum pudding made them feel, as one of the gentlemen laughingly remarked, "as if their jackets were buttoned." . . . They waited with great impatience for the crowning amusement of the day, "the children's tree."

All throughout the afternoon first one little head and then another popped in at the door to ask: "Isn't it 8 o'clock yet?" burning with impatience to see the tree.

When at last we reached the basement of St. Paul's Church the tree burst upn their view like the realization of Aladdin's subterranean orchard, and they were awed by its grandeur.

The orphans sat mute with astonishment until the opening hymn and prayer and the last Amen had been said, and then they at a signal warily and slowly gathered around the tree to receive from a lovely young girl their allotted present.

The President became so enthusiastic that he undertook to help in the distribution, but worked such wild confusion giving everything asked for into their outstretched hands, that we called a halt, so he contented himself with unwinding one or two tots from a network of strung popcorn in which they had become entangled and taking off all the apples he could when unobserved, and presenting them to the smaller children. . . .

We went home to find that General Lee had called in our absence and many other people. General Lee had left word that he had received a barrel of sweet potatoes for us, which had been sent to him by mistake. He did not discover the mistake until he had taken his share (a dishful) and given the rest to the soldiers. We wished it had been much more for them and him.

The night closed with a "starvation" party, where there were no refreshments, at a neighboring house. The rooms lighted as well as practicable, some one willing to play dance music on the piano and plenty of young men and girls comprised the entertainment. . . . The officers, who rode into town with their long cavalry boots pulled well over their knees, but splashed up to their waists, put up their horses and rushed to the places where their dress uniform suits had been left for safekeeping. They soon emerged, however, in full toggery and entered into the pleasures of the dance with the bright-eyed girls. . . .

So, in the interchange of the courtesies and charities of life,

to which we could not add its comforts and pleasures, passed. . . .
Christmas in the Confederate mansion.

3. SALLIE ANN BROCK PUTNAM

"For a Name and for a Ring"

> One of the numerous weddings mentioned by Mrs. Putnam
> was that of Miss Hetty Cary, "the toast of the town," and
> General John Pegram, who were married in St. Paul's church
> on January 19. According to their friend, Henry Kyd Doug-
> las, "One of the handsomest and most lovable men I ever
> knew was wed to the handsomest woman in the Southland—
> with her classic face, her pure complexion, her auburn hair,
> her perfect figure and her carriage, altogether the most beau-
> tiful woman I ever saw in any land."
>
> Three weeks later, to the day, General Pegram's coffin occu-
> pied the spot in the chancel where he had stood to be mar-
> ried. His widow knelt beside it.

We were now in the midst of winter—the cheerless season to
which we had looked forward with dread. It was the fourth year
of the war. The festivities of Christmas were rendered mournful
by the fall of Savannah. With saddened mien we turned our steps
towards the sanctuaries of God.

We left the temples of the Most High, and wended our way
back, many of us, not to the luxurious homes, where once the
festival was gladdened by the reunion of loved ones, but to the
humble, contracted lodgings which were all that remained to us,
to call "home." Instead of the sumptuous banquet, around
which we were wont to gather, we sat down to the poverty-
stricken board. We counted again the vacant chairs, and glanced
with eyes blinded by tears, upon the sombre living of woe, that
indicated whither had been borne our domestic idols.

With a brave attempt at cheerfulness, we decked our dwellings
with the evergreen, cedar, arbor-vitae, and holly, and here and

there, under the magical influence of the kind old patron saint of the holiday, the Christmas tree once more reared its cheery head, laden with a precious and incongruous burden of bon-bons and simple toys.

The New Year was ushered in with no better prospects. Day by day our wants and privations increased. The supply of provisions in the city of Richmond was altogether inadequate to the demand, and generally of a quality that would have been altogether unappetizing in seasons of plenty. Every fresh encroachment of the enemy increased this scarcity, and in a proportionate ratio, the prices at which articles of food were held. There was also a great want of fuel. Those formerly accustomed to well-heated houses, where comfort and luxury presided, now parsimoniously economized with a single ton of coal, or a single cord of wood to insure its lasting as long as possible, lest, when the last lump, or the last stick was consumed, no more could be obtained at any price.

In addition to our other miseries, robberies were fearfully on the increase. The fortunate possessor of a well-stocked larder or coal house was in constant danger from burglary. It finally became an almost universal fashion in Richmond to permit "every day to take care of itself." It was useless to lay up for the morrow, or to anticipate the rise in prices and provide against it, for the cunning housebreakers were still better at calculation, and would ever upset the best laid schemes by their successful midnight depredations.

During the war the "rebel capital" became famous for the large number of beautiful ladies who belonged to the city, or who found within its friendly walls refuge and security. While the god of war thundered from its ramparts, not less busy was the artful boy-god. As usual, the gossips thoroughly acquainted themselves with Cupid's victories. Ever and anon these *quidnuncs* whispered of interesting *affaires de coeur,* in which were associated the names of gallant officers and soldiers of our army

and of the fair and beautiful belles of the capital. That they
reckoned not without their host was made evident from the unusual number of weddings that were celebrated during the
winter. St. Paul's seemed to be the fashionable church for the
solemnization of these happy bridals. It appeared indeed that
many a fair young girl was only

> "Doffing her maiden joyousness,
> For a name and for a ring,"

ere long to cherish the memory of the early loved and the early
lost in the grave of the soldier. But the true sentiment of the
heart of Southern woman found expression in the language of a
noble daughter of Virginia, who, when she buckled the armor
on her patriot husband, remarked, "I had rather be the widow of
a brave man than the wife of a coward."

Of the numerous marriages which served as fruitful digres-
sions from the war topic, and brightened the usual gloom that
hung over the social circles of Richmond, we will mention particularly only one, rendered of thrilling interest from all the
associations connected with it. In January, the brave, gallant,
and chivalrous young Major-General John Pegram, of Richmond, led to the altar the fairest of the fair—the universally
acknowledged queen of society—the beautiful and accomplished
Miss C. A dense throng crowded the church to witness the
nuptials of the popular young officer and his magnificent bride.
Sincere congratulations were pressed upon them, and they set
forth on their matrimonial route with the brightest prospects
for happiness, and sustained by the prayers and best wishes of
numberless friends.

Three weeks had only passed when on the field of Hatcher's
Run this young officer—this happy young husband—was cut
down. Death, remorseless, cruel Death, claimed the warrior
bridegroom, and the snowy robe of the bride, the orange wreath,
and the misty veil, which had shaded, yet heightened her splen-

did beauty, were exchanged for the weeds of the widow, the sable robe of the heart's deepest affliction.

It is noticeable in connection with the scarcity of food and the high prices, that the class usually known as the poor was not the class which experienced the most serious inconvenience, and was reduced to the most dreadful misery. They were provided by the Common Council of the city with such staple articles of food as could be obtained, and in a quantity sufficient to secure them from suffering. They had furnished to them rations of corn-meal, sorghum syrup, and small quantities of bacon and flour. Starvation to them was not imminent, and the pauper class were indeed in more comfortable circumstances than persons who lived on salaries, or depended upon a moderate income for support.

Salaried officers with families dependent upon them found it extremely difficult, with the constantly increasing prices, and the depreciation of the currency, to bring their expenses within the limits of their income. In some instances we heard of those who subsisted solely on bread, and not enough of that to satisfy the cravings of hunger.

"Croakers" now began to multiply, and murmurs of dissatisfaction, deep but not loud, and mutterings of vexation and disapproval were sometimes heard from a certain class of malcontents, who, when the light of prosperity shone on our arms, were the first to hail the Confederacy, but who, like the fickle and inconstant people of France, in the time of the revolution, were ready to veer with every change of the political weathercock, and possessed not moral courage enough to sustain them under the dark clouds and beating winds of adversity. Like individuals, governments have their summer friends; and though we are proud to know that these exceptions in the Confederacy were exceedingly rare, still we are forced to admit, and mourn that we are compelled to admit, they did indeed exist.

Another and very obvious sign of weakness was the growing

want of confidence in our currency. The necessity for final re-
pudiation was currently entertained; and those who looked with
certainly to the establishment of the independence of the Confederacy, looked with equal certainty to the great financial crisis
which must follow. Ruin, bankruptcy, and the multitudinous
evils which follow in the train of all great political convulsions,
were predicted. But there were brave hearts that gave little heed
to these warnings, and clung to the phantom of Hope. . . .

There was, however, a marked change visible in the general
disrespect of the people for the circulating medium. This was
evident in a reckless expenditure of money, and a disposition to
indulge in extravagances, at whatever cost. The trousseau of a
bride, which might formerly have been procured at an expense
of a few hundred dollars, could now only be purchased at the
expenditure of as many thousands; yet there was no hesitancy
manifested at this time to indulge in what a year before we might
have considered reprehensible extravagance.

The simplest wardrobe of a lady at this time was enormously
expensive. For an ordinary calico, for which we formerly paid
twelve and a half cents per yard, (a New York shilling) we were
forced to pay from thirty to thirty-five dollars per yard. A nice
French merino or mohair dress cost from eight hundred to a
thousand dollars. A cloak of fine cloth was worth from a thousand to fifteen hundred dollars. A pair of balmoral boots for
ladies brought two hundred to two hundred and fifty dollars.
French kid gloves sold at from one hundred and twenty-five to
one hundred and seventy-five dollars per pair. Irish linens commanded from fifty to one hundred dollars per yard, and cotton
cloth, of inferior quality, varied from thirty to fifty dollars per
yard. We hardly dare trust ourselves to give the price of ladies'
hats, but they varied, from the difference in quality and material,
from six hundred to fifteen hundred dollars. . . .

Our dry goods were now principally obtained through the
blockade from Nassau. A very large capital was invested in this

trade, and it was carried on successfully and at comparatively little risk. The most important port to the Richmond market wàs Wilmington, North Carolina. But at the period which we are now noticing, this port was in the hands of the enemy;[1] and as the circle of our advantages gradually narrowed, the price of gold became higher and higher, and all articles of trade advanced in undue proportion. Day by day we congratulated ourselves on what we were fortunate enough to have, and were not forced to purchase of the remorseless tradesmen. . . .

4. NELLIE GREY

"Sometimes We Were Hungry"

"Nellie Grey" was not the real name of the lady who contributes the story to follow. "Out of deference to the wishes of living persons, her own and her husband's names were suppressed and others substituted" when her experiences as the wife of a Confederate officer were published after her death in 1903, under the title *A Virginia Girl in the Civil War.*

"Nellie Grey" was born in Norfolk, where her father was an officer in the Bank of Virginia. After his death, she and her mother and sister went to live with relatives in Petersburg. There, in 1861, at the age of seventeen, she married "Dan Grey."

Her husband became a major of cavalry with General W. H. F. Lee, and "Nellie" followed him when it was possible. On one occasion General Stuart gave her his photograph, on which he had inscribed, "To her who in being a devoted wife did not forget to be a true patriot."

In the winter of 1865 she came to live with her mother in Richmond. "Dan" was with General Lee before Petersburg.

I joined mother at the Arlington, prepared to make a joke of hardships and wring every possible drop of pleasure out of a

---

[1] Fort Fisher, below Washington, fell into Northern hands on January 15, 1865, which meant the loss of that great fort to the Confederacy.

winter in Richmond, varied, as I fondly imagined, by frequent if brief visits from Dan.

The Arlington was kept on something like the European plan, not from choice of landlady or guests but from grim necessity. Feeding a household of people was too arduous and uncertain an undertaking in those days for a woman to assume. Mrs. Fry before our arrival had informed her boarders that they could continue to rent their rooms from her, but that they must provide their own meals. We paid her $25 a month for our room— the price of a house in good times and in good money. During my absence . . . mother, to reduce expenses, had rented half of her room and bed to Delia McArthur, of Petersburg. I now rented a little bed from Mrs. Fry for myself, and set it up in the same room.

We had become so poor and had so little to cook that we did most of our cooking ourselves over the grate, each woman often cooking her own rations. There was an old Negress living in the back yard who cooked for any or all of us when we had something that could not be prepared by ourselves over the grate. Sometimes we got hold of a roast, or we would buy two quarts of flour, a little dab of lard, and a few pinches of salt and treat ourselves to a loaf of bread, which the old Negress cooked for us, charging ten dollars for the baking. But as a rule the grate was all sufficient. We boiled rice or dried apples or beans or peas in our stew-pan, and we had a frying-pan if there was anything to fry.

Across the hall from us Miss Mary Pagett, of Petersburg, had a room to herself. She worked in one of the departments, and in order that she might have her meals in time she went into partnership with us. Every morning she would put in with our rations whatever she happened to have for that day, and mother would cook it and have it ready when she came. Down-stairs under our room Mr. and Mrs. Sampson, their daughters Nan and Beth, and their son Don, all of Petersburg and old neighbors and friends of ours, lived, slept, cooked, and ate in two rooms, a big and a little one. They lived as we did, cooking over their grates.

Sometimes we all put what we had together and ate in company. When any of us secured at any time some eatable out of the common, if it was enough to go around we invited the others into breakfast, dinner, or tea, as the case might be. It must be understood that from the meal called "tea," the beverage from which the meal is named was nearly always omitted. Sometimes we would all get so hungry that we would put together all the money we could rake and scrape and buy a bit of roast or something else substantial and have a feast.

We all bought coal in common. Mother's, mine, and Delia's portion of the coal was a ton, and we had to keep it in our room—there was no other place to store it. We had a box in our room which held a ton, and the coal was brought up-stairs and dumped into that box. I can see those darkies now, puffing and blowing, as they brought that coal up those many steps. And how we had to scuffle around to pay them! For some jobs we paid in trade—only we had very little to trade off. How that room held all its contents I can't make out. Dan sent me provisions by the quantity when he could get any and get them through to me. He would send a bag of potatoes or peas, and he never sent less than a firkin of butter. The bags of peas, rice, and potatoes were disposed around the room, and around the hearth were arranged our pots, pans, kettles, and cooking utensils generally. When we bought wood, that was put under the beds. In addition to all our useful and ornamental articles we had our three selves and our trunks; such clothing as we possessed had to be hung up for better keeping—and this was a time when it behooved us to cherish clothes tenderly. Then there was our laundrying, which was done in that room by ourselves.

And we had company! Certainly we seemed to have demonstrated the truth of the adage, "Ole Virginny never tire." We had company, and we had company to eat with us, and enjoyed it.

Sometimes our guests were boys from camp who dropped in and took stewed apples or boiled peas, as the case might be. If we were particularly fortunate we offered a cup of tea sweetened with sugar. The soldier who dropped in always got a part—and the best part—of what we had. If things were scant we had smiles to make up for the lack of our larder, and to hide its bareness.

How we were pinched that winter! how often we were hungry! and how anxious and miserable we were! And yet what fun we had! The boys laughed at our crowded room and we laughed with them. After we bought our wood it was Robert E. Lee's adjutant who first observed the ends sticking out from under the bed; he was heartily amused and greatly impressed with the versatility of our resources.

"I confidently expect to come here some day and find a pig tied to the leg of the bed, and a brood or two of poultry utilizing waste space," said Colonel Taylor.[2]

He wasn't so far out of the way, for we *did* get hold of a lean chicken once some way or other, and we tied it to the foot of the bed, and tried to fatten it with boiled peas.

We devised many small ways for making a little money. We knit gloves and socks and sold them, and Miss Beth Sampson had some old pieces of ante-bellum silk that she made into neckties and sold for what she could get. For the rest, when we had no money, we went without those things which it took money to buy. With money a bit of meat now and then, a taste of sorghum, and even the rare luxury of a cup of tea sweetened with sugar, was possible. Without money, we had to depend upon the bags of peas, dried apples, or rice. . . .

One day we agreed to have a feast. The Sampsons were to bring their contributions, Miss Mary and Delia McArthur to put in theirs as usual, and mother and I to contribute our share,

---

[2] Colonel Walter H. Taylor was General Lee's Adjutant-General. After the war, he wrote *Four Years with General Lee.*

of course. Each of us had the privilege of inviting a friend to tea. Our room was chosen as the common supper-room because it had fewer things in it and was less crowded than the Sampsons'. The Sampsons, in addition to their coal-box, wood-pile, bags and barrels of provisions, had one more bed than we had, and also a piano. We had our tea-party and, guests and all, we had a merry time.

I never remember having more fun in my life than at the Arlington, where sometimes we were hungry, and while the country, up to our doors, bristled with bayonets, and the air we breathed shook with the thunder of guns.

For hungry and shabby as we were, crowded into our one room with bags of rice and peas, firkins of butter, a ton of coal, a small wood-pile, cooking utensils, and all of our personal property, we were not in despair. Our faith in Lee and his ragged, freezing, starving army amounted to a superstition. We cooked our rice and peas and dried apples, and hoped and prayed. By this time our bags took up little room. We had had a bag of potatoes, but it was nearly empty. There were only a few handfuls of dried apples left—and I must say that even in the face of starvation I was glad of that!—and there was a very small quantity of rice in our larder. We had more peas than anything else. . . .

There were hunger and nakedness and death and pestilence and fire and sword everywhere, and we, fugitives from shot and shell, knew it well, but, somehow, we laughed and sang and played on the piano—and never believed in actual defeat and subjugation. . . .

5. MARY CUSTIS LEE

"I Must Thank You Both"

On February 22, General Lee received a bag of socks from his wife, and on that same day he wrote from Camp Petersburg, "You will have to send down your offerings as soon as

you can, and bring your work to a close, for I think General
Grant will move against us soon . . . no man can tell what
may be the result. . . . "

The general's ominous warning caused Mrs. Lee no great
alarm. She went about her usual duties.

The first letter that follows was sent to the small daughter
of Mrs. Nottingham, a refugee from Northampton County,
who had carried fresh eggs, pickles and popcorn to General
Lee at Petersburg. She also helped weave cloth for her
brothers' clothes.

The second letter is to Colonel Francis Smith, superin-
tendent of the Virginia Military Institute, which had been
moved to Camp Lee at Richmond after Hunter burned the
buildings at Lexington. The two cadets who were invited to
visit the Lees were family friends.

Richmond, March, 1865.

My dear little friend:

General Lee gives me such a fine account of your industry
that I am tempted to send you this little basket of working ma-
terials, which I hope you will find useful in these hard times.

I have put in it a handkerchief for your Mamma, which she
must use for my sake & I must thank you both for your kind
attention to my husband.

Yrs most truly,
M. C. LEE

Richmond, March 30th, 1865

My dear Sir:

I write to beg the favour of you to allow my two young friends
Peyton Skipwith & John Cocke of Bremo, if still with you, to
visit us sometimes on Sunday, being the only day when we dine
sufficiently early for them to return in time to the Institute. I
shall take care that they attend church & shall be most happy if
you will grant them permission to visit us.

I will also take this occasion to thank you for your care of

our silver & papers & to inquire if you think they can remain
perfectly safe where they are until the close of the war, as I
should like to preserve the only relicks left us of our once happy
home. It would give me great pleasure if you could call & see me
when you come to town.

Yrs most truly & respectfully

M. C. LEE

6. MRS. WILLIAM A. SIMMONS

"The One Topic of Conversation Is Eating"

Many a woman followed her husband's regiment throughout the war. One was Mrs. Simmons, of Georgia, who left for
posterity a brief but unforgettable diary account of the last
days of the Confederate capital. At this time, her husband
was with General Longstreet's corps in the trenches below
Richmond.

Richmond, Va.

Friday, March 23, '65

Close times in this beleaguered city! Every day food supplies
are rising in price and becoming more scare, and our Confederate money is getting so reduced in value that it is a common
remark when one goes out to buy, "you can carry your money in
your market basket, and bring home your provisions in your
purse."

Indeed the stalls of the great market-house, so famous for
their abundant supplies of fish, flesh and fowl, are a sight now,
so empty are they. For many days nothing but "greens" is to be
seen there, and even our "bacon and greens" lacks the *bacon*. A
piece of fat meat is a luxury nowadays, corn meal sells at a
hundred dollars a peck and a barrel of flour this morning
brought $1,000.

The boarding-houses have suspended, the inmates keeping their rooms, but providing their own rations. The city is crowded with refugees. . . .

The one topic of conversation everywhere and on all occasions is "eating," even the ministers in the pulpit unconsciously preach of it. . . .

Sunday, March 25

A note from Gen. Lee was read in all the churches this morning, requesting the pastors to go out into the country around, and drum up provisions for the soldiers in the field. The army has not ten days rations at command and many of the men are in sad lack of clothing.

The rich Valley of Virginia, the beautiful Shenandoah, the granary of our army, is cut off from us. Alas for the day when the hero of the valley was taken from us—the beloved Stonewall Jackson, the idol of his soldiers, whose banner led them on to victory in every encounter! What will the morrow bring forth?

7. AGNES

"What Does All This Mean?"

Richmond was full of rumours of extravagant fortune—of peace negotiations and European recognition. "The report was credited for the space of three or four days by the most intelligent persons in the city," wrote journalist Edward A. Pollard, "that a messenger from France had arrived on the coast of North Carolina, and was making his way overland to Richmond, with the news of the recognition of the Southern Confederacy by the Emperor Napoleon. . . . It was difficult indeed to abandon altogether the idea that the happy accident of a victory somewhere might, after all, put a new aspect on affairs."

But our familiar friend "Agnes" is beginning to question

some unusual occurrences in the city. As usual, she keeps Mrs. Pryor posted. General Pryor, recently paroled by order of President Lincoln, was with his wife in Petersburg.

Richmond, March 28, 1865

I do hate to write you bad news just now when you should be so happy with our dear General, but, really and truly, I don't at all like the look of things here. Sheridan is at Ashland. And General Sherman has finished up North Carolina, and is in Virginia.

I made an excursion through some of the Main Street stores last week—and recognized some of Mrs. Davis's things. I learned that she had placed a great many articles at the dry-goods stores for sale and had sold her horses. And now comes the surprising news, that she has left the city with her family. What does all this mean? Some of the girls here have taken their jewelry to the Treasury Department, giving it to help redeem the currency. I am sure they are welcome to all mine!

8. VARINA HOWELL DAVIS

"Pray That As My Day Is, So May My Strength Be"

Mrs. Davis, her children, and her sister Margaret Howell, left Richmond on the evening of March 29 in a special car for Charlotte, North Carolina. They were under the charge of Burton N. Harrison, President Davis' secretary. Also with the party were Helen and Eliza Trenholm, daughters of the Secretary of the Treasury, on their way to South Carolina, under the escort of Midshipman James M. Morgan.

The following letter, evidently misdated by accident, was written by Mrs. Davis to her friend General John S. Preston, of Columbia, South Carolina, head of the Confederate conscript department in Richmond. The original letter is in the Confederate Museum at Richmond and bears the inscription, "Signed with a nom de plume in case of capture on the sea."

Richmond, April 1st [for March 29]

My dear [General Preston]—

My heart is sadder today than I can readily communicate to you at this distance. Affairs seem darker, the spirit of the people daily more depressed, women tremblingly come to me and beg me to say what I can to comfort them. All I can say is that my husband will never cry for quarter and all we can hope for is that the spirit of the people may enable him to defend the women and children of our unhappy land. The name of our enemies is legion and our poor people are fainting by the wayside. The physical man must be fed, and clothed, or the spiritual man, be he ever so elevated, must sink with the decay of the physique.

General Lee looks dispirited and wretched, says Congress does nothing to reinforce us, and unless reinforced it is impossible for us to achieve a victory over such overwhelming numbers, and fears he will be forced to abandon Richmond. Congress has fled, some announcing that they will never return to Richmond, others that the whole cause is gone.[3] Legislated for by such men in such temper, I am prepared to dread the latter evil. The only active measure of which I can hear, is the increase of their pay to half as much more than it was. Mr. Davis looks worn and exhausted, prays without ceasing and hopes for better than I can forsee arguing from the signs of the times.

Now, I am going to announce myself a great heretic but you know I am revolutionary, therefore, will excuse the expression of a habitude of free thought to me so dear and intimate. Our Constitution is framed for peace and nothing but a pure intelligence could be governed by it in times when the selfishness of man is so severely tested, nay even his heartstrings converted into an instrument upon which his physical nature may play. A strict construction of our Constitution is incompatible with the successful prosecution of a war. The cohesive power of a strong

---

[3] The Confederate Congress adjourned on March 18.

government is needed when the disintegrating tendency of misery is at work. The consent of the masses governed is only accorded to the government which confers at that time large blessings—faith is never displayed by the masses in things hoped for if they chance to be those everyday blessings which we call necessaries. I am disheartened with popular sovereignty, still more with State's sovereignty and fear both are fallacies, but nevertheless they are the only guarantees for Republican liberty. . . .

The supreme dread which has tortured me for many months —the separation from my husband—is now upon me. Mr. Davis says I must go out of Richmond in order that his mind may be free in the event of a siege. So I have turned my thoughts to financiering—that is a pretty word for a disgusting business as poor people have to do it. It means, with me, selling the pretty little pieces of china, cabinet glasses, sandalwood boxes, card-racks, little pictures etc. of which each one is a dear memorial of former happiness. My exquisite silver too must go and last and best all of my wardrobe not immediately necessary to me. This latter sacrifice I have not mentioned to my husband for he is possessed with the idea of selling his pretty fire-arms and his clothing and would do it if he thought I meant to sell mine. We have lived very poorly but I find that we cannot even exist thus without a heavy load of debt unless we make this sale. We have never as yet suffered the humiliation of any debt which we were not able to pay. Do let me vaunt myself a little to you, my friend, that I have so honest a man as my portion in life. He lives in the sight of God, and I fear thinks too little of man's verdict.

I am in the agonies of packing, and disposing of my earthly treasures here—so I have not much time to write even to you. . . .

It is a sore trial to leave husband, home and friends for an unknown quantity like the Confederacy; however, I shall have many lovely women to remember, sweet matronly examples of all the Christian virtues. They have sorrowed with me in my affliction and I have acquired a property in them which no enemy can confiscate. May God grant us a peaceful return to the dear home, but my heart misgives me.

I met with quite a reverse the other day. I had purchased our flour for the year through the kindness of a friend who is a mill-owner and unfortunately mentioned to Mr. Davis that I hoped to take it with me in lieu of gold which I had not. He told me decidedly it must be left in Richmond to feed the army as well from the necessity of the case as for an example to others. So I start *sans* everything for Charlotte, N.C., for the present. I have packed all my own linen, etc., to serve my needs there in place of buying new as I hope to go to housekeeping and the two armies will surely be able to cover as far north as Charlotte and I do not wish to go further from my husband than I can avoid. Excuse this scrawl; I am so depressed and so uncertain of our future that I cannot successfully arrange my thoughts. You will acknowledge that a young lady and four babies are not a very helpful family with whom to start out on the world. Pray that as my day is, so may my strength be, and have me in your heart.

9. MRS. WILLIAM A. SIMMONS
"Richmond Is To Be Evacuated"

> At 10:40 a.m., Sunday morning, April 2, Secretary of War Breckinridge received from General Lee, at Petersburg, a wire urging the evacuation of Richmond that night. Before noon, the evacuation of the city was a certainty.
> Mrs. William Simmons, who had followed her husband and his regiment for four years, faithfully followed him to Appomattox. She was near by when he stacked arms with General Lee. Then they set out on the long journey home to Atlanta.

Saturday, April 1st

My husband has just come thro' the lines from the trenches below Richmond, where Longstreet's Corps, the last force left on this side of the James, is encamped. He says orders have come for marching, in what direction we can only guess. The air is full of strange rumors, events are thickening around us. It is plain Gen. Lee cannot hold out much longer. With a force smaller than is reported and almost destitute it is impossible to hold our long lines, stretching below Petersburg, along which for a mile or two, at some places, there is not a sentinel on guard.

Sunday, April 2nd

When my husband attempted, early this morning, to rejoin his regiment, they had broken up camp and were marching away, the last force on the north side of the James gone. What does it mean?

Afternoon. This has been an eventful morning. While we were at church, in the midst of the service, a messenger came for Pres. Davis, who immediately left the house. An ominous fear fell upon all hearts and seemed to spread itself to all the church. Services were hastened to a close and as we walked home, the very air seemed heavy with impending ill.

Groups were gathered at street corners with bated breath discussing the situation. From official sources, we learned that a telegram from Gen. Lee had announced to Mr. Davis that his lines were broken, he could defend the city but a few days longer. Slowly between alternations of hope and fear, the conviction is settling down upon the stricken people that the long four years struggle is nearing its end,—Richmond is to be evacuated! The army is moving toward Amelia Court House and my husband must go with it. I cannot be cut off from him and left in the enemy's lines. His good horse John is here and we have a light wagon which he provided months ago for such an emergency. Yes, I will go.

Later. It is settled that we leave to-night.

10. SALLIE ANN BROCK PUTNAM
"The Direful Tidings"

As early as January, strange terms were heard in the city of Richmond. The words "submission," "surrender," "subjugation," "reconstruction" were intermingled with the word "evacuation."

Mrs. Putnam relied on the Army of Northern Virginia to save the Confederacy. As late as April 1, "the whole truth had not reached us," she wrote. "Destruction hovered over our fair city, yet happily we knew it not, and dreamed on in blissful unconsciousness of impending danger."

The morning of the 2d of April dawned brightly over the capital of the Southern Confederacy. A soft haze rested over the city, but above that the sun shone with the warm pleasant radiance of early spring. The sky was cloudless. No sound disturbed the stillness of the Sabbath morn, save the subdued murmur of the river, and the cheerful music of the church bells. The long familiar tumult of war broke not upon the sacred calmness of the day. Around the War Department, and the Post Office, news gatherers were assembled for the latest tidings, but nothing was bruited that deterred the masses from seeking their accustomed places in the temples of the living God. At St. Paul's church the usual congregation was in attendance. President Davis occupied his pew.

It was again the regular monthly return for the celebration of the sacrament of the Lord's Supper. The services were progressing as usual when a messenger was observed to make his way up the aisle, and to place in the hands of the President a sealed package. Mr. Davis arose, and was noticed to walk rather unsteadily out of the church. An uneasy whisper ran through the congregation, and intuitively they seemed possessed of the dreadful secret of the sealed dispatch—the unhappy condition of Gen.

Lee's army and the necessity for evacuating Richmond. The dispatch stated that this was inevitable unless his lines could be re-formed before eight o'clock that evening.

At the Second Presbyterian Church, Dr. Hoge, who had received information of the dire calamity impending over us, told his congregation of our situation, and the probability that never again would they meet there for worship, and in the thrilling eloquence of which he is so truly the master, bade them farewell.

The direful tidings spread with the swiftness of electricity. From lip to lip, from men, women, children and servants, the news was bandied, but many received it at first, as only a "Sunday sensation rumor." Friend looked into the face of friend to meet only an expression of incredulity; but later in the day, as the truth, stark and appalling, confronted us, the answering look was that of stony, calm despair. Late in the afternoon the signs of evacuation became obvious to even the most incredulous. Wagons were driven furiously through the streets, to the different departments, where they received as freight the archives of the government, and carried them to the Danville Depot, to be there conveyed away by railroad.

Thousands of the citizens determined to evacuate the city with the government. Vehicles commanded any price in any currency possessed by the individual desiring to escape from the doomed capital. The streets were filled with excited crowds hurrying to the different avenues for transportation, intermingled with porters carrying huge loads, and wagons piled up with incongruous heaps of baggage, of all sorts and descriptions. The banks were all open, and depositors were busily and anxiously collecting their specie deposits, and directors were as busily engaged in getting off their bullion. Millions of dollars of paper money, both State and Confederate, were carried to the Capitol Square and buried.

Night came on, but with it no sleep for human eyes in Richmond. Confusion worse confounded reigned, and grim terror spread in wild contagion. . . .

Into every house terror penetrated. Ladies were busily engaged in collecting and secreting all the valuables possessed by them, together with cherished correspondence, yet they found time and presence of mind to prepare a few comforts for friends forced to depart with the army or the government. Few tears were shed; there was no time for weakness or sentiment. The grief was too deep, the agony too terrible to find vent through the ordinary channels of distress. Fathers, husbands, brothers and friends clasped their loved ones to their bosoms in convulsive and agonized embraces, and bade an adieu, oh, how heart-rending!

At eleven o'clock on that night, Colonel ———, on General ———'s staff, came into the city and was married. In a few moments he left his bride, in the terrible uncertainty of ever again meeting.

At midnight the train on the Danville Railroad bore off the officers of the Government, and at the same hour many persons made their escape on the canal packets, and fled in the direction of Lynchburg.

11. ANNA HELEN HOLMES TRENHOLM

"I Was the Only Lady"

President Davis and his cabinet, with the exception of John C. Breckinridge, left Richmond on the night of April 2. Mrs. George Trenholm accompanied her husband, the head of a Charleston and Liverpool shipping firm which controlled more than fifty blockade-runners. He owned several plantations, a house in Charleston and a beautiful estate, "De Greffin," in Columbia, South Carolina.

For the sake of her children Mrs. Trenholm kept a brief

diary record of her husband's last days as Secretary of the Treasury. He resigned on April 27. He was arrested on June 14 and imprisoned at Fort Pulaski.

Sunday 2d, April 1865. We received notice to have everything ready to leave Richmond, that evening. We left the Depot at eleven o'clock, in an especial Car. I was the only Lady, there were about thirty Gentlemen, including the President and Suite.

Monday, 3d, April. Arrived in Danville at five o'clock, the next day, where there was an immense crowd to welcome the President. We were hospitably intertained at Mr. Sutherlin's.[4] Mr. Trenholm was quite sick from the effects of Morphine, as well as the pain in his head. . . .

---

[4] Major W. T. Sutherlin.

VII

THE ENEMY COME

April 2—May 1865

Before midnight of April 2, 1865, the city of Richmond was evacuated. At 8:15 the next morning, General Godfrey Weitzel and his Army of the James marched in. At 10:00, Secretary of War Stanton wired President Lincoln, "I congratulate you and the nation on the glorious news in your telegram just received. . . . "

By order of Stanton, a salute of a hundred guns, in honor of the capture of Richmond, was fired at midday on April 4 at each military post and arsenal in the United States. The New York *Herald* declared that the taking of Richmond was "one of the grandest triumphs that had crowned human efforts for centuries."

Said Mrs. Robert E. Lee, "They have achieved by starvation what they never could win by their valor; nor have they taken *a single town* in the South, except Vicksburg, that we have not evacuated. . . . "

On April 6, John B. Jones, the war-clerk diarist, wrote, "We are at their mercy, and prepared for our fate. I except some of our ladies, who are hysterical and want to set out on foot 'for the Confederacy.' "

Then, in succession, came Appomattox and the surrender of the Army of Northern Virginia on April 9; the assassination of President Lincoln at Ford's Theatre in Washington on April 14; the surrender of Joseph E. Johnston and the Army of the Tennessee near Durham, North Carolina, on the eighteenth; and the capture of President Davis by Federal cavalry at Irwinville, Georgia, on May 10.

1. FANNIE WALKER MILLER

"To My Horror"

> Fannie was eighteen years old when she received an ap
> pointment as "copying clerk" in the Bureau of War. She was
> the only woman employed in the department at that time,
> "and as copyist most of the correspondence fell to [her] lot."
> On April 1, she had "made merry over various April-fool
> jokes," and the merriment had lasted until "'late in the
> night."
> For several weeks in the Bureau, papers had been assorted
> and packed in long boxes, evidently for removal to some
> unknown place. This had not alarmed Fannie, who never
> dreamed that "a move of Grant was anticipated or that Rich
> mond would fall."

I was spending the day with my mother and sister, who were
matrons at Howard Grove Hospital, consequently was not in my
accustomed seat at dear old St. Paul; but others returned and
told us what had transpired, and as soon as I could gather my
things I proceeded to my home in the city.

As I reached the corner of Main and Third Streets, I met my
chief, Capt. R. G. H. Kean, with as much baggage as he could
conveniently carry. In reply to my question whether we should
follow, his reply was, "I cannot advise a lady to follow a fugitive
government," and with tears in his eyes he bade me farewell.

On reaching my home I found my aunt, an employee of the
Treasury Department, packing what things she could conveniently carry, preparing to follow with others of her department
the next morning. There was nothing left for me but to wait the
turn of affairs.

Taking my seat at the window, I fell to watching the excited
crowds passing, many of the men with such baggage as they could
carry, making their way toward the towpath, that being considered the safest avenue of escape. O, the horrors of that night! the

rolling of vehicles, excited cries of the men, women, and children as they passed loaded with such goods as they could snatch from the burning factories and stores that were being looted by the frenzied crowds; for to such straits had many been brought that the looting was not confined to the "poor white" or rabble. Delicately reared ladies were seen with sheets and shawls filled with goods, provisions, etc., even to boxes of tobacco. I remember one lady showing us as many as one dozen boxes of tobacco, a foot or more square, she had carried from some factory on Franklin, and she a delicate woman. She said the prospect of starvation and suffering of her almost blind husband and children stared her in the face and nerved her to the work.

No one dared to be down or think of sleeping, and as soon as it was light I started out with my aunt to communicate with the party with whom she was going. As I was about to descend the front steps the explosion caused by blowing up the magazine on a line to the rear of us occurred, and before I knew it I found myself flat. Glass was falling all around; but my aunt, nothing daunted, called to me to follow her, and we made our way to the Valentine House. While waiting for her conference to end, I looked down the street, and to my horror beheld a Negro cavalryman yelling: "Richmond at last!"

Seized with terror, I saw our chances for escape were hopeless, and together we started back home. On getting to my old headquarters, Mechanics Institute, I found the torch had been applied; but the mob were carrying out all available furniture, carpets, etc. As we neared home the smoke of the factories, etc., on Cary Street was almost blinding, to say nothing of the heat. All day and night we sat beside what of our belongings we could tie up in sheets ready to leave the building. Parties were kept on the roof with buckets of water and wet blankets, and we were saved. A guard was procured, and with some watching by turns while others slept we gradually adapted ourselves to the forlorn situation.

2. ELIZABETH L. VAN LEW

"Oh, Army of My Country!"

When the Federal army entered Richmond, General Grant sent his aide-de-camp, Colonel Parke, to protect the property of Elizabeth Van Lew. Later, Grant himself, like many other northern officials, called on the Van Lews. On one occasion Elizabeth gave a reception for Chief Justice Salmon P. Chase and his celebrated daughter Kate. Richmond was aghast. What they had only suspected was true, a Yankee spy had operated before their very eyes! It was not until after her death that a full story of her activities for the Federal government was revealed.

Grant appointed her Postmistress of Richmond for the full term of his presidential administration. Miss Van Lew died on September 25, 1900, and was buried in Shockhoe Hill Cemetery in Richmond. Massachusetts sent a memorial stone to be erected over her grave. An inscription reads, in part, "She risked everything that is dear to man—friends, fortune, comfort, health, life itself, all for the one absorbing desire of her heart—that slavery might be abolished and the Union preserved."

Sunday April 2, 1865. Toward the close of the day the young soldiers could be seen on horseback or on foot holding hurried farewells to their friends. Some said they must go, though they wished to stay and some said they would remain; but bodies of troops here and there without the town were hurried away.

I went to the front door of a neighbor—on the steps a woman was sitting in speechless acquiescence. We spoke of the news. She knew only the evacuation of the city. "The war will end now," I said. "The young men's lives will be saved."

"I have a son in the army about Petersburg," she replied.

I sympathized with her and assured her she might hope for his life, that there would be an end of the terrible words, "the last man must die," which were often spoken and acted upon.

She replied, "It would be better, anything would be better, than to fall under the U.S. Government." It was useless to talk with her.

Night came on. We could hear the hurried leaving. Word was sent us that our house was to be burned—some Confederate soldiers had said so. . . .

The bursting shells rent the air and lighted the windows. *Midnight.* The door bell rang—two fugitives came in from Castle Thunder. How alarmed now were the officials there. The wicked Wiley, deadly pale and trembling in every limb, unlocked by order the cell doors to make sure of the inmates—these prisoners were secured and carried through the streets to be hurried south. Some availing themselves of the confusion in the city, broke away from their keepers and at intervals found their way to our dwelling to be gladly welcomed. But with the terror yet upon us we were afraid to have a light in the room they were in. Some men I knew among the prisoners escaped from their guards and though they lived in Richmond wandered off about fifteen miles into the country so afraid were they of arrest. One feeble man was made to walk fifty miles before escaping but as the distance from Richmond increased the guards released their vigilance thinking more of self-preservation. One woman, confined as a spy, was obliged to walk thirty-two miles, when she succeeded in eluding them, and in due time made her appearance at our house.

The constant explosion of shells, the blowing up of the gunboats, and of the powder magazine, seemed to jar, to shake the earth, and lend a mighty language to the scene. All nature trembled at the work of arbitrary powers, the consummation of the wrongs of years; the burning bridges, the roaring flames added a wild grandeur to the scene.

Amid all this turmoil, quietly, noiselessly, the Federal army entered the city. There were wild bursts of welcome from the Negroes and many whites as they poured in. In an incredibly

short space of time by magic every part of our city was under the
most kind and respectful of guards. What a moment!

No wonder the walls of our house were swaying; the heart of
our city a flaming altar, as His mighty work was done. Oh! army
of my country, how glorious was your welcome!

3. NATHALIE

"The Victorious Army"

> On the morning of April 3, General Grant wired Major
> General Weitzel:
>
> "I do not doubt but you will march into Richmond unop-
> posed. Take possession of the city, establish guards, and pre-
> serve order until I get there. Permit no man to leave town after
> you get possession. The army here will endeavor to cut off the
> retreat of the enemy."
>
> At 11 A.M., General Weitzel telegraphed Secretary of War
> Stanton in Washington,
>
> "We took Richmond at 8:15 this morning. I captured many
> guns. The enemy left in great haste. The city is on fire in two
> places. Am making every effort to put it out. The people re-
> ceived us with enthusiastic expressions of joy."
>
> Nathalie, a lady of Richmond who prefers to remain forever
> unidentified, witnessed the entrance of the victorious army.

Stretching from the Exchange Hotel to the slopes of Church
Hill, down the hill, through the valley, up the ascent to the hotel,
was the array, with its unbroken line of blue, fringed with bright
bayonets. Strains of martial music, flushed countenances, waving
swords, betokened the victorious army. As the line turned at the
Exchange Hotel into the upper street, the movement was the
signal for a wild burst of cheers from each regiment. Shouts from
a few Negroes were the only responses. Through throngs of
sullen spectators; along the line of fire; in the midst of the

horrors of a conflagration, increased by the explosion of shells
left by the retreating army; through curtains of smoke; through
the vast aerial auditorium convulsed with the commotion of
frightful sounds, moved the garish procession of the grand army,
with brave music, and bright banners and wild cheers. A regiment of Negro cavalry swept by the hotel. As they turned the
street corner they drew their sabres with savage shouts, and the
blood mounted even in my woman's heart with quick throbs of
defiance.

4. NELLIE GREY

"We Covered Our Faces and Cried"

> Shortly after the events described by Mrs. Dan Grey in the
> following account, she received news of her husband. He had
> refused to surrender with General Rooney Lee, and was try-
> ing to make his way to Johnston's army. Many weeks later,
> "walking barefoot nearly all the way," he joined her in Rich-
> mond.
> "Those terrible, beloved days. They are the very fiber of
> us," wrote in 1903 the lady we know as Nellie Grey. "We are
> prosperous now, our heads are nearly white; little grandchil-
> dren cluster about us and listen with interest to grandpa's
> and grandmamma's tales of the days when they fought and
> bled and died together. They can't understand how such nice
> people as the Yankees and ourselves ever could have fought
> each other."

Exactly at eight o'clock the Confederate flag that fluttered
above the Capitol came down and the Stars and Stripes were run
up. We knew what that meant! The song "On to Richmond!"
was ended—Richmond was in the hands of the Federals. We
covered our faces and cried aloud. All through the house was the
sound of sobbing. It was as the house of mourning, the house of
death.

Soon the streets were full of Federal troops, marching quietly along. The beautiful sunlight flashed back everywhere from Yankee bayonets. I saw Negroes run out into the street and falling on their knees before the invaders hail them as their deliverers, embracing the knees of the horses, and almost preventing the troops from moving forward.

The saddest moment of my life was when I saw that Southern Cross dragged down and the Stars and Stripes run up above the Capitol. . . . As I tell this my heart turns sick with the supreme anguish of the moment when I saw it torn down from the height where valor had kept it waving for so long and at such cost.

Was it for this, I thought, that Jackson had fallen? for this that my brave, laughing Stuart was dead—dead and lying in his grave in Hollywood under the very shadow of that flag floating from the Capitol, in hearing of these bands playing triumphant airs as they marched through the streets of Richmond, in hearing of those shouts of victory? O my chevalier! I had to thank God that the kindly sod hid you from all those sights and sounds so bitter to me then. I looked toward Hollywood with streaming eyes and thanked God for your sake. Was it to this end we had fought and starved and gone naked and cold? to this end that the wives and children of many a dear and gallant friend were husbandless and fatherless? to this end that our homes were in ruins, our State devastated? to this end that Lee and his footsore veterans were seeking the covert of the mountains?

The Arlington is one-half of a double house, a veranda without division serving for both halves. Just before noon up rode a regiment of Yankees and quartered themselves next door. We could hear them moving about and talking, and rattling their sabers. But I must add that they were very quiet and orderly. There was no unnecessary noise. They all went out again, on duty, I suppose, leaving their baggage and servants behind them. They did not molest or disturb us in any way. After a while we heard a rap on the door, and on opening it three men entered.

They were fully armed, and had come, as they said, to search the house for rebels. The one who undertook to search our rooms came quite in and closed the door while his companions went below. Anxious to get rid of him quickly I helped him in his search.

Going to the bed I threw the mattress over so he could see that no one was concealed beneath.

"There's nothing for you to find," I informed him, as I pulled a bureau drawer open for his inspection.

I led the way into the next room to be searched, he following, asseverating in tipsy whispers, "Good Secesh as you is, sis," every few minutes.

We found little Ruf Pagett cleaning his gun.

"Better hide that, sonny," said our friend, glancing around. "That other fellow out there, *he'll* take it from you. But I won't take it from you. I won't take nothin'. I'm good Secesh as you is, bud. Hide your gun, bud."

Down-stairs our friends were having a harder time. The men who went through their rooms searched everywhere, and tumbled their things around outrageously. I could hear Mrs. Sampson quarreling. They went away, but returned to search again. She said she wouldn't stand it—she would report them. She saw General Weitzel and made her complaint, and he told her that the men were stragglers and had no authority for what they had done. If they could be found they would be punished. Before this time the fire had been brought under control. Houses not a square from us had been in flames. What saved us was an open space between us and the nearest house which had been on fire, and wet blankets. Mrs. Fry's son had had wet blankets spread over our roof for protection, and we had also kept wet blankets hung in our windows. At one time, however, cinders and smoke had blown into my room till the air was stifling and the danger great.

A niece of my husband's, a beautiful girl of eighteen, who had been ill with typhoid fever, had to be carried out of a burning house that night and laid on a cot in the street. She died in the street and I heard of other sick persons who died from the terror and exposure of that time.

As night came on many people were wandering about without shelter, amid blackened ruins. In the Square numbers were huddled for the night under improvised shelter or without any protection at all. But profound quiet reigned—the quiet of desolation as well as of order. The city had been put under martial law as soon as the Federals took possession; order and quiet had been quickly established and were well preserved. . . .

5. AGNES

"The Grewsome Story"

On the same day that Agnes reported to Mrs. Pryor in Petersburg, Assistant Secretary of War C. A. Dana informed his chief, Edwin M. Stanton, about the state of affairs in Richmond:

"General Weitzel finds much suffering and poverty among the population. The rich as well as the poor are destitute of food. . . . It is not true that Jeff. Davis sold his furniture before leaving. It is all in his house, where I am now writing. . . . Theater opens here tonight. Weitzel describes the reception of the President yesterday as enthusiastic in the extreme."

Unknown to Agnes, General Pryor had been arrested again, betrayed by one of the Negroes when the Federals came into Petersburg.

Richmond, April 5, 1865

My dear:—I am not at all sure you will ever receive this letter, but I shall risk it. First, I join you in humble thanks to God for the great mercy accorded both of us. Your General lives. My

Colonel lives. What words can express our gratitude? What is the loss of home and goods compared with the loss of our own flesh and blood? Alas! Alas! for those who have lost all!

I am sure you will have heard the grewsome story of Richmond's evacuation. I was at St. Paul's Sunday, April 1, when a note was handed to President Davis. He rose instantly, and walked down the aisle—his face set, so we could read nothing. Dr. Minnegerode gave notice that General Ewell desired the forces to assemble at 3 P.M., and also that there would be no further service that day. I had seen no one speak to the doctor, and I wonder at the acuteness of his perception of the state of affairs.

As soon as I reached the hotel I wrote a note to the proprietor, asking for news. He answered that grave tidings had come from Petersburg, and for himself he was by no means sure we could hold Richmond. He requested me to keep quiet and not encourage a tendency to excitement or panic. At first I thought I would read my services in the quiet of my little sky parlor at the Spotswood, but I was literally in a fever of anxiety. I descended to the parlor. Nobody was there except two or three children. Later in the afternoon I walked out and met Mr. James Lyons.[1] He said there was no use in further evading the truth. The lines were broken at Petersburg and that town and Richmond would be surrendered late at night—he was going out himself with the mayor[2] and Judge Meredith with a flag of truce and surrender the city. Trains were already fired to carry the archives and bank officials. The President and his Cabinet would probably leave at the same time.

"And you, Judge?"

"I shall stand my ground. I have a sick family, and we must take our chances together."

----

[1] Judge James Lyons of Richmond. His country home in the suburbs, "Laburnum," where he and "his handsome wife dispensed a large and graceful hospitality," was burned by his Negroes in March 1864.

[2] Joseph Mayo.

"Then seriously—really and truly—Richmond is to be given up, after all, to the enemy?"

"Nothing less! And we are going to have a rough time, I imagine."

I could not be satisfied until I had seen Judge Campbell, upon whom we so much relied for good, calm sense. I found him with his hands full of papers, which he waved deprecatingly as I entered.

"Just a minute, Judge! I am alone at the Spotswood and—"

"Stay here, my dear lady! You will be perfectly safe. I advise all families to remain in their own houses. Keep quiet. I am glad to know the Colonel is safe. He may be with you soon now."

With this advice I returned and mightily reassured and comforted the proprietor of the Spotswood. He immediately caused notice to be issued to his guests. I resolved to convey my news to the families I knew best. The Pegrams[3] were in such deep affliction there was no room there for anxious fears about such matters as the evacuation of cities, but I could see my dear Mrs. Paul, and Mrs. Maben, and say a comforting word at the Allan home, closed to all the world since poor John fell at Gettysburg. Mrs. Davis was gone and out of harm's way. The Lees were sacred from intrusion. Four members of that household—the General, "Rooney," Custis, and Robert—were all at the post of danger.

Late in the afternoon three hundred or more prisoners were marched down the street; the Negroes began to stand about, quietly observant but courteous, making no demonstration whatever. The day, you remember, was one of those glorious days we have in April, and millions on millions of stars watched at night, looking down on the watchers below. I expected to sit by my window all night as you always do in a troubled time, but sleep overtook me. I had slept, but not undressed, when a loud explo-

---

[3] Twenty-three-year-old Colonel William Pegram had been killed on April 1, 1865, at Five Forks; his brother, John Pegram, had fallen on February 6.

sion shook the house—then another. There were crashing sounds of falling glass from the concussion. I found the sun had risen. All was commotion in the streets, and agitation in the hotel. The city government had dragged hogsheads of liquor from the shops, knocked in the heads, and poured the spirits into the gutters. They ran with brandy, whiskey, and rum, and men, women, and boys rushed out with buckets, pails, pitchers, and in the lower streets, hats and boots, to be filled. Before eight o'clock many public buildings were in flames, and a great conflagration was evidently imminent. The flames swept up Main Street, where the stores were quickly burned, and then roared down the side streets almost to Franklin.

The doors of all the government bakeries were thrown open and food was given to all who asked it. Women and children walked in and helped themselves. At ten o'clock the enemy arrived—ten thousand Negro troops, going on and on, cheered by the Negroes on the streets.

So the morning passed—a morning of horror, of terror! Drunken men shouted and reeled through the streets, a black cloud from the burning city hung like a pall over us, a black sea of faces filled the street below, shells burst continuously in the ashes of the burning armory.

About four in the afternoon a salute of thirty-four guns was fired. A company of mounted dragoons advanced up the street, escorting an open carriage drawn by four horses in which sat Mr. Lincoln and a naval officer, followed by an escort of cavalry. They drove straight to Mr. Davis's house, cheered all the way by Negroes, and returned the way they came. I had a good look at Mr. Lincoln. He seemed tired and old—and I must say, with due respect to the President of the United States, I thought him the ugliest man I had ever seen. . . .

The next day I persuaded one of the lads in the hotel to take a walk with me early in the morning, and I passed General Lee's house. A Yankee guard was pacing to and fro before it—at which I felt an impulse of indignation, but presently the door opened, the guard took his seat on the steps and proceeded to investigate the contents of a very neatly furnished tray, which Mrs. Lee in the kindness of her heart had sent out to him.

I am obliged to acknowledge that there is really no hope now of our ultimate success. Everybody says so. My heart is too full for words. General Johnston says we may comfort ourselves by the fact that war may decide a *policy*, but never a *principle*. I imagine our *principle* is all that remains to us of hope or comfort.

Devotedly,

AGNES

6. JENNIE D. HARROLD

"The City Under Martial Law"

> Jennie Harrold, the little girl whom we have met before, never forgot those strange days of April in a topsy-turvy world. She had witnessed the unfurling of the first Confederate flag in the new capital.

I remember when President Davis, Cabinet, the bank treasurer, clerks and valuables left. The train gave an unearthly whistle (it seems I can hear it now) as it left the bridge over James River. The bridge was burned behind them as several others were, which set fire to the town. The shells at the State Arsenal exploded and a piece struck our house at Fourth and Main and knocked out fifty panes of glass at once. My little sister was sick in bed and later lost the use of her limbs from fright.

I remember when the order came from General Lee that Richmond would be evacuated at daylight. We had an early breakfast, drinking coffee without counting the cups, supposing strength would come (notwithstanding it was made of parched wheat with a few grains of the genuine thrown in for decency's sake).

Soon our house took fire and we decided to move uptown to our Uncle's, Mr. Phil Paul Winston's. I had a bag over my shoul-

der containing a new calico dress, costing $25 a yard, a new
alpaca dress and a wheat straw hat. I had this made at a cost of $60
and had narrow purple ribbon trimming at $25 per yard. Under
one arm I had my pet dog, Frank.

We shortly returned to my home and as the city was under
Martial Law, citizens were provided with a guard upon application. We had a boy about sixteen years of age from Brooklyn,
who informed us that his name was Harry Bluff. He told us he
was almost starved and we provided him with the best lunch we
had, but he looked with wide open eyes and said, "Do you think
I would eat a thing you Rebs gave me? Why, you would poison
me." We were equally afraid of his gun. . . .

Like most others, we had only Confederate money. Two faithful servants of our Uncle, Major Tom Doswell, came to my
mother and said, "Miss Thomasia, I expect to have more money
than you have now, in silver and gold, so we wish to give you
each 25 cents to start up life with." As there were several in the
family, it helped out, according to heads. . . .

7. JUDITH BROCKENBROUGH McGUIRE

"Dearer Than Ever, in Its Captivity and Ruin"

> From Richmond, Mrs. McGuire and her husband go to
> "Westwood," in Hanover County, the home of her brother,
> Dr. Brockenbrough.
> The last heartbreaking entry in her journal is dated May
> 4. Two years later, the diary was published anonymously as
> "By a Lady of Virginia." It was dedicated to her grandchil-
> dren, nephews and nieces, and has gone into several editions.
> Mrs. McGuire wrote also a *Life of Lee* for young people.

Tuesday night, [April 18]. I try to dwell as little as possible on
public events. I only feel that we have no country, no government, no future. I cannot, like some others, look with hope on
Johnston's army. He will do what he can; but, ah, what can he
do? Our anxiety now is that our President and other public men

may get off in safety. O God! have mercy upon them and help
them. For ourselves, like the rest of the refugees, we are striving
to get from the city. The stereotyped question when we meet is,
"When and where are you going?" Our country relatives have
been very kind. My brother offers us an asylum in his devastated
home at W[estwood]. While there we must look around for some
other place, in which to build up a home for our declining years.
Property we have none—all gone. Thank God we have our facul-
ties; the girls and myself, at least, have health. . . . The Northern
officials offer free tickets to persons returning to theirs homes—
alas! how few of us have homes! Some are confiscated, others
destroyed. . . .

[*April*] *20th.* The cars on the Central Raliroad will run to-
morrow, for the first time, under Federal rule, and the day after
we will use our passports and free tickets to leave the city—
dearer than ever, in its captivity and ruin. . . .

W. [*April*] *24th.* On Saturday evening my brother's wagon
met us at the depot and brought us to this place, beautiful in
ruins. . . . We all try to be cheerful as we can. The governess
having returned to her home in Norfolk, I shall employ myself
in teaching my bright little niece here and the dear children at
S.H.[4] and feel blessed to have so pleasant a duty. . . .

[*April*] *28th.* . . .We have no mail communication, and can
hear nothing from General Johnston. We go on as usual, but are
almost despairing. Dear M., in her sadness, has put some Confederate money and postage stamps into a Confederate envelope,
sealed it up, and endorsed it, "In memory of our beloved Confederacy." I feel like doing the same, and treasuring up the
buttons, and the stars, and the dear gray coats, faded and worn

---

[4] "Summer Hill," home of the family of her deceased nephew, Captain
Newton.

as they are, with the soiled and tattered banner, which has no
dishonouring blot, the untarnished sword, and other arms,
though defeated, still crowned with glory. But not yet—I cannot
feel that all is over yet.

8. EMMIE SUBLETT

"I Never Dreamed of the Yankees Getting to Richmond"

> Thirteen-year-old Emmie was the daughter of John T.
> Sublett. Some years after the war, she married William Leslie
> Jennings. Emily Anderson, the friend to whom she sends the
> following letter, became Mrs. George A. Haynes.
> "Waverly Place" had been used as a hospital for a small
> number of Confederate soldiers.

Waverly Place, April 29, 1865

My darling Emilie—
    . . . I never dreamed of the Yankees getting to Richmond sure
enough, but the wretches are here. . . .
    The Yanks came in at fifteen minutes before eight A.M. and
first of all placed the *horrible stars and stripes* (which seemed to
me to be so many bloody ashes) over our beloved capitol. O, the
horrible wretches! I can't think of a name horrible enough to
call them. It makes us fifty times more Southern in our feelings
to have them here, though they have behaved very well indeed,
no private property has been touched and no insults have been
offered to any of the citizens. They say they can't get anything to
report the Richmond girls for, to save their lives. They all behave with such perfect dignity and coolness, always go out thickly
veiled and never notice the Yanks in the least. I've nearly broken
my neck holding such a high head, never condescending to look
at one when I meet him. Our paroled prisoners are coming
slowly in; poor fellows! they are all so sad! Gen. Lee is completely

crushed; I never saw anything like it. I do feel so sorry for him.
I saw a little piece of the apple tree under which he surrendered;
they say it was cut down to the roots, every soldier wanting a
piece. . . .

Brother, we hear, is in Charlotte, N.C., but we can't hear anything definitely from him. O God when will we ever meet again!
not on earth I am afraid. Emilie, are we ever to have any more
pleasure? It seems to be a dreary life for one who is just setting
out in life as you and I are.

The Yanks are very lenient to us at present, but they are drawing the ropes tighter and tighter every day. I believe there is
some villainy at the bottom of it all. I am so sorry Lincoln was
killed I don't know what in the world to do, because I believe
the whole South will be punished for it. Johnson will be such
an awful President; he is a perfect old tyrant.

You know Lincoln came to Richmond Tuesday the 4th and
was paraded through the streets in a vehicle very much like an
ambulance, only a little nicer, but *very common indeed,* attended
by a body guard of about one hundred horsemen and dashed
through the streets like the horses were wild. The *"monkey
show"* came right by here, but we wouldn't let them see us looking at them, so we ran in the parlor and peeped at them.

I reckon Johnston has certainly surrendered. Today's paper
says so and they have been firing salutes and marching the soldiers over the streets all day yesterday and today. . . .

P.S. Tell any one any thing you choose in this letter, but it is
for your eyes alone.

9. MARY A. FONTAINE

"A Grief Which Was Terrible"

> Mrs. Fontaine lived with her father, the Reverend J. L.
> Burrows, an eminent Baptist minister of Richmond, whose
> home was near the Capitol Square, the City Hall and other

public buildings. Her husband was a prisoner of war. Since the fall of the city, Dr. Burrows had been "completely broken down" and had lost twenty pounds in weight. "He was always so hopeful that the suddenness of the change prostrated him," she said.

The horrors of the arrival of the enemy are described by Mary Fontaine in a letter to her cousin, Mrs. Marie Burrows Sayre.

Richmond, Va. April 30, 1865

My dear Cousin,

. . . We Richmond people have grown calm somewhat. The young ladies keep themselves quietly at home, doing nothing to expose themselves to insults; and in all cases declining controversy with the U.S. officers, which I heartily approve. The question is closed for the present, and no lady ought to permit a discussion at all, because they have the advantage of success and law, and it is not a fair contest. For my own part, I tread my own path utterly ignoring them. I do not seem to see them, careful only not to expose myself to insult.

I hardly dare venture a description of the first few days of April, but will attempt to give you an idea. Sunday, the 2nd, was one of those unusually lovely days that the Spring sometimes brings, when . . . invalids and convalescents venture out in the sunshine; when the churches are crowded as never before. So it was on this Sunday. I have never seen a calmer or more peaceful Sabbath morning, and alas! never a more confused evening. During service messengers tiptoed into the churches after prominent military and civil officers, and when the congregations were dismissed everybody asked, "What is it?" but no one could tell.

Presently there were rumors that General Lee's line was broken, and the enemy had reached the R.R. & Richmond must fall, etc. etc. We ladies were not contented except in the yard & all were in the streets with troubled faces. Major Williamson came to prepare to leave, then, one by one, the gentlemen hurried up with orders to leave that night. Then Mr. Davis, oh, so

bowed & anxious, came, & when he told us he feared Richmond
must be evacuated by midnight, the truth was forced upon us.
We turned to our rooms to prepare those who were to leave. Mrs.
Williamson gave herself to a grief which was terrible.

All through that long night we worked & wept, & bade farewells, never thinking of sleep; in the distance we heard the shouts
of the soldiers & mob as they ransacked stores; the rumbling of
wagons, & beating of drums, all mixed in a confused medley. Just
before dawn explosions of gunboats & magazines shook the city,
& glass was shattered, & new houses crumbled beneath the shocks.
Involuntarily I closed the shutters, & then everything had become still as death, while immense fires stretched their arms on
high all around me. I shuddered at the dreadful silence. Richmond burning & no alarm. It was terrible. I cannot describe my
feelings as I stood at a window overlooking the city in that dim
dawn. I watched those silent, awful fires, I felt that there was no
effort to stop them, but all like myself were watching them, para-
lyzed & breathless.

After a while the sun rose as you may have seen it, a great, red
ball veiled in a mist. Again the streets were alive with hurrying
men & women, & the cry of "Yankees" reached me. I did not
move—I could not—but watched the blue horseman ride to the
City Hall, enter with his sword knocking the ground at every
step, & throw the great doors open, & take possession of our beautiful city; watched two blue figures on the Capitol, white men.
I saw them unfurl a tiny flag, & then I sank on my knees, & the
bitter, bitter tears came in a torrent. . . .

About eight o'clock, after some thirty Cavalrymen had taken
possession of Richmond, hoisted their flag, etc., the Artillery
came dashing up Broad street, positively the fat horses came
trotting up that heavy hill, dragging the cannon as tho. they
were light carriages, the trappings were gay, & I commenced to
realize the fearful odds against which our gallant little army had

contended. Then the Cavalry thundered at a furious gallop. We haven't been used to that, you know, & it startled us; indeed I imagined that there never was such riding before, unless at Bull Run. Then the Infantry came playing "The Girl I Left Behind Me," that dear old air that we heard our brave men so often play; then the Negro troops playing "Dixie." . . .

Then our Richmond servants were completely crazed, they danced & shouted, men hugged each other, & women kissed, such a scene of confusion you have never seen. Imagine the streets crowded with these wild people, & troops by the thousands, some loaded with plunder from the burning stores, whole rolls of cloth, bags of corn, etc., chairs, one old woman was rolling a great sofa; dozens of bands trying to drown each other it seemed; gorgeously dressed officers galloping furiously about, men shouting & swearing as I never heard men do before; the fire creeping steadily nearer us, until houses next to us caught & we prepared to leave; & above all, inconceivably terrible, the 800,000 shells exploding at the laboratory. I say imagine, but you cannot; no one who was not here will ever fully appreciate the horrors of that day. I have heard persons say it was like their idea of the judgment day; perhaps it may be. So many shells exploding for five hours would be fearful at any time; the heavens were black as with a thunder cloud, great pieces of shells flying about, oh! it was too awful to remember, if it were possible to be erased, but that can not be. By night things quieted down; there were brigade headquarters in the house; so we were protected from stragglers; and the oppressive stillness & darkness (there was no gas) was as fearful as the confusion had been. . . .

We had a number of sudden marriages last Sunday. An order being issued Saturday that after Monday all persons marrying must take the oath before procuring licenses, there was considerable confusion created among certain Confederate officers, who were looking forward to marriage in the Spring. Such walking was done on Saturday to get licences then, & such fixing up of old white dresses. . . .

I have not one cent, & no prospects of any unless I go to work. You all don't understand how poor we are here, not even a friend to borrow from, for all are alike. . . .

P.S. Don't let a Yankee see this.

P.S. Mr. Fontaine is still in prison. . . . I have not seen him for a year.

10. ANITA DWYER WITHERS

"Such Fright, Anxiety and Dread"

> After four years as a "Lady of Richmond," Mrs. John Withers bade farewell to her friends and set out on the long journey home to San Antonio, Texas. Shortly after her arrival, she brought her diary to a close.

[*April 1865*]. . . . My Husband sometimes advised me to go to North Carolina or some other part of the Confederacy, but I refused, believing it best to remain in Richmond, thinking it would be the easiest way I could reach my home.

I never spent *two such* nights in my life as I did the one of the evacuation and the one following, such fright, anxiety and dread I never before experienced. I felt sick for a week afterwards. . . .

I heard from my dear Husband only once after we parted in Richmond. He tells me to go home as soon as practicable. I started three weeks after the evacuation. Mr. G. T. Williams was my escort as far as New York. He was very attentive. We reached the city of N. York the very day that President Lincoln's remains passed through the city, the place seemed gayer and more crowded than ever. . . .

[*May 1865*]. I remained in New Orleans two weeks waiting to see if they could allow me to go by Galveston,—through the kindness of Gen'l Wilcox and Judge Hancock I succeeded in getting permission.

I remained in Houston about ten days waiting for my brother to come for me. . . .

Sunday June 4th. I reached my dear home, my Mother of course was delighted to see me once more after a separation of nearly five years. . . .

June 8. . . . I have not heard one word from my dear Husband, I trust he may soon get here.[5]

June 18th, Sunday. I went to the old church at ten o'clock. We had good rain on our return home. . . .

Poor Gen. Wilcox[6] came to say farewell to me, he is about to start for Mexico with several other officers—they flee from their country on account of President Johnson's proclamation.

11. SALLIE ANN BROCK PUTNAM

"Our President a Captive"

> Prayers for Jefferson Davis, who was making his way from Virginia into North Carolina, South Carolina and Georgia, were forbidden in the churches of occupied Richmond. "I have seen your dispatch to Colonel Hardie about the matter of prayers," wrote President Lincoln on April 12 in a message to General Weitzel. "I do not remember hearing prayers spoken of while I was in Richmond, but I have no doubt you have acted in what appeared to you to be the spirit and temper manifested by me while there."
>
> Before the closed churches were opened again in the city, Lincoln was dead and Jefferson Davis a prisoner.

---

[5] Captain John Withers reached his Texas home on August 14, 1865.

[6] General Cadmus Marcellus Wilcox. He did not go to Mexico, after all.

With heart-sickening anxiety, with forebodings too dreadful to be whispered, we listened for tidings from our beloved, our unhappy and fugitive President. We were painfully aware that his enemies were in pursuit of him. Various rumors were` in circulation. His escape across the Mississippi was reported; and the doors of Mexico were said to have opened to him.

On a bright Sabbath morning, after the middle of May, the voices of newsboys in the familiar cry, "Extra! Extra!" drew us to the doors and windows; and our hearts were chilled, and our complexions paled, as in trembling agony, we heard proclaimed, "The capture of Jeff. Davis!"

Thus was announced the fate of the unfortunate chief representative of our lost cause. What Southern heart cannot recall the sickening, the palsying weakness of that moment? Our chastisement seemed heavier than weak human nature could endure.

Our President a captive, the members of his Council fugitives or prisoners, our cause perished, our country ruined, our land desolated, our armies overpowered! We were left to muse on the mutability of human events, to glance mournfully backward on the Past, and to gaze with steady, cold, dead calmness on the altered Present. We were driven to reflect on the strange and mysterious dealings of the wonder-working hand of God, and wiping the film from the eyes of faith, to steer clear of the wrecking reefs of infidelity. . . .

The occupation of Richmond by our enemies occurred at a peculiarly interesting period in the ecclesiastical division of the year. It was the last week of the Lental season, the week which commemorates the passion of our Saviour.

In the diocese of Virginia, the clause in the prayer for the "President of the United States, and all others in authority," had been altered by order of the Bishop, to correspond to our status under the Confederacy. The Bishop being absent, it could not then be conveniently changed, and owing, as they felt they then owed, political allegiance only to the President of the Confederate States, and with no instruction at that time from their diocesan, to make use of the prayer differently, the Protestant Episcopal ministers of Richmond could not conscientiously use the unamended prayer of the Prayer-book. They were therefore required by the military authorities of the city to close their churches. It was the most rigorous and aggravating feature of our peculiar situation, and was felt to be a direct blow upon the very root of the tree of religious liberty.[7]

The vast armies of our conquerors, on their homeward march, now began to pour through the streets of Richmond. Day after day, as we witnessed the passage of the countless, and as they seemed to us interminable legions of the enemy, against which our comparatively little army had so obstinately, and all but successfully held out for four years, the question that arose in our minds, was not why we were conquered at last, but "how we could have so long resisted the mighty appliances which operated against us." Our pride, our glory in our countrymen was heightened, and we felt indeed, "the South is the land for soldiers," and though our enemies triumphed, it was at a price that was felt by them.

12. MARY CUSTIS LEE

"Despise the Shame"

> News came to Richmond that Jefferson Davis was in chains at Fortress Monroe. "I know of no one so much to be pitied," Mrs. Lee said of the prisoner's wife.

[7] On April 19, 1865, General Godfrey Weitzel wrote to Secretary of War Edwin M. Stanton: "The clergy in Richmond were notified that any prayers for the Rebel Government or officials, or for the success of the rebellion, would be considered as treason, and punished as such. As in the ritual in use in the Episcopal churches here there was a form of prayer for the rebel authorities they were ordered to omit it. No orders were given as to what would be preached or prayed for, but only as to what would not be permitted." (*O.R.I.*, XLVI, 696)

Enclosed with the following letter to Jefferson Davis was a copy of Mrs. Lee's favorite hymn, "Jesus, I my cross have taken, all to leave and follow Thee." The lines of the third verse are:

"Perish earthly fame and treasure;
Come disaster, scorn and pain;
In Thy service pain is pleasure;
With Thy favor loss is gain."

[*Richmond, May 1865*]

My heart has prompted me my dear friend ever since I knew of the failure of our glorious cause to write to you and express my deep sympathy, how much more since I learned your captivity, your separation from your beloved family and incarceration in a solitary dungeon. If you knew how many prayers and tears had been sent to Heaven for you and yours, you could realize that you were not forgotten. We did so long to hear that you could reach in safety some foreign clime where you could enjoy the repose and consideration which seems to be denied you in your own country. Oh why did you delay and fall into the hand of those whose only desire is to humiliate and destroy you. The only consolation I can now offer you besides our deep attachment and remembrance of you, is contained in the words of my favorite hymn which I have transcribed for you. As a Christian I feel confident that you have fortitude "To bear the cross and *despise the shame"* and ever to *pray* for your persecutors. As I know not if this letter will be allowed to reach you I will not say more. You can imagine all we would say and feel, and know that one sentiment animates the hearts of your true friends and among them believe there is no one truer than yours etc.,

MARY C. LEE

If you are allowed to write let me know if you receive this; where your family have gone and if I can do anything for them.

Postlude

THEY FACED THE FUTURE
May 1865—December 1870

> At Clouded Dawn of Peace
> They Faced the Future
> Undismayed by Problems
> and Fearless of Trials
> in Loving Effort to Heal
> Their Country's Wounds
> and with Conviction
> That from the Ashes of Ruin
> Would Come Resurrection
> of Truth
> with Glorious Vindication.
>
> —From the inscription by William E. Gonzales on the
> Confederate Women's Monument, Columbia, S. C.

1. AGNES

"I Shall Not Repine"

Indeed, the lively Agnes had herself "pretty well in hand" when she wrote the following letter to Mrs. Pryor. On the eve of departure from Richmond to a new life in New York, she shows her sympathy, courage, and independence, and a determination to remember the past which adversity could not shake.

Richmond, May, 1865

My Dearest: What could I do without you? Now don't flatter yourself that I need now, or ever did need, those beautiful moral reflections in well-chosen language by means of which you have striven to educate me. But you are an unmitigated blessing when "feelings are too many for me"—when, in short, I boil over.

Now when a kettle boils over it puts out the fire, and then we go tea-less to bed. How nice it would be for the kettle if some convenient utensil were at hand to receive its excited bubbles.

I am aggrieved and indignant at the sermons people are preaching to us. And I have caught a young brother in a flagrant theft. All Richmond is in a state of beautiful admiration at a sermon it listened to last week on the uses of our great misfortune. War was declared to be a blessing. "The high passion of patriotism prevents the access of baser passions. Men's hearts beat together, and woman is roused from the frivolousness and feebleness into which her nature is apt to sink. Death, insult, carnage, violated homes, and broken hearts are all awful. But it is worse than a thousand deaths when a people has adopted the creed that the wealth of nations consists, not in generous hearts, in primitive simplicity, in preference of duty to life; not in MEN, but in silk, cotton, and something that they call capital. If the price to be paid for peace is this—that wealth accumulates and men decay, better far that every street in every town of our once noble country should run blood."

Now all this is very fine, but very one-sided. . . .

I feel impatient at this attempt to extort good for ourselves out of the overwhelming disaster which brought such ruin to others; to congratulate ourselves for what is purchased with their blood. Surely, if for no other reason, for the sake of the blood that has been split, we should not hasten to acquiesce in the present state of things. If I catch my Colonel piously affirming too much resignation, too prompt a forgetfulness of the past, I'll—well, he knows what I am capable of saying!

But, now that I have safely boiled over, I will tell you my news. We cannot remain here. We are literally stripped to the "primitive" state my reverend brother thinks so good for us. We are wofully in need of "silk, cotton, and something they call capital," and we'll never get it here. And so my Colonel and I are going to New York. He has secured a place in some publishing house or other. I only wish it were a dry-goods store.

Of course our social life is over. I have taken my resolution. There are fine ladies in New York whom I used to entertain in Washington. Just so far as they approach me, will I approach them! A card for a card, a visit for a visit. But I imagine I shall not be recognized. I am content. There will be plenty to read in that publishing house. I shall not repine. All the setting, the *entourage,* of a lady is taken from me, but the lady herself has herself pretty well in hand, and is quite content if she may always be

Your devoted

AGNES

2. MARY BOYKIN CHESNUT

"To Look on Our Desolated Country and Be Strong"

"Nothing is left to us now but the bare land, and the debts contracted for the support of hundreds of Negroes during the war," said Mrs. Chesnut when they returned to Mulberry Plantation. She brought her diary to a close and stored it away.

She and General Chesnut built a home called "Sarsfield" near Mulberry. He resumed the practice of law in Camden, South Carolina, and, in 1868, was a delegate to the Democratic National Convention at New York City. Mrs. Chesnut continued to correspond with Mrs. Jefferson Davis and other friends of Confederate days for the rest of her life.

The general died on February 1, 1885, and the next year his wife followed at the age of sixty-three. They are buried at the Chesnut Cemetery, Knight's Hill, near Camden. Inscribed on her gravestone are the words

"Rest and drink thy fill
Of pure Immortal streams."

Mrs. Chesnut bequeathed her diary to her friend Isabella D. Martin. After the war, Miss Martin had kept a girls' school in Columbia, and the sad-faced, black-robed Mary Chesnut became a familiar sight to her pupils.

"She had love of companionship, native wit, an acute mind . . . and a searching insight into the motives of men and women," Miss Martin wrote. "Her heart was of the warmest and tenderest."

June 1st 1865. . . . We came, for three days of travel, over a road that had been laid bare by Sherman's torches. . . . No living thing was left, no house for man or beast. . . .

Went up to my old house, "Kamtchatka." The Trapiers live there now. In those drawing-rooms where the children played Puss in Boots, where we have so often danced and sung, but never prayed before, Mr. Trapier held his prayer-meeting. I do not think I ever did as much weeping or as bitter in the same space of time. I let myself go; it did me good. I cried with a will. He prayed that we might have strength to stand up and bear our bitter disappointment, to look on our ruined homes and our desolated country and be strong. And he prayed for the man "we elected to be our ruler and guide." We knew that they had put him in a dungeon and in chains. Men watch him day and night. By order of Andy,[1] the bloody-minded tailor, nobody above the rank of colonel can take the benefit of the amnesty oath, nobody who owns over twenty thousand dollars, or who has assisted the Confederates, and now, ye rich men, howl, for your misery has come upon you. You are beyond the outlaw, camping outside. Howell Cobb and R. M. T. Hunter have been arrested. Our turn will come next, maybe. A Damocles sword hanging over a house does not conduce to a pleasant life.

June 12th. Andy, made lord of all by the madman, Booth, says, "Destruction only to the wealthy classes." Better teach the

---

[1] President Andrew Johnson.

Negroes to stand alone before you break up all they leaned on,
O Yankees! After all, the number who possess over $20,000 are
very few.

. . . My husband will remain quietly at home. He has done
nothing that he had not a right to do, nor anything that he is
ashamed of. He will not fly from his country, nor hide anywhere
in it. These are his words. He has a huge volume of Macaulay,
which seems to absorb him. Slily I slipped Silvio Pellico in his
way. He looked at the title and moved it aside. "Oh," said I, "I
only wanted you to refresh your memory as to a prisoner's life
and what a despotism can do to make its captives happy!" . . .

We are shut in here, turned with our faces to a dead wall. No
mails. A letter is sometimes brought by a man on horseback,
traveling through the wilderness made by Sherman. All railroads
have been destroyed and the bridges are gone. We are cut off
from the world, here to eat out our hearts. . . .

July 26th. I do not write often now, not for want of something
to say, but from a loathing of all I see and hear, and why dwell
upon those things? . . .

I am reading French with Johnny[2]—anything to keep him
quiet. We gave a dinner to his company, the small remnant of
them, at Mulberry house. About twenty idle Negroes, trained
servants, came with leave or license and assisted. So there was no
expense. They gave their time and labor for a good day's feeding.
I think they love to be at the old place.

August 2d. Dr. Boykin and John Witherspoon[3] were talking
of a nation in mourning, of blood poured out like rain on the
battle-fields—for what? "Never let me hear that the blood of the
brave has been shed in vain! No; it sends a cry down through
all time."

---

2 Captain John Chesnut, her husband's nephew.

3 Of Society Hill plantation, husband of Mrs. Chesnut's cousin, Betsy, who
had been murdered, reportedly by slaves, in September 1861.

3. SARA RICE PRYOR

"I Shall Not Fall"

During the military occupation of Petersburg by Sheridan, Mrs. Pryor was a prisoner "in two rooms for ten days." Shortly afterward she and her children went to a small house belonging to her brother, outside the city. The story to follow begins in the summer of 1865.

After her husband's departure to seek his fortune in New York, Mrs. Pryor moved back to Petersburg. She burned the old fortifications for warmth, gave music lessons to neighboring children, and waited for the day when she might join her husband. In December 1865 the Boston *Post* reported, "The Rebel Pryor has opened an office in New York for the practice of the law, but he has not yet *had a rap.*" But in less than three months he could joyfully retort, "The Rebel Pryor has had a rap at last—a rap with no uncertain significance. I have had a call from a *bona fide* client." In May 1867 Mrs. Pryor and the children joined him.

As the years went by, he became a distinguished jurist. In 1890, he was appointed judge of the Court of Common Pleas, and, six years later, a justice of the Supreme Court of New York.

Mrs. Pryor won recognition for her stories and essays and for her books, *The Mother of Washington and Her Times,* published in 1903, *Reminiscences of Peace and War,* 1904, and *My Day: Reminiscences of a Long Life,* 1909.

She died in 1912, at the age of eighty-two.

When I reached Cottage Farm I found a home that no soldier, however forlorn, could have envied me. A scene of desolation met my eyes. The earth was ploughed and trampled, the grass and flowers were gone, the carcasses of six dead cows lay in the yard, and filth unspeakable had gathered in the corners of the house. The evening air was heavy with the sickening odor of decaying flesh. As the front door opened, millions of flies swarmed forth.

"If this were I," said Mrs. Hartsuff,[4] as she gathered her skirts as closely around her as her hoops would permit, "I should fall across the threshold and die."

"I shall not fall," I said proudly; "I shall stand in my lot."

Within was dirt and desolation. Pieces of fat pork lay on the floors, molasses trickled from the library shelves, where bottles lay uncorked. Filthy, malodorous tin cans were scattered on the floors. Nothing, not even a tin dipper to drink out of the well, was left in the house, except one chair out of which the bottom had been cut, and one bedstead fastened together with bayonets. Picture frames were piled against the wall. Every one was empty. One family portrait of an old lady was hanging on the wall with a sabre-cut across her face.

"Now, what in the world are you going to do?" asked Mrs. Hartsuff.

"The best I can," I said. . . .

I sent Abram to the quartermaster, and borrowed a team to haul away the filth and the dead animals. . . . Before night we were comparatively clean, having had a score or more scrubbers, and as many out-of-door laborers at work.

My husband returned to us,[5] and we commenced our new life of hopeless destitution. Not before October could I get my consent to eat a morsel in the house. I took my meals under the trees, unless driven by the rains to the shelter of the porch.

My dear General had not remained in Richmond. There was no hope there for immediate occupation. His profession of law, for which he had been educated, promised nothing, for the very good reason that he had forgotten all he ever knew in his later profession of editor and politician. The latter field was closed to him forever. There was nothing for a rebel to earn in editing a newspaper. . . .

---

[4] The wife of General George L. Hartsuff, at that time the commanding Federal officer in Petersburg.

[5] In March 1865 General Pryor was released from Fort Lafayette for exchange by Lincoln's personal order. He was arrested again when Federals entered Petersburg on April 2, 1865.

We suffered terribly during the ensuing months for want of something in which we might occupy ourselves. We sat silently, looking out on a landscape marked here and there by chimneys standing sentinel over the blackened heaps where our neighbors had made happy homes. A few books had been saved, only those for which we had little use. A soldier walked in one day with a handsome volume which Jefferson Davis, after inscribing his name in it, had presented to the General. The soldier calmly requested the former owner to be kind enough to add to the value of the volume by writing beneath the inscription his own autograph, and, his request granted, walked off with it under his arm. "He has been at some trouble," said my husband," and he had as well be happy if I cannot!"

As the various brigades moved away from our neighborhood a few plain articles of furniture that had been taken from the house were restored to us, but nothing handsome or valuable, no books, pictures, *bric-à-brac,* or house-furnishings of any kind— just a few chairs and tables. I had furnished an itemized list of all the articles we had lost, with only this result.

We had news after a while of our beloved mare, Lady Jane. A letter enclosing her photograph came from a New England officer:

"To Mr. Pryor:

"Dear Sir: A very fine mare belonging to you came into my camp near Richmond and is now with me. It would add much to

her value if I could get her pedigree. Kindly send it at your earliest convenience, and oblige

"Yours truly,

——— ———

"P.S. The mare is in good health, as you will doubtless be glad to know."

Disposed as my General was to be amiable, this was a little too much! The pedigree was not sent.

A great number of tourists soon began to pass our house on their way to visit the localities near us, now become historic. They wished to stand on the site of General Lee's headquarters, to pluck a blade of grass from the hollow of the crater, to visit the abattis, lunettes, and fortifications of both lines, especially Fort Steadman, Fort Gregg, and Battery 45, where the lines were broken the last of March and on April 2.

These tourists, men and women, would pause at the well, some on horseback, others in the dilapidated landaus or buggies for hire in Petersburg. Uncle Frank, with his flow of courteous language . . . would usually meet and discourse to them, earning many a *douceur* by drawing from the well the cold water for which it was famous. Abram's family was abroad in the fields, where the old man had planted corn in June—too late to hope for other harvest than the fodder to feed the horse the quartermaster had given him at my earnest request. Under the impression that we were still working our Negroes, some of the tourists would dismount and harangue Abram at length upon his "rights." The old man would listen respectfully, shaking his gray head dubiously as they rode off.

"Recollect, boy," said one of these travellers to Aleck, "the white woman in that house is now *your slave!*"

Aleck was standing beneath my window, amusing himself by tying up a rosebush. He looked up, simply advising me, "Let 'em go 'long," and resumed his work in training the rosebush.

Sometimes the tourists would ask permission to call on us, claiming some common acquaintance. My husband was inclined to resent this. Their sympathetic attitude was offensive to him. Like the Douglas he had endured much, but—

> "Last and worst, to spirit proud
> To bear the pity of the crowd:"—

this was more than he could endure.

We were perfectly aware that they wished to see *us*, and not to gain, as they affected, information about the historic localities on the farm. Still less did they desire ignobly to triumph over us. A boy, when he tears off the wings of a fly, is much interested in observing its actions, not that he is cruel—far from it! He is only curious to see how the creature will behave under very disadvantageous circumstances. . . .

Our friends in town were in too much poverty and sorrow to visit us. A deadly silence and apathy had succeeded the storm. It was a long time before the community waked up from this apathy—not, indeed, until the cool, invigorating weather of autumn. The blood-soaked soil and the dead animals emitted sickening odors until the frosts came to chain them up.

A bachelor friend occasionally visited us and invited the little boys to accompany him upon relic-hunting expeditions to the narrow plain which had divided the opposing lines on that fateful April morning, just three months before. Ropes were fastened around extinct shells, and they were hauled in, to stand sentinel at the door. The shells were short cylinders, with one pointed end like a candle before it is lighted. Numbers of Minié-balls were dug out of the sand.

One day Mr. Kemp brought in a great curiosity—two bullets welded together, having been shot from opposing rifles. . . .

I had no garments to mend or to make, no household to manage. The sultry days were begun and rounded by hours of listless endurance, followed by troubled sleep. A bag of army "hardtack" stood in a corner, so the children were never hungry. Presently they, too, sat around us, too listless to play or talk. A great army of large, light brown Norway rats now overran the farm. They would walk to the corner before our eyes and help themselves to the army rations. We never moved a finger to drive them away. After awhile Aleck appeared with an enormous black-and-white cat.

"Dis' jest a little mo'n I can stand," said Aleck. "De Yankees has stole ev'rything, and dug up de whole face o' the yearth . . . but I ain' obleedged to stan' sassyness fum dese outlandish rats."

Aleck had to surrender. The very first night after the arrival of his valiant cat there was a scuffle in the room where the crackers were kept, a chair was overturned, and a flying cat burst through the hall, pursued by three or four huge rats. The cat took refuge in a tree . . . and left the field to the enemy.

Of course there could be but one result from this life. Malaria had hung over us for weeks, and now one after another of the children lay down upon the "pallets" on the floor, ill with fever. Then I succumbed and was violently ill. Our only nurse was my dear General; and not in all the years when he never shirked duty, or lost a march, or rode on his own horse when his men had a toilsome march or if one of them failed by the way, and never lost one of the battles into which he personally led them,—not in all those trying times was he nobler, grander, than in his long and lonely vigils beside his sick family.

After we recovered, my dear husband was ill—ague and fever had fastened on him. When he, too, grew better, he would sit for days in hopeless despair, looking out on the desolate landscape.

General Hartsuff and his wife often visited us. They were terribly afraid of fever, and would send in messages from the gate while we were so ill. But after we had recovered, General Hartsuff came himself—and finally sent Captain Gregory, the commissary-general, to see me, and to reason seriously with me about the necessity of sending General Pryor away. He had never been pardoned. There were men in power who constantly hinted at punishment and retribution. General Pryor would die here. He should go to New York, go by sea, shake off the chills that shook him so relentlessly every third day, meet friends (many Southerners were in New York), and something might result for his benefit.

This idea grew in our minds as feasible, if only we had the money. It had never occurred to me to make a second attempt (one had failed) to sell my watch. I now took it to a banker in

Petersburg, added to it a cherished antique cameo set in diamonds which had never left my finger since it was given me, like Shylock's turquoise from his Leah, when my husband was a bachelor. Leaving these in pledge, I received three hundred dollars. I bought some quinine forthwith, ordered a suit of clothes to replace the threadbare Confederate gray, and sent Roger A. Pryor, the sometime "rebel," to New York. . . .

A difficult task lay before him. Ruined in fortune, his occupation gone, his friends dead or impoverished, his health impaired, his heart broken, he had yet to win support for a wife and seven children, and that in a hostile community. Only two things were left to him—the ability to work and the willingness to work. . . .

He accepted a position on the *Daily News* which yielded him twenty-five dollars a week. Meanwhile he must learn New York law. . . .

4. VARINA HOWELL DAVIS

"I, Varina Davis"

On May 3, 1866, Mr. Davis arrived at Fortress Monroe, Virginia. Before she was allowed to enter the cell of "the Rebel Davis," she signed this statement in the presence of witnesses:

"I, Varina Davis, wife of Jefferson Davis, for the privilege of being permitted to see my husband, do hereby give my parole of honor that I will not engage in or assent to any measures which shall lead to any attempt to escape from confinement on the part of my husband or to his being rescued or released from imprisonment without the sanction and order of the President of the United States, nor will I be the means of conveying to my husband any deadly weapons of any kind."

Permission to join her husband was a small but important victory. It was the result of a year of hard campaigning in her fight for his ultimate release.

What happened to her in that year may be glimpsed in letters to Horace Greeley, editor of the New York *Tribune;* to Mrs. John Tyler; to Mrs. Howell Cobb; and to Andrew Johnson, President of the United States.

Mrs. Davis remained with her husband at Fortress Monroe. He was released in Richmond on May 13, 1867, and they joined their children in Montreal; later, they went to England. After living for several years in Memphis, they settled at "Beauvoir," near Biloxi, Mississippi. After the death of Mr. Davis, on December 6, 1889, she devoted her time to writing a tribute to him. *"Jefferson Davis: a Memoir by His Wife"* was published in 1890.

She died in a New York hotel on October 16, 1906, and was buried in Hollywood Cemetery in Richmond. An editorial in the *Confederate Veteran* of December 1906 paid her this tribute:

"In that epic period from 1861 to 1865 and in the tragic years which immediately followed she was a luminous figure, courageous, brave, patient, and hopeful. . . .

"In her extreme old age her condition was pathetic. With sisters, brothers, husband and children all dead, save one, Mrs. J. A. Hayes, in distant Colorado, she spent her last years quite alone. . . . Always and to everybody a gracious, brilliant, queenly, kind-hearted old lady, she passed away honored and beloved by all who knew her great worth. . . .

"She accepted the saddest decree of fate unmurmuringly, and won the admiration of the whole country as well as the adoration of the people of the South. . . ."

Savannah, Georgia
June 22nd, 1865

Honorable Horace Greeley,

Sir—Not that you may blush for your people, but only to give you an idea of how I am tormented in my imprisonment here, I send you an article clipped out of the Savannah *Republican*— one of the many which have been published for my benefit daily, about the man of all others I most reverence. How can the honest men and gentlemen of your country stand idly by to see a gentleman maligned, insulted, tortured and denied the right of trial by the usual forms of law? Is his cause so strong that he must be done to death by starvation, confined air, and manacles? With all the Archives of our government in the hands of your government, do they despair of proving him a rogue, falsifier, assassin and traitor—that they must in addition guard him like a wild beast, and chain him for fear his armed hands will in a casemated cell subvert the government? Shame, shame—he is not held for the ends of Justice but for those of torture.

There is not a man I will venture to say among the better class of your people who in his heart believes Mr. Davis guilty of the crime so falsely imputed to him. Is no one among you bold enough to defend him? Will no one of influence stand forth and demand where the money is with which he was found running off to a foreign country? Where the elaborate disguise in which he was arrayed? What benefit he expected to accrue to him from the assassination of a kindly man about whom he knew nothing, and the substitution of a bitter enemy in his place? Where are the commissions which authorized the hotel burnings—the St. Albans raid— and all the other "villainies" of which he is accused? Is reiteration to be substituted for the truth? What counsel has he been allowed to see; is it intended to precipitate his counsel unprepared upon a mass of undigested matter thoroughly sifted and *expurgated* of all vindicatory matter, by the prosecuting counsel?

Even now I see extracts of his letters to me in the papers; letters which were never written—and which they profess to have taken from me at Fortress Monroe. I will tell what they did take. My husband under circumstances of brutality, my friends and protectors, servants, money, clothing and liberty—last not least my good name and that of my family. When I reached Savannah my children had to be clothed by contributions from our poor dear impoverished people, until I could have some clothing made for them. In the next lexicon a free Confederate woman "under no restraint" means a woman confined to a town in which she never set foot before, free to pay the heavy expenses of a large family at an expensive hotel. Magnanimity means refusal to prosecute an honorable man upon untenable and villainous charges, but to pardon him as guilty, and so on to the bitter end.

Now I have important documents which I could cite if necessary. I have not got them with me but I could produce them if needs be. I have also important evidence which I could give if summoned. *I demand to be summoned upon Mr. Davis' trial,* if the means used to slay him do not succeed before that time. I know you can feel for the sorrows of the oppressed. Will you ask why I alone am denied the privilege of sending a word of affectionate greeting to my husband—why he is debarred from the fresh air which is accorded Mr. Stephens upon the plea of delicate health? Is it because Mr. Davis *believed* in the cause he advocated; is it because he served, for love, the country of his birth instead of holding office in it for expediency's sake?

Will you take pity upon a helpless distracted woman and find out how Mr. Davis is for me, and put the exact state of his case in your paper; so that I may see it? . . . If he is on a monitor where is his cell? Is his food such as will support the life of a man of such delicate constitution? How is he? Let me implore you to cry aloud for justice for him, with that I shall be content. With the hope that you will not show this letter but feel for me and aid me I am

Very respectfully yours,
VARINA DAVIS

Savannah, Ga., July 24, 1865

Mrs. John Tyler
My dear Friend,

My mother will hand you this letter or send it to you. She goes now to New York for the purpose of taking my poor little children to school in Canada. As I am a prisoner in Georgia until Mr. Stanton sees fit for me to go out of the country, I have thought it better to send them out from under Yankee influence. . . . As we are very poor economy is a great item in our calculations, so I must beg of you to get them a cheap and quiet place if you can by your superior knowledge of the New York locality. They do not know any one and are quite unused to a large city. Will you take the trouble to be their cicerone?

In what a maze of horrors have we been groping for these two months. As for me, I sometimes wonder if God does not mean to wake me from a terrific dream of desolation and penury, to a rectified conviction of freedom achieved and government established on the "best and surest foundation."

I cannot trust myself to speak of my husband. I feel so sure your sympathies are with me that I can say to you that the light is gone from my house and the strength with it. Where is your family? I hope safe. . . . Do write to me of yourself and yours. What concerns you cannot fail to be interesting to me.

Please present my respectful remembrance to Mrs. Gardiner[6] and believe me

Affectionately yours,
VARINA DAVIS

Mill View, near Augusta, Ga.
Sept. 9th, 1865

To Mrs. Howell Cobb.[7]

My Very Dear Friend, I have been waiting from day to day to find out when I should obtain leave to quit Georgia; and that

---

[6] At this time, Mrs. Tyler was with her mother, Mrs. David Gardiner, in New York. The Tylers and the Davises were close and long-time friends.

[7] *Née* Mary Ann Lamar, of Georgia. Her husband rose to the rank of Major General in the Confederate Army. He was arrested on May 25, 1865, and released three days later. He died suddenly in New York on October 9, 1868.

point ascertained, to decide and write to you at what time I could be able to go to see you at your home to which you invite me in your sweet affectionate way; but the authorities so far do not vouchsafe to me an answer and I do not like to leave here until it is received. I am so racked by anxiety, so unhappy between hopes and fears. At present released from imprisonment "within the city limits of Savannah," I am permitted to go at large in the State of Georgia. Think what a roaring lion is going loose in Georgia seeking whom she may devour—one old woman, a small baby, and nurse; the Freedmen's Bureau and the military police had better be doubled lest either the baby or I "turn again and rend them."

But I will not talk of these things lest I say more than is right. Let me tell you rather of the "leniency," "humanity" or what not which has been evinced towards me. I am now allowed to correspond with my dear husband under the supervision of the Atty. General strictly upon family matters, and the permission has relieved me of the dreadful sense of loneliness and agonizing doubt and weight of responsibility. I may ask his advice instead of acting upon my own suggestions, and above all I may know from him how he is. I know, dear friend, you will rejoice with me over this change in my unhappy circumstances and pray with me that God may bless me yet more by softening their hearts to let us meet. He writes in such a spirit of pious resignation and trust in God's faith with those who put their dependence upon him that he has comforted me greatly.

The children who were so large as to remember their father and the Confederacy I was forced to send out of the country. Their sensibilities were so wounded that I felt it could not be well for them to share my durance, and so sent them to Canada with my mother who will put them in school there.

Mr. Schley's[8] family who reside about five miles from Augusta are very kind to me and urge my remaining here a few weeks

---

[8] Mr. George Schley.

longer. Then after a short visit to Mrs. Burt[9] (if I can get permission to go to Abbeville) I will return and pay you . . . a short
visit. I so much desire to see you before I leave the country. I
want to see your children and your kind husband once more. . . .

My dear old friend, may God add all unto you which now
seems denied to our poor people, and if it is not his blessed will
be assured you will ever have the most affectionate sympathy of
your sincere friend. . . .

Savannah January 1866

His Excellency the President:

Sir: Please receive my thanks for permission transmitted to
me through Mr. Attorney-General Speed to go to Canada. But
before I proceed there will you reconsider your decision not to
permit me to see my husband? He is suffering and wretched. I
fear an utter failure of his health if kept long in the state in
which he now is. I have never desired to be either defiant or rude
to you, but have greatly suffered, and perhaps may have appeared both in my unstudied expressions.

Will you exert your great power and exercise this clemency
to me, the most helpless and wretched of all those over whom
you rule? I look to you for protection and aid, in common with
the people of our Southern country. I cannot feel that you will
refuse it. May I hope once more to sit near my sick husband? I
cannot do anything for him in his great peril and agony but
speak to him of my love and despair. Will you not let me do this?
Neither is he nor am I responsible for the silly efforts for his
escape, which are alleged to have been on foot, and which I
deprecate as much as any one. Then do not, Mr. President, let
me be the helpless sufferer. I will take any parole, do anything,

---

9 Mrs. Armistead Burt was a niece of John C. Calhoun. She and her husband had entertained Mrs. Davis in Abbeville, South Carolina, as she fled
south from Richmond. On May 2, the Confederate Cabinet held a meeting
in the Burt home.

if you will only let me see him. Will you not? I pray God daily
to spare you for a long life. May I not hope that you will permit
me to thank God for your clemency also?

With the hope that you will grant my prayer, offered with
tears enough to float it to you if they were as many as the throbs
of agony which bring them forth, I am, sir, regretful of the past,
if in it I have unwittingly offended you.

> Very respectfully and
> prayerfully, yours,
> VARINA DAVIS

Mr. President, please decide this matter yourself. For the love
of God and his merciful Son do not refuse me. Let me go to him
and admire and bless your name every hour of my life.[10]

5. MARY CUSTIS LEE

"Such Acts of Atrocity"

> General and Mrs. Lee left the house on Franklin Street in
> Richmond in early June to accept the hospitality of their
> friends the Palmores. For many months they lived in a small
> cottage on the estate of Mrs. Elizabeth Randolph Cocke, at
> Bremo on the James River.
>
> "Miss Em" is, of course, Miss Emily Mason who would soon
> travel abroad. *Southern Poems of the War,* which she edited,
> was published in 1867. She wrote a life of Robert E. Lee which
> was issued in 1872.
>
> Soon after writing this letter, Mrs. Lee accompanied her
> husband to Lexington, Virginia, where he had accepted an
> offer of the presidency of Washington College.

---

[10] President Johnson made no reply to this appeal. For ten days, Mrs.
Davis waited for one in New York and then proceeded on her way to
Montreal to join her children, whom she had not seen for a year.

When she heard rumors that Mr. Davis was near death, she telegraphed
the President, "Is it possible that you will keep me from my dying husband?"
Then, at last, the permission was granted, and she set out at once for
Fortress Monroe.

Bremo 23d Nov. 1865

My dear Miss Em

. . . The Palmore's were indeed kind during all our sojourn there. Virginia, though so devastated cannot yet forget her wonted generosity and hospitality, & I shall never forget all their kindness. Of course we are full of complacency at Mr. Beecher's approval of Genl Lee's course, but when he exalts Dahlgren into a hero & martyr we have less respect for his judgement.

I hope my dear Miss Em you will not forget me in my distant home but write me all that is going on in the great world tho' alas we have little concern with that now. I feel very anxious & uneasy about Mr. Davis & all who are yet confined without even the semblance of justice.

Perhaps you know Burton Harrison of Richmond the private Sec. of Mr. Davis, a fine handsome young man who had committed no offence greater than the whole South was guilty of. He was put in the Penitentiary in Washington in a cell just large enough to contain his bed where he lay for three weeks without one ray of light & finding his health was giving way under such treatment they brought him out & promenaded him by the graves of Mrs. Surratt[11] & others who had been executed in the meantime. When such acts of atrocity are perpetrated at the seat of government under the very eyes of our ruler, what can we expect.

Poor Mrs. Mallory, I do feel for her, she was so devoted to her husband.[12] I am glad you were able to go & see him. It must have been such a comfort to him. Write me of all your plans. . . .

Yours affectionately
M. C. LEE

---

[11] Mrs. Mary E. Surratt was hanged on July 7, 1865, after conviction of complicity in the murder of President Lincoln.

[12] Mr. Mallory was imprisoned at Fort Lafayette. Other Cabinet members who were imprisoned were Mr. Seddon, Mr. Hunter, and Mr. Trenholm at Fort Pulaski; Mr. Reagan and Mr. Stephens at Fort Warren.

6. ISABEL MAURY

"Yankee Rule"

Commander Matthew Fontaine Maury, who headed the Torpedo Bureau in Richmond, had gone to England on behalf of the Confederacy in the winter of 1862. When war ended, Molly, one of his daughters, and other members of his family joined him there. The Maurys returned to Virginia in 1868, and the Commander accepted the chair of Physics in the Virginia Military Institute at Lexington.

In the meantime, Isabel or "Bel" Maury, one of the numerous cousins, kept Molly posted on the news from Richmond.

Richmond January 1, [1866]

My Dearest Molly,

. . . Saturday before Christmas we were all busy preparing a tree for the children. It was beautiful. On the top were two flags, our Confederate and our battle flag. Gen. Lee, bless his soul, was hung immediately below. . . . Of course, we had egg-nog Christmas night, but no company. . . . Today, being New Year's day we had numerous calls, though very unexpected to us, as Southern people do not generally receive. Ma said they did once, when she was a young lady, but since—it hasn't been customary. My only objection is that the Yankees not only do it, but abuse the custom, and I want to do entirely different from them. We are a distinct and separate nation, and I wish our customs to be as distinct as we are.

Pa is very gloomy—so many without money, without employment, and no prospect for business. Then the Yankees are taxing us, what our people cannot pay, to pay their war debt. Yes, we are drained to pay for being reduced to this slavery. Oh! Molly I feel sometimes I would like to get from under their rule. Do you know a *nice* fellow who wants a *nice* wife?—then tell him if he will deliver her from Yankee rule, here she is!

No Molly, I would rather abide my fate with one of our noble Confederate soldiers, wait on him, help him battle with *poverty,* and the degradation he has been reduced to by an overwhelming number, but Molly I must begin the New Year by trying to submit more humbly to His will who loveth whom He chasteneth. I know it is all for our good, tho Molly I must confess I am blind. I pray faith may open my eyes and better reconcile me to our lot. Molly it is not myself as an individual I deplore, I could not be so ungrateful for we have a home and other comforts still left us, but the numbers of penniless men and women without any prospects for work, the widows and orphans—oh Molly, it makes my heart ache.

The poor servants too, how they must suffer. Mammy came back the other day, with tears in her eyes and begged help, "for God's sake." Molly you know how comfortable she was here. We got her a good home and I am sure we will never let her want bread when we have it. She told us of hundreds in her condition—and they cannot get work and Southern people haven't the means to help them. Tell me of Yankee philanthropy! They do not care what comes of them, and they say so! . . .

Anne Greenhow has a French teacher, a very nice gentleman who has been in Europe fifteen years. He amuses me talking of the beaux. He says those of his old friends who were not killed have gone off, and nobody but boys are left, more truth than poetry I believe. . . . If we have no Confederate beaux we will not have Yankees. . . .

BEL

7. VIRGINIA TUNSTALL CLAY

"My Husband Is My World"

Mrs. Clement Clay and her husband were in LaGrange, Georgia, when news came of the assassination of President Lincoln. On May 10, 1865, she wrote, "We received the President's proclamation offering reward of $100,000 for my dear husband's arrest as the murderer of Lincoln." Senator Clay immediately surrendered to Federal authorities at Macon. Mrs. Clay resolutely accompanied him to Fortress Monroe. Then she devoted her time and energy to securing his release. She appealed to the President, and to former Washington friends and acquaintances, not once, but many times.

On April 17, 1866, more than three months after the following letter to President Johnson was written, Clement Clay was freed. Once more the Clays went home to Huntsville, where they lived until his death in 1882. In 1887, Mrs. Clay married Judge David Clopton, of Montgomery.

"Beloved of the South," she was called when she died on June 23, 1915, in her ninety-third year.

Washington City, January 11, 1866

To His Excellency, President of the United States:

... How true it is that all conditions of life, however seemingly extreme, are capable of augmentation! I have thought and so told you, that for eight months past I have been, and God knows with what cause, at the nadir of despair; that my cup, bitterer than the waters of Marah, was brimming, my heart breaking. A letter received two evenings ago announces the death of my husband's beloved mother, wife of ex-Governor Clay. Deeply distressing to me; oh! Mr. Johnson, what a blow to my husband, your unhappy prisoner! He was her idolized son, her first-born. . . .

How can I summon nerve to tell him the news? I cannot write so great a grief, nor can I tell it and leave him in his gloomy prison to struggle with it alone! Will you not pour in the oil of healing? I beg of you, permit me to bear with me, along with my "weight of woe," the antidote. Issue the order for my husband's release on his *parole d'honneur,* with bail if desired, and let him once more see our father, who lies (now) on a bed of illness. . . .

Mr. President, you hold many noble prisoners in your forts, but Mr. Clay's case is *sui generis.* General Grant, the whole-hearted soldier, in his letter to you in his behalf, says, "His manly surrender is to me a full and sufficient guarantee that he will be forthcoming at any time the civil authorities of the land may call for him." Even Mr. Stanton, who is not considered partial to so-called "Rebels," told me, in my only interview, that "he was not my husband's judge," as if he, Pilate-like, were willing to wash his hands of innocent blood. I replied tremblingly, "I would fain not have you for his accuser, Sir." To which he rejoined, not unkindly, "I am not his accuser, Madam." I thanked God for even that cold comfort as harbinger of better days.

And now, Sir, may I ask you who are those opposed to my husband's release on parole? I have yet to find the first man, Federal or other, who does not express admiration for the high sense of honour and chivalric faith, for the prompt and manly surrender; and astonishment at the detention. To-day we might have been far away in some peaceful spot, united at last, and happy, but for that sense of unsullied honour, which, "feeling a stain like a wound," remained to wipe it out. Can you longer refuse him the privilege?

The law supposes all men innocent till proven guilty, and if it will allow me, I, alone, can disprove, *in toto,* the testimony of the conspiracy case, implicating him. Mr. Clay, always delicate, is dying daily. He told me he was resigned to God's will and perfectly willing to perish in those four walls if his country would be benefited thereby. Mr. President, my husband is my world, my all, and "dear to me as are the ruddy drops that visit this sad heart." Give him to me for a little while, at least long enough to gladden the dim eyes of the eager and aged watcher at home and close them; and he shall return to you, on his honour and my life, at any moment called for by the Government. Let me bring him to you to prove to you the truth of my statement in point of health, and to afford him the right of personal appeal. . . . That God may incline you to grant my prayer and soften "the hearts of our enemies," restore Peace indeed to the land, and bless and guide and guard you in public and

private life to your journey's end, is the prayer of her who hopefully, trustfully, and truthfully subscribes herself,

Your friend,

V. C. CLAY

8. ANGELA MORENO MALLORY

"I Went to Fort Lafayette"

Mrs. Mallory and her young children had fled to friends
in LaGrange, Georgia, before the evacuation of Richmond.
She was there while her husband was heading south with
President Davis, and she welcomed him at LaGrange after he
had left the President at Washington, Georgia, on May 2,
1865.

Only a few days later, he was arrested and taken off to Fort
Lafayette. Mrs. Mallory and the children went to their
daughter Margaret Bishop in Bridgeport, Connecticut.

In July, she visited him in his cell at Fort Lafayette in the
presence of a guard. In Washington, she pleaded with President Johnson for his release. A second appeal to the President
in December proved in vain.

The letter to Mrs. Clement C. Clay tells of her last visit to
Fort Lafayette with her daughters Maggie and Ruby.

Mr. Mallory was released on parole to Bridgeport, on
March 10, 1866; months later, he was granted permission to
return to the South. The beautiful home in Pensacola had
fared badly during their absence. Many scars from Federal
occupation remained, and Mr. Mallory's valuable law library
had been destroyed.

He died on November 12, 1873. He willed his estate to his
"darling wife, Angela S. Mallory . . . as an act of justice to
her devotion and duty as wife and mother."

Bridgeport [Connecticut], 7th Feb. 1866

My Dear Friend,

I regretted very much to have to leave Washington without
seeing you and offering you my deep sympathy in the great

bereavement which has befallen your dear husband and your-self, in the loss of his dear Mother. Do present my love and that of my dear husband to him and tell him not to give way to feel-ings of dismay for this world is a place where our souls are pre-pared and refined by sorrows and care to make us acceptable to our heavenly Father. He is our only hope, therefore we must trust Him, and carry our troubles with patience, hope and confi-dence. These last words were the ones used by our good President on the occasion of my interview with him in behalf of my hus-band and they have been words of comfort indeed to me.

I returned to New York last Wednesday night and on reaching the city, I went at once to Fort Lafayette. I found my dear hus-band suffering from an attack of Gout, which until now has always confined itself to his foot and ankles; now it has gone into his knee and he has had several violent attacks of palpitation of the heart, which are produced by the Gout. Oh it makes my soul sink within me when I see my husband languishing in a prison, and I cannot help him out. I would not be surprised if some morning when Gen. Burke goes into Mr. Mallory's room to see that he has not escaped, if he finds nothing but his body there, for his soul cannot be detained by earthly prisons.

Mr. Mallory suffers all the excruciating torments . . . without a word of complaint. Those around him, who do not know him believe that he does not suffer much, but I who have for seven-teen years witnessed the great suffering which he undergoes know that he cannot bear it much longer. I went to see him on Thursday, Saturday and Sunday. Maggie and Ruby accompanied me on Sunday. . . .

Maggie and Ruby join me in much love to you. Do let me know what your prospects are of getting your husband's re-lease. . . .

Your most sincerely attached
friend and fellow sufferer,
ANGELA M. MALLORY

9. MARY ELIZABETH RANDOLPH

"I Did Not Walk About the City"

Late in 1864, Mrs. George Wythe Randolph accompanied her sick husband to France, where he hoped to regain his health. He died in 1867, shortly after their return to Virginia. As will be seen, Mrs. Jefferson Davis was remembered devotedly by her friends in Paris. The "forget-me-nots" were sent as a memento of happier days. The pattern for them was selected by Mary Preston, of Columbia and Richmond, who had married Dr. John Darby in September of 1864 in "the handsomest wedding party I ever saw," according to Mrs. Chesnut.

Mary Elizabeth Randolph, who had entertained statesmen and warriors of the Confederacy, and who "had money, beauty and talent," was without a home in Richmond.

Edge-Hill, September 29th [1866]

Dear Mrs. Davis

I sent you through Mrs. Caskie[13] a box of jewelry Mrs. Norman Walker asked me to bring over. It was thought best not to put it up in paper, for the customs-bond officers are sometimes very troublesome. Mrs. Walker was not at all pleased with the "forget-me-nots" they have made in Paris and the pattern selected by Mrs. Darby who, by the way, was looking handsomer than I ever saw her. . . . The family will probably return to America this year.[14]

We reached N.Y. the fourth of this month and passed a week in Richmond. I did not walk about the City; my heart was sad and I felt so much not having a home to go to that my visit was a sad one, though my friends gave us such a kind welcome we felt truly grateful for all the kind feelings manifested.

---

[13] Mrs. James Caskie, of Richmond.
[14] General John S. Preston had taken his family abroad in May 1865.

My husband's health is so bad we are quite at a loss as to what
we had best decide upon for our future plans. We are now on a
visit to his eldest brother and will remain among his friends
until January. I hope to take a couple of rooms in Richmond
next year but it is uncertain about our having the means to live
there.

We anxiously watch for some bright spot in your husband's
fate. I cannot but hope he may be released from his prison life
this fall. My husband joins me in kind remembrance to him and
yourself. Did you receive a letter I wrote you from Paris last
spring? I should be glad to hear from you sometimes.

Very sincerely your friend

M. E. RANDOLPH

10. LOUISE WIGFALL

"There Is Nothing Like One's 'Ain Countrie' "

Senator Wigfall and his family began their slow journey
from Richmond home to Marshall, Texas, several weeks before the evacuation. But there was no peace or safety for "the
hero of Fort Sumter" in Texas. The family fled to Galveston
and sailed for England.

Halsey returned to the United States to find work in
Louisiana and Arkansas and in his father's Colorado mine.
Homesick Louise longed to "spend a winter in America and
feel once more as I used to feel." In 1870, she visited her
friends the Izards in Baltimore. The next year, she was married there to Daniel Giraud Wright, a young lawyer of the
city and an ex-Confederate soldier. Her father, mother and
sister Fanny followed her to Baltimore to make it their home.
But, before long, her father went back to Texas, where he
died in 1874. Fanny married B. Jones Taylor.

Dr. Giraud Wright became a judge. Louise was president
of a chapter of the United Daughters of the Confederacy in
Baltimore, and, in 1905, her memoirs of the war years were
published.

Here are letters from Louise, the Confederate exile in London, to Halsey. Many years later, in 1892, he was appointed U.S. Consul at Leeds.

Gloucester Place, Portman Square
London, November 23d, 1866

Dearest Brother,

. . . Since you left us we have heard of so many shipwrecks and horrible accidents at sea that I must confess that I was much relieved to hear that you had arrived safely at New York. I hope you went from there by rail and are now in New Orleans. . . . I think both Mamma and Papa are in better spirits than they were some time ago, and I hope affairs are brightening. . . .

The Opera was here for two weeks a short time since, and General McRae[15] took a box for us to hear Titiens in "Figaro." You know she is now the first Prima Donna in Europe. . . . The old General did the thing quite in style, a very comfortable box and a nice carriage. The house was very well filled, and we had the felicity of seeing the Duke of Edinburgh and some other members of the Royal Family, or they might have been merely persons of distinction, with him. The royal box was quite full. Mamma says the only thing she remarked about the young Prince was his large red hands and his wearing no gloves, which last was certainly singular.

Nov. 22. Mamma and I made an excursion a few days ago to see the Mannys. Mary has returned from Scotland, and we had a very pleasant visit, talking over old times. . . . They told us that the Walkers[16] found it rather dull at the Isle of Wight. . . .

If you have time in New Orleans, you must find out the Keiths. They were very polite to us in Richmond, and I know liked you very much. You will see doubtless the elegant "Bro Ned" if he

---

[15] General William McRae, of North Carolina.
[16] Norman Walker and wife, of Richmond.

has not left to visit his friend Prince Carl at Berlin. You will
enjoy seeing your old friends. There is nothing like one's "Ain
Countrie," even though enslaved. Goodbye, my dear Brother,
and God bless you.

I am your devoted sister,
LOUISE

57 Gloucester Place, Portman Square
London, June 29, 1867

. . . We have had a considerable break lately in our usual
monotony by several Confederates arriving and nice little
changes in our arrangements. Mrs. Perkins, the wife of Judge
Perkins of La., came over some weeks ago, and with her quite a
party—her daughters, Evelyn Bayley, Miss Virginia Tayloe, a
Miss Jenkins of Baltimore, and Mary Triplett, a beautiful girl
from Richmond (who was at school with me when there but who
has grown up since the war). She is a niece of Mrs. Bolling. They
all lived in that handsome brown-stone house on Franklin St.[17]
. . . They brought a great deal of news, and Mary Triplett
gives a droll account of things in Richmond. They all agree in
one thing: that there are no Yankees in society at all. Mary
Haxall[18] is as gay as ever, and I am afraid has not given up her
old propensity for flirting. . . . Judge Perkins and his party, with
the exception of Mary Triplett, who, I believe, stayed with her
aunt in Paris, are going after the Emperor's fete, to travel on the
Continent—through Switzerland, Germany, and down the
Rhine again to Paris. . . .

We are having a little touch of warm weather just now, and
I expect you are suffering with the heat in N. Orleans. . . .

Your devoted Sister,
LOUISE

---

[17] The Triplett family, the Haxalls and the Bollings were all related
and all played a prominent part in the social life of Richmond.
[18] Mary Haxall married Alexander Cameron in the fall of 1870. He was
a Scotsman living in Richmond, and, according to Louise, "the match is a
good one in all respects."

79 Gloucester Place, Portman Square
London, July 29, 1868

. . . It seems to strike you with wonder that I should care to go back to America on a visit. You forget, my dear Brother, how unpleasantly stupid, and wearying very often has been our life for the last two years. . . . I should like before my youth slips quite away to enjoy myself a little as girls generally do. And if it is convenient, and all things are agreeable, I should like very much to spend a winter in America and feel once more as I used to feel. . . . I have only selected Baltimore as the place of my sojourn as that is the only place to which I have been invited.[19] Papa's affairs are not yet settled, although we hope for that happy consummation daily. . . .

We had a great surprise the other night. The servant came up and announced "An American friend." The door opened, and in walked General Johnston.[20] Papa was not at home, and when at last he came in without any warning of the arrival, you should have seen the greeting! General Johnston stayed till after one o'clock talking with Papa, and left the next day for Scotland from which he has not yet returned. He has come over on some business about a wonderful gun, which if successful, will make his fortune. He will be back before long and may be in England some little time. I believe there is some talk of his being here with us. Mrs. Johnston is not with him. . . .

Your devoted Sister,
LOUISE

11. MARY CUSTIS LEE

"The Glorious Old Times of the Confederacy"

Mrs. Lee remained unconquered by the defeat of the Confederacy. As may be seen from her letters, she was never re-

---

[19] Louise actually visited Josephine Izard, whose mother was Rosetta Ella Pinckney Izard, widow of Ralph Stead Izard of Charleston.
[20] General Joseph E. Johnston.

signed to it, and she was unforgiving to those who dealt unjustly with her countrymen.

Some of her deepest convictions were expressed to Mrs. Davis, who was at Fortress Monroe with her husband, and to the wife of Brigadier General R. H. Chilton.

Lexington   February 6th, 1867

You must excuse me, my dear Mrs. Davis, for applying to you for an autograph of your noble husband so ardently desired by a little lady in England that I have promised to endeavor to procure it. The application was made to me by a gentleman in New Orleans and all the General's & Custis' papers having been destroyed & captured they cannot furnish one. . . . And if you have a picture of Maggie or any of your children I will beg it for my album. I have a very handsome one sent me by a young Virginia girl at school in London & on the *first* page large enough to contain four photos I have two of yourself & one of Mr. Davis & the other space I have reserved for Maggie.

I need not tell you how often we think of you all & how much we are rejoiced at even the slight amelioration in your condition. God grant it may be an earnest of better things! I hear of you often through the Caskies. . . . I was also very glad to learn that your sister was with you. The Genl, Custis & the girls desire to unite in warm regards to *you all.* I am still confined mostly to my chair & through the kindness of friends have many comforts, but my heart yearns for the home & scenes of my past life. I feel as a stranger & exile always looking forward to some change in my condition. It may be only the last change I shall ever experience. Much as I long to go there I dread to witness the plunder & desecration of my once cherished & beautiful home. I only wish I had set the torch to it when I left, or that it was sunk in the bottom of the Potomac rather than used as it now is.[21] But I need not trouble you with my sorrows who have so

---

[21] Mrs. Lee is speaking of Arlington.

much harder ones to bear. I pray that our God may comfort you all & incline the hearts of your enemies & persecutors to accord you the justice you deserve. . . .

Yrs most truly & affectionately,

M. C. Lee

[*Lexington*] *March 10th, 1867*

The Genl has afforded me an opportunity, my dear Mrs. Chilton, of writing to you which I gladly avail myself of, not only as it aids him but enables me to renew a little the pleasant and friendly intercourse we enjoyed in Richmond in the glorious old times of the Confederacy. . . . Miss Em[22] is very busy about her orphans and ought to succeed, you know of course she anticipates a trip to Europe, she deserves such an enjoyment after all her labors. Indeed there is little to keep us in our poor down trodden country *now* but the hope of helping to raise her up and our *malignant* enemies will deprive us of that if possible. It is bad enough to be the victims of tyranny but when it is wielded by such cowards and base men at Butler, Thaddeus Stevens, and Sumner, it is indeed intolerable. The country that allows such *scum* to rule them must be fast going to destruction and we shall care little if we are not involved in the crash. God only knows what our future may be. It is dark enough now but He can cause the light to shine out of darkness.

I am the only person in the house except the girls occasionally who reads the papers. The Genl and Custis will not look at them, better perhaps for their tempers and peace of mind but I always like to know the worst and never desire any evil to be hidden from me. Indeed confined as I am constantly to the House and to my chair, I should have little to employ me if I did not read and we have but few books. . . .

---

[22] Miss Emily Mason did go to Europe and visited Paris and Rome. Before going, she spent much time enlisting aid for Confederate orphan children.

The College is steadily increasing in numbers and I hope will be established on a firm basis but they are much in need of buildings as most of the new professors are obliged to board. . . . The Genl and Custis are much engrossed with their respective duties and I see but little of them except at night and at meals.

I am glad to hear you have a comfortable home but I know you long sometimes for the banks of the Potomac and James. I confess I do. These mountains seem to shut out all I used to know and love yet I am thankful we have found an asylum here and such kind people. We read the most fearful accounts of the destitution and famine in the Carolinas, Georgia and Alabama which I cannot but hope may be exaggerated yet I know the *best* is bad enough.

You must remember us all to the Genl and the girls when you write. . . .

> Believe me most truly yrs
> M. C. LEE

Lexington   May 6th 1867

I was very glad to hear from you my dear Mrs. Chilton. . . . Mildred is still in Richmond and enjoys the sojourn there greatly. The Bazaar which has drawn there a number of persons from Baltimore has proved I am told quite a success tho' I have not yet heard the result. It closes this week.

Do you see the Richmond papers and have you read Underwood's charge to his grand jury five of whom are *negroes*. It is the most remarkable piece of composition I ever read, the most *false* and *vindictive* and that such a creature should be allowed to dispense justice is a perfect farce. I think his meanness and wickedness have affected his brain and John Minor Botts[23] is little better and certainly must have lost all self respect 'ere he would stand

---

[23] A Virginia Unionist leader who was one of those to sign President Davis' bail.

foreman for such a jury. . . . I wonder our people, helpless and disarmed as they are can bear it.

Oh God how long? He seems indeed to have hidden His face from us and yet what hope can we have but in His mercy. All nature is shining out in beauty showing His power and love while our souls are sad and dark. This is want of faith and trust, but I seem to have cast all hope and buoyance since the surrender of a cause of the failure of which I never entertained a doubt.

But I will not dilate upon my sorrowful feelings. Being confined generally to the House I have more time for reflection. . . . The Genl is well and in good spirits. . . . The Genl, Custis and the girls unite with me in much love to you and yours. . . .

Yrs. affecly.

M. C. LEE

12. JULIA GARDINER TYLER

"The South's Dear General Lee"

General Lee died at Lexington on October 12, 1870. Among the hundreds of letters of sympathy to Mrs. Lee was one from Mrs. Tyler, whose sons, eighteen-year-old Gardiner and sixteen-year-old Alexander, had been with the General at Appomattox.

In the summer of 1863, Mrs. Tyler, aboard the Confederate government steamer, the *Lee,* ran the blockade at Nassau. She carried with her a "few bales of cotton." Later in the year, she and the young children fled to her mother on Gardiner's Island. After the war they returned to Sherwood Forest.

She died on July 10, 1889, in the Exchange Hotel at Richmond, where her husband had passed away in 1862. The handsome Tyler monument in Hollywood Cemetery bears the name of Letitia Christian, John Tyler's first wife, and that of Julia Gardiner, his second wife, who were buried beside him.

Sherwood Forest
October 14 1870

Dear Mrs. Lee

I can express but faintly the loss I feel today on the announcement of the death of your noble husband, the South's "dear
General Lee." No one I am sure will approach you with words of
sympathy which come more entirely from the heart than do
mine. I feel as if the grave had closed over one of the dearest and
best friends of my own family. I regarded him tenderly for the
pure perfection of his character. The casket was worthy, it
seemed to me so often, of the gem it contained. He combined in
mind and person those traits which attract and win the apprecia-
tion of young and old.

My Husband esteemed him at his full value and my dear
Gardiner, who saw more of him than any of the young members
of my family during and since the close of the war, paid him ever
a beautiful "homage." He, Gardiner, is at present at a household
in Virginia just preparing to enter upon the practice of the law,
and I know what a gloom is upon him at this news.[24]

Dear Mrs. Lee, I trust you and your daughters will be able to
bear up under your bereavement—be thankful that so many feel
it in common with you which should, I think, help to sustain
you. Oh, it is a blessing to be thankful for, to have had such a
Husband and Father spared to you so long.

I earnestly pray for you—

Your friend
JULIA G. TYLER

13. MARY CUSTIS LEE

"For Him I Do Not Now Weep"

Before Mary Custis Lee joined her General "where parting
and sorrow are unknown," she paid a last visit to Arlington.

---

[24] Gardiner Tyler became judge of the 14th judicial circuit of Virginia.
He was a member of the U. S. House of Representatives from 1893 through
1897.

"I rode out to my dear old home," she wrote to a friend, "but so changed it seemed but as a dream of the past." She never again saw her war-time home in Richmond.

Her daughter Agnes died in October 1873. Less than a month later, the South sorrowed over a brief announcement in the Lexington *Gazette and General Advertiser*, Friday, November 7, 1873:

"Mrs. Mary Custis Lee died at her home in Lexington on the night of the 5th of November, near the hour of twelve.

"The funeral services will be held in the Lee Memorial Chapel today (Friday) at 12 o'clock, and the remains will be deposited in the vault of the Chapel, in accordance with her wish.

"The places of business will be closed during the services."

Major Cooke, of Matthews, Virginia, had been a member of General Lee's staff. In his opinion, "The General died of a broken heart."

Lexington, 31 Dec., 1870

To Major Giles B. Cooke:

I will not let the year close, my dear sir, without replying to your kind letter of sympathy. It has been most truly gratifying to me in my deep sorrow to know that so many have mingled their tears with mine, that the prayers of many of God's servants have been offered for me. For him I do not now weep. He has entered into his rest, the glorious rest of Heaven. Few persons could know what an humble consistent Christian he was and how fast for the last few years he had been ripening for glory. From the moment he was seized with the last fatal attack, I saw from the appearance of perfect calm and resignation in his whole bearing and countenance that he knew his hour had come. He never evinced the slightest anxiety, restlessness, or impatience, and had evidently taken his leave of earth. It was a sublime spectacle and could only have been exhibited by a true Christian. That we may be prepared to meet him in the world where parting and sorrow are unknown is my prayer for all, especially those who knew and loved him.

Yours most faithfully,
MARY CUSTIS LEE

Bibliography and
Acknowledgments

BIBLIOGRAPHY

PROEM (Washington, D.C. November 8, 1860—April 22, 1861)
1. "Where Will It All End?"
   Mrs. Eugene McLean, "When the States Seceded," *Harper's Monthly Magazine*, CXXVIII (January 1914), 282-288.
2. "Straws Tell Which Way the Wind Blows"
   Mrs. Jacob Thompson to Mrs. Howell Cobb, December 15, 1860. "The Correspondence of Robert Toombs, Alexander H. Stephens, and Howell Cobb," *The Annual Report of the American Historical Association for the Year 1911*, Vol. II, edited by Ulrich B. Phillips. Washington, D.C.: 1913, 522-24.
3. "Tremendous Event"
   Mrs. Roger A. Pryor, *Reminiscences of Peace and War*. New York: The Macmillan Company, 1904.
4. "Were Ever Circumstances So Complicated?"
   Emily Mason to her brother Robert Mason, December 31, 1860. Kate Mason Rowland papers, Confederate Museum, Richmond, Virginia.
5. "God Grant They May Succeed"
   Mrs. Eugene McLean, "When the States Seceded." (*See* 1.)
6. "I Have Despaired of the Union"
   Mrs. Robert Toombs to Alexander H. Stephens, January 1, 1861. American Historical Association. (*See* 2.)
7. "Madness of Coercion"
   Emily Mason to her brother Robert Mason, January 6, 1861. Kate Mason Rowland papers. (*See* 4.)
8. "Speed the Parting Guest"
   Mrs. Eugene McLean, "When the States Seceded." (*See* 1.)
9. "The Saddest Day of My Life"
   Mrs. Virginia Clay-Clopton, *A Belle of the Fifties: Memoirs of Mrs. Clay of Alabama*. New York: Doubleday, Page & Company, 1904.
10. "A Final Adieu"
    Varina Howell Davis, *Jefferson Davis: A Memoir by his Wife*. New York: Belford Company, 1890.
11. "This Peace Convention"
    Julia Gardiner Tyler to her mother Mrs. David Gardiner, February 3, and February 4, 1861.

Lyon G. Tyler, *The Letters and Times of the Tylers*. Richmond, 1885.

12. "Soldiers in Every Ward"
Emily Mason to her sister Mrs. I. S. Rowland, February 4, 1861. Kate Mason Rowland papers. (*See* 4.)

13. "All Is Suspense"
Julia Gardiner Tyler to her mother, February 13, 1861. Lyon C. Tyler, *The Letters and Times of the Tylers*. (*See* 11.)

14. "Abraham Lincoln Is Here"
Mrs. Eugene McLean, "When the States Seceded." (*See* 1.)

15. "The End Has Come"
Mrs. Virginia Clay-Clopton, *A Belle of the Fifties*. (*See* 9.)

16. "We Leave for Richmond"
Mrs. Eugene McLean, "When the States Seceded." (*See* 1.)

Chapter I. GAY CAPITAL. (May-December 1861)

1. "Richmond Was One Great Camp"
Varina Howell Davis, *Jefferson Davis: A Memoir by His Wife*. (*See* "Proem," 10.)

2. "I Can Scarcely Realize That We Are At War"
Mrs. D. Giraud Wright, *A Southern Girl in '61: The Wartime Memories of a Confederate Senator's Daughter*. New York: Doubleday, Page & Company, Inc., 1905.

3. "It Makes the Heart Beat and the Eyes Fill"
Lyon G. Tyler, *The Letters and Times of the Tylers*. (*See* "Proem," 11.)

4. "I Am In Richmond"
Mary Boykin Chesnut, *A Diary from Dixie*, edited by Isabella D. Martin and Myrta Lockett Avary. New York: D. Appleton and Company, 1905.

5. "Our Glorious Victory"
Mrs. D. Giraud Wright, *A Southern Girl in '61*. (*See* 1, 2.)

6. "Cheers and Shouts Rent the Air"
Sally Tompkins to her sister Ellen, July 22, 1861. Archives Division, Virginia State Library, Richmond.

7. "The Trains Began to Bring in the Wounded"
Mrs. Eugene McLean, "A Northern Woman in the Confederacy," *Harper's Monthly Magazine*, CXXVIII (February 1914), 440-451.

8. "The Day the Grand Battle Was Fought"
Anita Dwyer Withers, diary, May 4, 1860-June 18, 1865. Southern Historical Collection, University of North Carolina Library, Chapel Hill, North Carolina.
9. "The Lovely, Joyous, Hopeful Days of Summer"
Mrs. Fannie A. Beers, *Memories: A Record of Personal Experience and Adventure During the Four Years of War*. Philadelphia: J. B. Lippincott Company, 1888.
10. "Drums Beating . . . Banners Flying"
Mrs. D. Giraud Wright, *A Southern Girl in '61*. (See 1, 2.)
11. "No One Was Singular in Being Homeless"
Catherine Cooper Hopley, *Life in the South: From the Commencement of the War, by a blockaded British subject*, 2 vols. London: Chapman and Hall, 1863.
12. "There's Bound to Be Somethin' Goin' On"
Mrs. Virginia Clay-Clopton, *A Belle of the Fifties*. (See "Proem," 9.)
13. "Hospitable Old Town"
Constance Cary Harrison, "A Virginia Girl in the First Year of the War," *The Century Illustrated Monthly Magazine*, XXX (August 1885), 606-614.

Chapter II. SOUND THE ALARM (January-August 1862)

1. The Death of a Confederate Congressman
Lyon G. Tyler, *The Letters and Times of the Tylers*. (See "Proem," II.)
2. "I Am Called to the Work"
Mrs. Fannie A. Beers, *Memories*, (See I, 9.)
3. "They Shan't Get To Richmond"
Judith Brockenbrough McGuire, *Diary of a Southern Refugee During the War, by a Lady of Virginia*. Richmond, 3rd ed., 1889.
4. "Richmond Went Dinnerless"
Clara Minor Lynn papers, Confederate Museum, Richmond.
5. "Heavy Firing on the River"
Judith Brockenbrough McGuire, *Diary of a Southern Refugee*. (See II, 3.)
6. "The Enemy's Gun-Boats Are Ascending the River"
Varina Howell Davis, *Jefferson Davis*. (See "Proem," 10.)

7. "God Help Us"
Judith Brockenbrough McGuire, *Diary of a Southern Refugee.*
(*See* II, 3.)

8. "Our President Did Me the Honor"
Rose O'Neal Greenhow, *My Imprisonment and the First Year of Abolition Rule in Washington.* London: Richard Bentley, 1863.

9. "The Roar of the Guns Grew Louder and Louder"
Elizabeth L. Van Lew, journal. Archives Division, Virginia State Library, Richmond.

10. "Our Success Is Glorious"
Mrs. D. Giraud Wright, *A Southern Girl in '61.* (*See* 1, 2.)

11. "Beautiful Yet Awful"
Judith Brockenbrough McGuire, *Diary of a Southern Refugee.*
(*See* II, 3.)

12. "The Hospital Was Filled to Overflowing"
Mrs. Roger A. Pryor, *Reminiscences.* (*See* "Proem," 3.)

13. "Give Me the Privates"
Jennie D. Harrold, *Reminiscences of Richmond from 1861-65.*
Manuscript Division, Confederate Museum, Richmond.

Chapter III. THE SECOND AUTUMN AND WINTER
(September 1862-April 1863)

1. "The Radiant Image of Peace"
Sallie Ann Brock Putnam, *Richmond During the War: Four Years of Personal Observation, by a Richmond Lady.* New York: G. W. Carleton & Co., 1867.

2. "In the Secret Corps"
Loreta Janeta Valazquez, *The Woman in Battle: A Narrative of the Exploits, Adventures and Travels of Madame Loreta Janeta Velazquez, Otherwise Known as Lieutenant Harry T. Buford, Confederate States Army,* edited by C. J. Worthington, Hartford, Connecticut: T. Belknap, 1876.

3. "My Dear Friend"
Mary Boykin Chesnut to Mrs. Louis T. Wigfall, October, 1862.
Mrs. D. Giraud Wright, *A Southern Girl in '61.* (*See* I, 2.)

4. "The Suffering Among the Poor Was Great"
Mrs. D. Giraud Wright, *A Southern Girl in '61.* (*See* I, 2.)

5. "The Bloody Battle-Field So Near"
Kate Mason Rowland, diary in manuscript, Confederate Museum,
Richmond.
6. "A Sort of Court is Still Kept Up"
Mrs. Roger A. Pryor, *Reminiscences*. (*See* "Proem," 3.)
7. "The Blockade"
Judith Brockenbrough McGuire, *Diary of a Southern Refugee.*
(*See* II, 3.)
8. "Your Patriotic Labour"
Mary Custis Lee papers, Confederate Museum, Richmond.
9. "Our Starving Women and Children"
Agnes to Mrs. Roger A. Pryor April 4, 1863. Mrs. Roger A. Pryor,
Reminiscences. (*See* "Proem," 3.)
10. "My Bonnet is Finished"
Anita Dwyer Withers, diary. (*See* I, 8.)
11. "The Girls Wore Homespun Dresses"
Mrs. Mark Valentine, "A Girl in the Sixties in Richmond," *Con-
federate Veteran*, XX (June 1912), 279-281.
12. "Watch Over Charley"
A Calendar of Confederate Papers, edited by Douglas S. Freeman,
Confederate Museum, Richmond, 1908.

Chapter IV. HOPE ON, HOPE EVER (May-December 1863)

1. "They Are Within Three Miles of Richmond"
Mary Boykin Chesnut, *A Diary from Dixie*. (*See* I, 4.)
2. "The Sick and Wounded Are Pouring In"
Kate Mason Rowland, diary. (*See* III, 5.)
3. "Now What?"
Mrs. Louis T. Wigfall to Halsey Wigfall, May 11 and May 17,
1863. Mrs. D. Giraud Wright, *A Southern Girl in '61*. (*See* I, 2.)
4. "Hood's Division Passed Through"
Louise Wigfall to Halsey Wigfall, May 15, 1863. Mrs. D. Giraud
Wright, *A Southern Girl in '61*. (*See* I, 2.)
5. "Wishing You Much Success"
Mary Custis Lee papers. (*See* III, 7.)
6. "Remember New Orleans"
Kate Mason Rowland, diary. (*See* III, 4.)
7. "On the Day Vicksburg Fell"
Anita Dwyer Withers, diary. (*See* I, 8.)

8. "Willy and John Are Safe"
Emma Mordecai to her sisten Ellen, July 12, 1863. Mordecai papers, Southern Historical Collection, University of North Carolina Library, Chapel Hill, North Carolina.
9. "The Blood of the Bravest and Best"
Mary E. Rowland to Mary Pettigrew, July 13, 20, 23, 1863. Pettigrew papers, Southern Historical Collection, University of North Carolina Library, Chapel Hill.
10. "My Mind Is So Full of One Thing"
Mary Cantey Preston to Mary Boykin Chesnut, September 18, 1863. Williams-Chesnut-Manning papers. South Caroliniana Library, University of South Carolina, Columbia, South Carolina.
11. From Chimborazo Hospital
Phoebe Yates Pember to Mrs. Jeremy F. Gilmer, October 20, 1863. Phoebe Yates Pember papers, Southern Historical Collection, University of North Carolina Library, Chapel Hill.
12. "Threats"
Elizabeth L. Van Lew, journal. (*See* II, 9.)
13. "I Was Besieged with Company"
Belle Boyd, *Belle Boyd: In Camp and Prison*. London: Saunders, Otley & Company, 1865.
14. "We Bought a Servant Yesterday"
Anita Dwyer Withers, diary. (*See* I, 8.)

Chapter V. BUT RICHMOND WAS SAFE (January-June 1864)

1. "Something Told Her He Would Never Get Back"
Judith Brockenbrough McGuire, *Diary of a Southern Refugee*. (*See* II, 3.)
2. "We Go On As Before"
Mary Boykin Chesnut, *A Diary from Dixie*. (*See* I, 4.)
3. "Beware"
Elizabeth L. Van Lew, journal. (*See* II, 9.) *See also* Elizabeth L. Van Lew to General Benjamin F. Butler, January 30, 1864. *War of the Rebellion: Official Records of the Union and Confederate Armies,* Series I, XXXIII, 520.
4. "Champagne Is $350 a Dozen"
Agnes to Mrs. Roger A. Pryor, January 30, 1864. Mrs. Roger A. Pryor, *Reminiscences*. (*See* "Proem," 3.)

5. "109 Prisoners Escaped"
   Elizabeth L. Van Lew, journal. (*See* II, 9.)
6. "I Could Not Reconcile the Two Ulrics"
   Varina Howell Davis, *Jefferson Davis*. (*See* "Proem," 10.)
7. "The Battle Raid Interferes"
   Virginia Nicholas Sanders to Mrs. John Hunt Morgan, March 1, 1864. John Hunt Morgan papers, Southern Historical Collection, University of North Carolina Library, Chapel Hill.
8. "The City Might Be Shelled"
   Clara Minor Lynn papers. (*See* II, 4.)
9. "We Went to Church"
   Anita Dwyer Withers, diary, (*See* I, 8.)
10. "My Precious Husband Left Me"
    Virginia Tunstall Clay, diary, 1859-1866, Manuscript Division, Duke University Library, Durham, North Carolina.
11. "I Feel Very Uneasy"
    Mrs. Angela Moreno Mallory to Mrs. Virginia Tunstall Clay, May 6, 1864. Clement Claiborne Clay papers, Manuscript Division, Duke University Library, Durham.
12. "Oh, the Yearning for a Deliverance"
    Elizabeth L. Van Lew, journal. (*See* II, 9.)
13. "I Am Not Rebellious"
    Varina Howell Davis papers, Confederate Museum, Richmond.

Chapter VI. CLOUD OF SORROW (June-December 15, 1864)

1. "The Safest Place in the Confederacy"
   Sallie Ann Brock Putnam, *Richmond during the War*. (*See* III, 1.)
2. "This Abode of Misery"
   Mason Smith Family Letters, 1860-1868, edited by Daniel E. Huger Smith, Alice R. Huger Smith, Arney Robinson Childs. Columbia: University of South Carolina Press, 1950.
3. "Camp Winder Hospital"
   Emma Mordecai, diary, May 1864-May 30, 1865. Southern Historical Collection, University of North Carolina Library, Chapel Hill.
4. Hospital Scenes
   Emily V. Mason, "Hospital Scenes, "*Our Women in the War; The Lives They Lived; The Deaths They Died*. Charleston, South Carolina: The News and Courier Book Presses, 1885.

5. "The Band on the Square Played"
Kate Mason Rowland, diary. (*See* III, 5.)
6. "They Carried Him to Hollywood"
Cornelia Peake McDonald, *A Diary with Reminiscences of the War and Refugee Life in the Shenandoah Valley, 1860-1865,* edited by Hunter McDonald. Nashville, Tennessee: Cullom & Ghertner, 1934.
7. "No. 707 Franklin Street"
Mrs. Sally Nelson Robins, "Mrs. Lee During the War," *Gen. Robert Edward Lee,* edited by R. A. Brock. Richmond: Royal Publishing Co., 1897.

Chapter VII. NEVER CRY FOR QUARTER
(December 16, 1864-April 2, 1865)

1. "The Tree Was a Lovely Holly"
Alice West Allen, "Recollections of War in Virginia," *Confederate Veteran,* XXIII (June, 1915), 269.
2. "Christmas in the Confederate White House"
Mrs. Jefferson Davis, "Christmas in the Confederate White House," New York *Sunday World,* December 13, 1896.
3. "For a Name and for a Ring"
Sallie Ann Brock Putnam, *Richmond during the War.* (*See* III, 1.)
4. "Sometimes We Were Hungry"
A Virginia Girl in the Civil War, 1861-1865: being a record of the actual experience of the wife of a Confederate officer, edited by Myrta Lockett Avary. New York: D. Appleton & Company, 1903.
5. "I Must Thank You Both"
Mary Custis Lee to "a little friend," March, 1865; to Colonel Francis Smith, March 30, 1865. Rose Mortimer Ellzey MacDonald, *Mrs. Robert E. Lee.* Boston: Ginn & Company, 1939.
6. "The One Topic of Conversation Is Eating"
Mrs. William A. Simmons, diary, Confederate Museum, Richmond.
7. "What Does All This Mean?"
Agnes to Mrs. Roger A. Pryor, March 28, 1865. Mrs. Roger A. Pryor, *Reminiscences.* (*See* "Proem," 3.)
8. "Pray That As My Day Is, So May My Strength Be"
Varina Howell Davis to General John S. Preston, April 1, 1865. Varina Howell Davis papers, Confederate Museum, Richmond.

9. "Richmond Is To Be Evacuated"
Mrs. William A. Simmons, diary. *(See* VII, 6.)
10. "The Direful Tidings"
Sallie Ann Brock Putnam, *Richmond during the War.* (*See* III, 1.)
11. "I Was the Only Lady"
Mrs. George A. Trenholm, diary in manuscript, South Caroliniana Library, University of South Carolina, Columbia.

Chapter VIII. THE ENEMY COME (April 2-May 1865)

1. "To My Horror"
Mrs. Fannie Walker Miller, "The Fall of Richmond," *Confederate Veteran,* XIII (1905), 305.
2. "Oh, Army of My Country"
Elizabeth L. Van Lew, journal. (*See* II, 9.)
3. "The Victorious Army"
"Nathalie," Norfolk *Virginian,* n.d. Reprinted, Edward A. Pollard, *The Lost Cause: A New Southern History of the War of the Confederates.* New York: E. B. Treat & Co., 1866.
4. "We Covered Our Faces and Cried"
A Virginia Girl in the Civil War, edited by Myrta Lockett Avary. (*See* VII, 4.)
5. "The Grewsome Story"
Agnes to Mrs. Roger A. Pryor, April 5, 1865. Mrs. Roger A. Pryor, *Reminiscences.* (*See* "Proem," 3.)
6. "The City Under Martial Law"
Jennie D. Harrold, *Reminiscences of Richmond from 1861-65.* (*See* II, 13.)
7. "Dearer Than Ever In Its Captivity and Ruin"
Judith Brockenbrough McGuire, *Diary of a Southern Refugee.* (*See* II, 3.)
8. "I Never Dreamed of the Yankees Getting to Richmond"
Emmie Sublett to Emily Anderson, April 29, 1865. Manuscript Division, Confederate Museum, Richmond.
9. "A Grief Which Was Terrible"
Mrs. Mary A. Fontaine to Mrs. Marie Burrows Sayre, April 30, 1865. *A Calendar of Confederate Papers,* edited by Douglas S. Freeman. (*See* III, 12.)
10. "Such Fright, Anxiety and Dread"
Anita Dwyer Withers, diary. (*See* I, 8.)

11. "Our President a Captive"
Sallie Ann Brock Putnam, *Richmond during the War*. (*See* III, 1.)
12. "Despise the Shame"
Mary Custis Lee to Jefferson Davis, May, 1865. Mary Custis Lee
papers, Confederate Museum, Richmond.

POSTLUDE (May 1865-December 1870)

1. "I Shall Not Repine"
Agnes to Mrs. Roger A. Pryor, May 1865. Mrs. Roger A. Pryor,
Reminiscences. (*See* "Proem," 3.)
2. "To Look at Our Desolated Country and Be Strong"
Mary Boykin Chesnut, *Diary from Dixie*. (*See* I, 4.)
3. "I Shall Not Fall"
Mrs. Roger A. Pryor, *Reminiscences*. (*See* "Proem," 3.)
4. "I, Varina Davis"
Varina Howell Davis to Horace Greeley, June 22, 1865. Varina
Howell Davis papers, Confederate Museum, Richmond; Varina
Howell Davis to Julia Gardiner Tyler, July 24, 1865. Manuscript
Division, Virginia State Library, Richmond; Varina Howell Davis
to Mrs. Howell Cobb, September 9, 1865, *The Annual Report of
the American Historical Association*, Vol. II, 1911. (*See* "Proem,"
2); Varina Howell Davis to President Andrew Johnson, January
1866. *War of the Rebellion: Official Records of the Union and
Confederate Armies*, Series II, Vol. VIII, 874-75. Washington,
1880-1901.
5. "Such Acts of Atrocity"
Mary Custis Lee to Miss Emily Mason, November 23, 1865. Mary
Custis Lee papers, Confederate Museum, Richmond.
6. "Yankee Rule"
Isabel Maury to Molly Maury, January 1, 1866. Confederate Museum, Richmond.
7. "My Husband Is My World"
Mrs. Virginia Clay-Clopton, *A Belle of the Fifties: Memoirs of
Mrs. Clay, of Alabama*. (*See* "Proem," 9.)
8. "I Went to Fort Lafayette"
Mrs. Angela Moreno Mallory to Mrs. Clement C. Clay, February
7, 1866. Clement Claiborne Clay papers, Manuscript Division,
Duke University Library, Durham.

9. "I Did Not Walk About the City"
Mrs. George Wythe Randolph to Mrs. Jefferson Davis, September 29, 1866. Varina Howell Davis papers, Confederate Museum.

10. "There is Nothing Like One's 'Ain Countrie'"
"Confederate Exiles in London, 1865-70: the Wigfalls," contributed by Sarah Agnes Wallace. *South Carolina Historical Magazine,* LII (1951), 76-77; 70-81; 143-44; 202-203.

11. "The Glorious Old Times of the Confederacy"
Mary Custis Lee to Mrs. Jefferson Davis, February 6, 1887, and Mary Custis Lee to Mrs. R. H. Chilton, March 10, May 6, 1867. Mary Custis Lee papers. Confederate Museum, Richmond.

12. "The South's Dear General Lee"
Julia Gardiner Tyler to Mary Custis Lee, October 14, 1870. Manuscript Division, Virginia State Library, Richmond.

13. "For Him I Do Not Now Weep"
Mary Custis Lee to Major Giles B. Cooke, December 31, 1870. *Confederate Veteran,* XXXVII (May, 1929), 183.

ACKNOWLEDGMENTS

The Confederate Museum in Richmond, once the White House of the Confederacy, was an appropriate and rewarding point to begin the search for extant writings of the ladies of Richmond. Here Miss India W. Thomas and Miss Eleanor S. Brockenbrough, whose vast knowledge of the subject is astonishing, kindly and graciously introduced me to their rich collections of letters, diaries, and papers, including those of Mrs. Davis and Mrs. Lee.

I want to thank again Mr. John W. Dudley and Milton C. Russell, of the Virginia State Library, for suggestions and help; Mr. John Melville Jennings, Director of the Virginia Historical Society; Mr. Robert Waitt, Jr., of Richmond Civil War Centennial Committee; Mrs. Ralph Catterall, of the Valentine Museum; Miss Mattie Russell and Miss Jane Robinson, of the Manuscript Department, Duke University Library; Mr. Robert E. Stocking, of the Alderman Library, University of Virginia; Dr. David C. Mearns and Russell M. Smith, of the Library of Congress; Dr. James W. Patton and Mrs. Wesley H. Wallace, of the Southern Historical Collection, University of North Carolina Library; Mr. E. L. Inabinett and Mrs. George Rembert, of the South Caroliniana Library, University of South Carolina; Mr. Peter A. Brannon, Director, Albama Archives and History, Montgomery, Alabama; Dr. Bell I. Wiley, Emory University, Atlanta, Georgia; Mr. J. W. G. Gourlay, Miss Sidelle Ellis and the staff of the Clemson College Library, South Carolina; Dr. Robert Tucker and the library staff of Furman University, Greenville, South Carolina; and Mr. N. L. Armistead, of Richmond.

In addition, I wish to acknowledge the gracious consent of *Harper's Magazine,* the South Carolina Historical Society, the American Historical Association, the City of Richmond, the University of South Carolina Press, and Mr. Hunter McDonald of Nashville for permission to use important selections.

Index

INDEX

357

C

Cabell, Dr., 189
Cabell, Edward C., 95
Cabell, William Preston, 204
Calhoun, John C., 318n
Cameron, Alexander, 330n
Cameron, Mary Haxall, 330n
Campbell, 32
Campbell, John A., 156, 286
Carrington, H., 176
Carter, Robert Shirley, 241
Cary, Archibald, 91
Cary, Constance, 91, 195, 196
Cary, Hettie, xii, 91, 196, 253
Cary, Jennie, 91
Cary, Monimia Fairfax, 91
Caskie, James, 153, 241
Caskie, Mrs. James, 153, 327n
Cass, Lewis, 23n, 25
Chandlers, 49
Charleston *Courier,* 94
Chase, Kate, 278
Chase, Salmon P., 278
Chegary, Madame, 44
Chesnut, Cheves, 142, 143
Chesnut, John, 305n
Chesnut, James, Jr., 19, 43n, 65, 66, 68, 303
Chesnut, Mary Boykins, xii, 19, 65, 83, 142, 143, 162, 163n, 168, 169, 180, 194, 217, 305n, 327
Cheves, Langdon, 142
Chilton, R. H., 332
Chilton, Mrs. R. H., 333, 334
Christian, Letitia, 335
City of New York, 186
Claiborne, Mrs. H. A., 101
Clark, Dr., 99
Clarkson, Capt., 227
Clay, Virginia Tunstall, 25, 36, 48, 211, 213, 322, 323, 324, 325
Clay, Jeannie, 173n
Clay, Clement C., 19, 22, 37, 38, 39-40, 43, 52, 87, 88, 211, 323, 324
Clopton, David, 323
Cobb, Howell, 22, 304

Cobb, Mary Ann, 22, 313, 316n
Cocke, Elizabeth Randolph, 319
Cocke, John, 263
Cohen, Mr., 176
Coles, Captain, 102-103
Collier, Henry W., 37
Congress, 105, 117
Conrad, Jeanetta Emily, 153, 171
Cooke, Giles B., 337
Cooper, James Fenimore, 43
Cooper, Mrs., 174
Cooper, Samuel, 28n, 72
Corse, Montgomery D., 107n
Couch, Deborah, 128-129, 229
Coxe, Major, 241
Crittenden, John J., 31n, 35, 47
Cullen, Charlotte, 176
Cumberland, 105

D

Dabney, Sarah, 135
Dahlgren, John A., xi, xiv, 203, 204, 206, 320
Dahlgren, Ulric, 190, 203, 204-205, 206
Dana, Charles A., xv, 284
Daniel, John M., 145n
Darby, John T., 180, 327
Darby, Mrs. John, 327
Davis, George, 191
Davis, Jeff, Jr., 41, 246, 247
Davis, Jefferson, 20, 21, 22, 29, 33, 39, 41-42, 43, 44, 48, 52, 59, 64, 68, 69, 73, 74, 75, 82, 83, 86, 87, 90, 93, 95, 103, 111, 116, 120, 159, 160, 164, 184, 190, 197, 205, 210n, 212, 217, 242, 246, 267, 268-269, 270, 271, 273, 275, 284, 285, 287, 288, 297, 298, 299, 300, 308, 312, 314-315, 325, 334
Davis, Joseph Emory, 217
Davis, Joseph Robert, 41, 68-69, 210, 212
Davis, Maggie, 41, 246, 247
Davis, Samuel, 41